PLAY BY PLAY

PLAY BY PLAY

Calling the Wildest Games in Sports—from SEC Football to College Basketball, the Masters and More

VERNE LUNDQUIST

WITH GARY BROZEK

wm

WILLIAM MORROW
An Imprint of HarperCollinsPublishers

PLAY BY PLAY. Copyright © 2018 by Verne Lundquist. All rights reserved. Printed in the United States of America. No part of this book may be used or reproduced in any manner whatsoever without written permission except in the case of brief quotations embodied in critical articles and reviews. For information, address HarperCollins Publishers, 195 Broadway, New York, NY 10007.

HarperCollins books may be purchased for educational, business, or sales promotional use. For information, please email the Special Markets Department at SPsales@harpercollins.com.

A hardcover edition of this book was published in 2018 by William Morrow, an imprint of HarperCollins Publishers.

FIRST WILLIAM MORROW PAPERBACK EDITION PUBLISHED 2019.

Library of Congress Cataloging-in-Publication Data has been applied for.

ISBN 978-0-06-268443-1 (pbk.)

19 20 21 22 23   LSC   10 9 8 7 6 5 4 3 2 1

For Nancy,

Your warmth and generosity, along with your kindness
and your sense of humor, have made the path we have taken together
so wonderful that it's almost beyond my ability to describe.
You've still got the greatest smile I've ever seen.
I love you.

CONTENTS

PREFACE

History has a funny way of sneaking up on you. One day you're sitting at a radio control board in Austin on November 22, 1963, having your boss shouting at you to put him on the air, and then seemingly seconds later you're talking with your bosses about winding down your days covering South Eastern Conference football. No, it doesn't happen that fast, but it sure feels like it in retrospect. At first you're eager to get on the air to make a name for yourself, and then before you know it, you're contemplating how to exit gracefully, avoid hanging on too long.

So when Sean McManus and I had those first conversations in the spring of 2016 about my ending my seventeen-year relationship with America's premier football conference, I was ready to figure things out with him. I was grateful to Sean and the rest of the management team at CBS for allowing me to have some input into how my career would wind down. Corporations don't always do that, and I understood and appreciated another unique opportunity they were offering me. I was also pleased that they'd let me know early on in the process that Brad Nessler would be filling my role. Not that my opinion carried a lot of weight, but I agreed wholeheartedly with the choice. Brad is a great sportscaster, had worked with my partner and friend Gary Danielson before, and I was familiar with his outstanding work.

I am proud of what we built at CBS in covering the SEC all those Saturdays, and it was comforting to know that the games would be in great hands, in the booth, in the truck, and back in New York. After the announcement was made that the '16 season would be my last, I went about my business as usual preparing for another great season of NCAA football. At our annual pre-season seminar, I made it clear to everyone that business as usual was how I wanted things to go. This was no farewell tour; this was no victory lap. The games were the thing, the student-athletes and their coaches and families the storyline.

Everyone nodded and agreed.

Seems like some people had a different idea, and as the season went on they wanted to recognize my years covering the SEC. I was okay with that; just so long as what people chose to do for me didn't interfere with all of us getting the job done in telling the most compelling stories we could about a game and a league we all loved.

I don't mind telling you that as I sit here in my office back home in Steamboat Springs, Colorado, many of the mementos I received from that last year are hung on the walls or have taken a prominent place elsewhere in the room. Jerseys, footballs, plaques, and other memorabilia mean so much to me. I'm an avid collector (okay, I'm a rat-packer and have copies of rosters and other things dating back to my first days in radio), so these things mean a lot to me. More than that, much more, in fact, they are a reminder of the wonderful people I met along the way. I've been blessed that people seem to like me in this world. I know that I was called Uncle Verne by SEC Football fans, and sometimes derisively. But I consider that a warm compliment. I like being in people's homes and I never take that for granted.

When I think of all the names and faces, it can get pretty crowded in here—Archie and Peyton Manning, Steve Spurrier and Jeremy Foley, Lou Saban and Joe Namath. Heck, the entire University of Georgia band is crammed in here spelling out "Yes Sir!" I apologize in advance for not listing and naming everyone and every school that showed me such great kindness. That would take up an entire book on its own. I am enormously grateful and humbled by the time and attention that went into those various salutes. I could not have imagined back in my first days in radio in Austin, and before, that I'd receive that kind of a send-off for simply doing something that I so dearly love to do.

That last season was a memorable one on the field as well. I thoroughly enjoyed revisiting some of my favorite haunts from Auburn, Alabama to College Station, Texas and all points in between as our crew crisscrossed the conference. From Alabama's stirring 48–43 victory over Ole Miss to Tennessee's last-second win over Georgia to the double-overtime thriller between Texas A&M and Tennessee, the games stayed center stage and dramatic.

As hard as it may be for some to believe, there's more to my story than just SEC football—a lot more. For more than fifty years I've had a front-row seat to some of the greatest sporting events America has witnessed. I've been blessed to be present at events where something truly significant has broken out in front of me. You go into a broadcast with high hopes every week, every event, every night that something special will break out, and if you're really, really lucky, it will. In my case, I've been really lucky a half dozen times or more. Then you hope that you're up to the moment and capture it with words that are appropriate to the significance of the event. I'm very proud of the fact that for the most part, I have done that.

I have always seen myself as a teller of stories and not the story itself. My role as a play-by-play man is to relate the facts so that those watching can know where we are in the unfolding story of the game. If that means time, score, down, and distance in football, how much time is left on the shot clock in basketball, and not a whole lot more, I'm okay with that. I was never on the scene to make headlines or have my calls of a game go down in history. I leave the history-making to the athletes and coaches, the other true participants in the games and contests I've covered. I suppose, like the old adage that a baseball umpire has done his job if no one notices his presence, then that has been my life's ambition. To tell the story but not be the story.

To a degree this book is the exception to that rule. After more than fifty years I think I've earned the right to step out from behind the camera and have my say about what went on behind the scenes of some of the events I've covered in that span. I've no interest in spoiling your memories of the things that happened or diminish your sense of what some of the most famous athletes and broadcasters of the day were like. That doesn't mean that I won't be honest, but I also live by the example my minister father and my gracious mother set. If you can't say something nice about someone, don't say anything at all.

I've met and worked with some fascinating and some frustrating figures, and have been witness to history on the playing fields and in the streets. Consider the recollections that follow postcards from my past. I was there, but my heart and my head were always filled with thoughts of you all back home listening and watching. I loved the sense that I was sharing and that we were all bound together in a community. I'm of the generation of Americans whose lives and whose viewership weren't quite so fragmented by choice as they are today. Things change; I know that and I'm fine with that. I'm just happy for one more opportunity to share with you again, to take on my role as storyteller. I hope you enjoy reading this as much as I have enjoyed writing it.

CHAPTER ONE

Names and Tunes

As any competent play-by-play man would, I've always considered myself duty bound to get the names right. I suppose that I ought to do the same here. I was born in Duluth, Minnesota, in July 1940 and was christened with the name Merton LaVerne Lundquist, Jr. For some reason "Uncle Merton" doesn't have the same ring to it, does it? "Uncle LaVerne" would cause all kinds of confusion. Why my father, Merton LaVerne Lundquist, Sr., bequeathed that hefty name on me I'll never know. Obviously, he was of good Swedish stock and he likely figured I'd grow up stout and strong as a result of toting that name around. That's not quite the same as the legendary Johnny Cash and his song "A Boy Named Sue," but that's okay.

It could have been worse. Both my parents—my mother, Arda Christine, was Norwegian—came from a long line of really weird names, I mean really weird. My paternal grandfather was Ebenezer. My paternal grandmother was Edla. My dad was the oldest of five; he was Merton. There were also Clinton, Orvin, Roland, and Leona.

Dad was born in Kansas. His people were all farmers, wheat farmers, and they tried to eke out a living in the Dust Bowl days. He and my grandparents had some ambition for him beyond struggling.

He was fortunate and smart enough to attend Augsburg College in Minneapolis. He had his sights set on becoming a Lutheran minister. Between completing his four-year degree and starting seminary, he attended the Lutheran Bible Institute. It was while there that he met my mother. By the time I came along in 1940, they'd been married for a year. I'm an inveterate pack rat, and I must have inherited that trait from my parents. At some point years later, they showed the receipt for my delivery—twenty-five dollars. After serving as a student pastor for three months in Duluth, Minnesota, we settled in to live in Rock Island, Illinois, where my father attended seminary at Augustana College. He graduated on D-Day, June 6, 1944, and was assigned to Zion Lutheran Church in Everett, Washington.

My earliest memories are of the cramped parsonage we lived in. It was adjacent to one of the two churches he served, the one in downtown Everett. The other was in nearby Lake Stevens. My father was very present in my formative years since his office was just a few steps from our home.

One Friday afternoon in 1947, I stepped out of the parsonage with my father to run a weekly errand with him. The state of Washington was still dominated by the logging industry, and the smell of fresh-cut cedar and spruce battled, and took a whipping from, the chemical odors coming from the pulping operations at Weyerhaeuser Timber and others. Eyes blinking against the stench, we headed to the studios of radio station KRKO at the outskirts of town. The studios were in a small, squat, garage-like building, and out in front stood a large tower, the transmitter that broadcast the signal throughout much of Snohomish County at 1380 on your radio dial. As part of KRKO's programming they did public service announcements, and my dad was there to deliver the church notes. The First Baptist Church was hosting a potluck dinner; the Luther League—our church's youth group was meeting at seven thirty Sunday night, that sort of thing. We stepped into the cozy quarters of the radio station, and my eyes were instantly drawn to a man wearing headphones behind a glass partition. In front of him hung a microphone that craned out from a large black metal console with illuminated dials, switches, and other mysteries. I was enthralled. I could smell superheated dust and cigarettes. A man wearing spectacles and a white shirt and black tie sat squinting at some copy as he read the news. I saw his lips moving but it took a few seconds for the sound to come out of a nearby speaker. The Cleveland Indians had signed Larry Doby. Following Jackie Robinson's breaking of the color barrier, Doby would be the first African American to play in the American League.

To that point, radio had figured largely in my life. I know that many of you might not be old enough to recall pre-Internet and pre-smartphone existence, but once upon a time the only moving images we saw on-screen were in a movie theater. For news, sports, and entertainment, we relied on sound waves only. Though my father made very little money, we did have two radios. A smaller version about the size of a toaster oven sat on a kitchen counter. A larger wooden console Motorola radio stood in the living room. The furniture there was arranged around the radio so that, strangely but typically, we could have a good view of the cabinet and its speakers. Ralph Edwards's *Truth or Consequences*, *The Roy Rogers Show*, and, of course, *The Jack Benny Program* were all popular in our household.

Of equal interest to me was the Mutual Radio Major League Baseball game of the day. The play-by-play man was Al Helfer, a name that likely won't ring many bells, though he was one of the giants of his day. At the time guys like Red Barber and Mel Allen, who were the first two recipients of the National Baseball Hall of Fame's Ford C. Frick Award—the greatest honor a baseball announcer can receive—had huge followings in New York. That was their local market. Al Helfer's voice went nationwide, reaching many more people.

Radio always fascinated for its ability to bring distant events near to us, into our living rooms and kitchens. As I sat there and listened to live sporting events, it was difficult for me to fathom the technology that it took that allowed me to hear simultaneously what was going on thousands of miles from my home in Everett. On a Saturday morning, I could tune in and listen to a man in South Bend, Indiana, describe the arc of a football field goal attempt. Fridays I could hear a man describe another arcing ball—a long drive over the Green Monster in Boston's Fenway Park. I'd sit there and visualize the path those balls traveled through sunlit skies, the roar of the crowd tickling my stomach, and marvel at the world we lived in.

Family legend has it that—and I have to believe it to be true because my parents would never lie—my interest in play-by-play men began long before I pursued any job in the field. We were only thirty miles from Seattle and today Everett has been subsumed into the large Seattle metro area, but back then it seemed like a far-flung outpost. We weren't so far away that we couldn't tune into KRKO to listen to the Seattle Rainiers' broadcasts. The Rainiers were a Triple-A minor league affiliate of the Chicago White Sox. They played in the Pacific Coast League along with teams like the Hollywood Stars, the Los Angeles Angels, and the Portland Beavers. KRKO was part of the Seattle Rainiers baseball broadcasting network. We got the broadcast each night of the season, and Leo Lassen's voice became as familiar to me as anyone's in my circle of family and friends. According to my folks, I would stand in the kitchen with an upturned broom in my hands serving as a microphone and imitate Leo Lassen in my high-pitched pipsqueak squeal.

I enjoyed sports of all kinds and participated in as many of them as I could. As much as I loved listening to baseball games, my passions were unrequited. In Everett and later on as we moved to Austin, Texas, in 1952, I played a fair amount of sandlot and organized ball. I was the unlikely combination of catcher and second base. I was a little guy, only reaching five feet three inches in height by the time I started high school. I couldn't hit a lick, especially breaking balls.

I once struck out fourteen times in a row. Upon making contact, a weak dribbler to the pitcher, I received a standing ovation from the guys in the dugout. The writing was in the batter's box dirt, and any dreams I had of playing the game seriously were swept away well before they could fully form.

That was no real heartbreak, really. Basketball captured my imagination and passion in a way that baseball didn't. Baseball was great to listen to, but its stop-and-start nature didn't entice me the way that the more continuous action of basketball up and down the floor did. I liked its combination of set plays and improvisation. I also developed a fondness for the game because of my exposure to another, more enticing phenomenon coming on the scene in my last days in Everett. A block away from our church/home on Colby Avenue was a Sylvania store. They sold radios primarily and, toward the end of our eight-year stay in Everett, televisions. The vast majority of people in Everett couldn't afford a luxury item like a television, which was about one-third the price of a new car.

Recognizing this, the owners of the Sylvania store put a DuMont console model at the front of the place. It faced out toward the sidewalk and the large glass storefront afforded a view of the roughly ten-inch screen. Undeterred by that small view, each Friday or Saturday night somewhere between ten and twenty Everett residents gathered to catch a glimpse of the flickering black-and-white spectacle. Of course, I was as fascinated as everyone else and was grateful for every opportunity afforded to me to gather there with the others. They were few and far between, what with schoolwork and the rest, but that indelible vision of the future was powerful. I can't say that I was wise enough to predict just how much impact that device would have on the world generally and me specifically. Still, the same principle applied to television as it did the radio. It brought the world and its people and events closer to me.

Most often when I got to go and watch, it was to see the Uni-

versity of Washington Huskies basketball team take on one of their
Pacific Coast Conference rivals. They had two stars. Bob Houbregs
went on to play in the early days of the National Basketball Association. But the guy I really admired, because he was relatively small
and quick like me, was Joe Cipriano. "Slippery Joe" went on to coach
the University of Nebraska Cornhuskers and one of my earliest jobs
in television in Austin was covering the University of Texas (UT)
Longhorns. I idolized this guy as a young man and not too many
years later, when Nebraska played at Texas I was interviewing him at
the Villa Capri Hotel in downtown Austin a few hours before tip-off.
Small world.

Sports and broadcasting are, obviously, intertwined in my mind.
During my formative years, my imagination was captured by another
larger-than-life figure who ran up the middle of our living room on
Saturdays. His exploits were captured by another great storyteller.
I became initially a fan of Southern Methodist University running
back Doak Walker through the descriptions of Bill Stern. He was
the play-by-play man on national radio college football broadcasts.
Later on, I'd get to meet them both, and Doak played a big role in
my development as a broadcaster. In his football-playing days, Doak
won the coveted Heisman Trophy as the nation's best player in 1948.
Doak was truly a do-it-all player. This was the World War II era,
when many young men who otherwise might have played in college
put in their time in the military. In fact, Doak left SMU for the
1946 season to serve in the Merchant Marine. When he won the
Heisman in 1948, he gained 532 yards on 108 carries for a 4.9 per-
carry average—not huge numbers, but you have to keep in mind
that he also threw for six touchdowns as a halfback and went 26 for
46 with 304 yards gained on those passes. He also caught 15 passes
for 279 yards and three touchdowns. Defensively, he was responsible
for three interceptions. On special teams, he had a 42.1-yard average
punting the ball. He also was the team's placekicker. Along with his

11 offensive touchdowns, his kicking brought his points total to 88. He also served as the team's punt and kick returner. Given all that, his name came up quite a bit during Bill Stern's calling of the game. No wonder I idolized Walker.

During the fall football season, a group of friends and I would gather on a vacant lot next to the church to play tackle football. We'd be out there for an hour and more. We played without pads, but I had my own uniform: blue jeans, tennis shoes, and a T-shirt. On the back of my shirt I'd stencil in Doak's number, 37. If anybody else showed up and had that number, I'd get real angry. That was my number. That was Doak's number.

Doak went on to enjoy a brief but outstanding five-season professional football career with the Detroit Lions. In that span he earned All-Pro honors and won two NFL championships. He was later inducted into both the college and pro football halls of fame. Eventually an award for the best collegiate running back was given his name. I've had the privilege of being present for a number of those presentations in Dallas. That meant a huge amount to me, especially given our later association. Doak was a quintessential Texan. Handsome as a Marlboro Man, so polite that he wrote a thank-you note to the Associated Press for naming him an All-American, he was the proverbial man that every woman wanted to date and every man wanted to be best friends with. I idolized him as a youngster and treasured his friendship later on. Not everyone lives up to their press billing (Doak's likeness appeared on nearly fifty magazine covers, including mainstream ones like *Look* and *Life*) but Doak was that rare public figure.

Our family's 1952 move to Austin was fortunate, and Texas has figured large in my life. I left behind some good friends, but I gained a whole lot more in return. Austin, of course, had no professional sports teams. The world was hung from one prong of a Texas Longhorn bull. So, at the end of sixth grade, when my father was reassigned to Austin, I became steeped in UT sports. By that time I was the oldest of four children. My three younger brothers all had been born while in Washington State. Today I think back and imagine we were a handful for my mother, but you wouldn't have known it from her demeanor. She was always as calm as could be, and no matter what her sons got up to, school activities or some such, dinner was always on the table at six thirty. The vast majority of the time, we were all gathered together for that meal.

After our move to Austin, I attended University Junior High School, on the campus of the University of Texas. That name was quite a mouthful, so we called it UJH. Lessons come in many forms, and I quickly sized up my chances of playing football at UJH—they were as small as I was. Still, I wanted to be involved, so I got myself a job as one of the water boys for the squad. I know that position can make you the butt of jokes and the object of derision, but I never experienced any of that. I wasn't too proud to admit that I wasn't capable of playing the sport. I wasn't so vain to believe that contributing to the well-being of the team was beneath me. In my family, being of service was a noble calling, and my parents would never cotton to any form of sloth. Be of use was a lesson instilled in all of us. Though it wasn't one of the seven deadly sins, not carrying your weight, be it with a water bucket or some other way, was no way to live your life. For those reasons, I also ran for school office and became a cheerleader my senior year in high school.

I also got a chance to play basketball at UJH. I made the squad but only saw playing time in the waning seconds when the outcome, good or bad, was already well in hand. I was okay with that. I had no delusions of grandeur. I loved being a part of the team and worked hard in practice. I briefly "ran" track and field. I finished seventh out of eight runners in a 100-yard dash. As hard as I tried to churn my legs on that cinder track, I produced more of a dust cloud than forward propulsion. So be it. I gave it my all. The lessons were adding up: I had no future as a professional athlete or even a collegiate one.

That didn't diminish my interest in sports; it simply put things in perspective. Besides, I wasn't so single-minded that my only interests were sports. I sang in the school choir. I wrote a weekly column for the school's newspaper.

During the fall term of eighth grade all UJH students had to take a course that was broken up into three parts—home economics, typing, and speech. Now, why they put those three together I couldn't tell you. Speech actually came first and a lot of my classmates dreaded the thought of speaking publicly. Growing up in a pastor's family, listening to my dad preach every Sunday, watching him interact and ad lib conversations and speeches, I had no fear of an audience. I never had it. In that class my teacher, Mrs. Marguerite Burleson, had us get up in front of the rest of the group and perform various exercises. I'd see my classmates go pale and bug-eyed and I felt sorry for them. I didn't want to show them up, but I had to do my best and outshone them with my calm performances.

Two or three weeks after the six-week segment had started, Mrs. Burleson took me aside after class and said that she had gotten a call from Radio House at the University of Texas. Back then UT had no television department. But they did have Radio House and undergraduates could major in radio. Part of the program entailed radio students tape-recording half-hour dramas every Tuesday night. These dramas would later be distributed by the university to public broadcasting stations throughout Texas and perhaps even beyond that. She said they needed an adolescent, a person with a boy's voice, to come over that night to take part in this taping with the college student actors. If I was interested, I would go and play the role of a ten-year-old Indian boy. I said, Oh, my gosh, yes. I got my dad to take me to Radio House, and we were there for three hours taping this recorded play.

To me, the production wasn't amateurish at all. This was the big time as far as I was concerned. The studio was so well equipped and

I was on the other side of that glass partition I'd seen at KRKO back in Everett. I was enthralled by the sound effects guy, who supplemented the voice acting. He sat in front of a small sandbox and used hollowed-out pineapples, coconuts, and other things to simulate the sound of horses galloping or trotting as need be. He used all kinds of other tools to produce more sounds and I was fascinated. They liked my performance enough to ask me back for the next week. And so, for the next year, I went over there every Tuesday, and in the process I got hooked on radio as a participant rather than solely as a listener.

But the following September, I learned a valuable lesson about the business: you're only as good as your next performance. Upon returning to school, I heard from Mrs. Burleson that the students at Radio House wanted me back for the next season of recordings, and I showed up that first Tuesday night raring to go. I got the script and I was playing the son of a West Texas farmer, a boy of about ten years of age. No problem. We started the session, and I followed along, thinking about this young man and wondering how to play him. When it came for my first line, I opened my mouth and said, "Well, I don't know, Dad. I'm not so sure—" I startled myself with the screeching sound that came out with those two S-words. I looked around the room and the rest of the actors sat there with their mouths open and their eyebrows raised. I gave it one more shot, but it was no good; my voice was in the process of changing.

I was done performing at Radio House.

Not completely, however. At the end of that school year, my ninth, my dad told me to get my church clothes on. We were going out for the evening. He didn't tell me where we were going, but as it turned out, we were invited to the awards banquet for the radio department students. I was presented with a diploma and a note of thanks from Radio House at the University of Texas. As I sit here writing this, I can look up and see that piece of parchment framed on the wall of my office. It was signed by the two administrators of the program—Gale

Long and Gale Adkins. I don't know if those two men understand the impact they and their program had on a young boy's life. As I said before, I'm a rat packer, but much of what I've kept has been stored away. I only put on display the things that really, really matter to me. Thank you, Radio House. Thank you, University of Texas.

Once I got bit by the performing bug, I could find no way to soothe the itch other than to sing in the church and school choir and act in a few of the school's dramas. I only ever sang one solo and that was a gut-twisting experience. I swear my knees knocked so much I sounded like a one-man band.

Even though I stopped being on-air every week, my passion for radio kept growing, even more so after we got a transistor radio. Inexpensive and portable, the transistor radio meant I no longer had to sit in the kitchen listening to games, which felt life-changing in itself. Instead I could go into the room I shared with my brothers, where together we'd spend many nights in bed listening to baseball and other sports broadcasts.

Crucially, I also was able to tune in to music via clear-channel stations from some of the larger and more influential markets. I pulled the covers over my head and by the dim glow of the dial I'd bring in WLS out of Chicago, Pittsburgh's KDKA, and WCCO out of Minneapolis–St. Paul. Again, the romantic notion of being able to bring different lives and different experiences and points of view was at the forefront of my mind. It also exposed me to something increasingly popular with American teenagers of the time—rock and roll.

It may come as a surprise but Uncle Verne sang in a rock-and-roll group in high school. The four of us dressed and styled ourselves as cutting-edge rockers—we wore flat tops with ducktails. That act of hair semi-rebellion set us apart from our parents. In most yearbook photos of the era, students looked like adults, with their dour expressions and trim haircuts and shirts and ties. We even called ourselves the Flat Tops in honor of our more hirsute appearance. We made a bit of a name for ourselves at school. Our manager was a disc jockey at KTBC—a station where I later worked—who was able to book us at what we used to call teen canteens on Friday nights. Our lead singer, Dan Showalter, had a wonderful voice, and the other two and I mostly sang backup, which consisted of variations on "doo-wa-doo" or "bee-bop bee-bop." We did covers of popular tunes of the day. One of them was the Monotones' "Book of Love," on which my great contribution was a series of background "who's." We also broke hearts with our tender rendition of "Earth Angel."

It makes for a great story that we were on the express train to greatness only to be derailed by our lead singer impregnating his girl-friend. He dropped out of school to marry her and to go to work to support her and the child they were expecting. The part about great-ness isn't true; the rest is. The band dissolved and like my athletic dreams, fame and fortune as a recording artist eluded me.

Still, my love of music remained. In the spring of 1957, as my six-teenth year was waning, a friend of mine by the name of Perry Moss drove a small group of us to San Antonio in his beat-up Chevrolet. At that time you could get a Texas driver's license at age fourteen, so Perry had been behind the wheel for a while and our parents all trusted him. Chuck Berry opened the show and his guitar playing electrified us. I'd heard him on the radio, but as any music lover knows, there's something special about a live performance. He was followed on-stage by Fats Domino. His rhythm-and-blues inflected songs were wonderful and his two hits, "Ain't That a Shame" and "Blueberry Hill," stirred the soul. Next out was Frankie Lymon and the Teenagers. They were one of the first boy bands, each of the five still in their teens when they recorded their big hit, "Why Do Fools Fall in Love." Frankie's boy soprano climbed to places I would never be able to reach. Finally, a young man with a guitar and a haircut that put all of ours to shame stepped out onstage and gave a lip-sneering, hip-gyrating performance I'll never forget. Elvis Presley was in the house. I'd see him much later on, during his so-called Fat Elvis stage, and he was a mere shadow, albeit a large one, of his former self as a performer.

On the drive home, my mind was filled with possibility and wonder. Music has always had a transformative and inspirational power. I had vague notions of what I wanted to do with my life. Ill-defined dreams of there being something beyond the city limits of Austin. At the time, Austin wasn't the musical universe it is today. It was the state capital and home to a major university. Its boom years were ahead of it. And though I couldn't have known it then, the same was true for me. Whatever dreams I had weren't anything I had penned myself; like so many other young people of my generation, I pulled together a vision of my future from the lyrics others had written. That view of a self was something I kept private. I was a minister's son, and obligation and call and duty to others and to my God sat in balance to my performing and radio fantasies. Which way that scale would tip was apparent to me, and I don't think I understood then what doubts lingered and how I would eventually give in to desire.

CHAPTER TWO

Finding My Direction

Like many young people then and now, I struggled a bit with the idea of what to do with my life. I knew that I wanted to go to college, of course, that was a given, but what to study was problematic. I say that in hindsight because at the time, the decision wasn't all that difficult. I admired my father and his work as a minister. A lot of people admired him. So, I entered college with the idea that I would eventually follow his path and become a minister. In retrospect, I can see I made that decision partly out of desire and partly out of a sense of obligation or doing the right thing. Countless oldest sons have followed their father's example and taken up the same line of work. Maybe I was doing the right thing; maybe I was doing the easy thing.

Regardless, I enrolled at Texas Lutheran College (now University) in Seguin. Seguin is the seat of Guadalupe County, about an hour's drive from Austin. I lived on campus and was close enough that I could go home as needed or desired on weekends. I didn't do that very often. Much of my motivation for going to TLC was to get away from home. I wanted to experience more independence, that is, dormitory life, so I opted not to go to the University of Texas. It was, and is, an incredibly fine institution. As you will see, much of my life later on would be shaped by its influence, but being a so-called townie held little appeal for me. Broadcasting had brought the world to me and enlarged my vision of what was possible. Fifty miles south of Austin wasn't that far, but at least it was a start.

Similarly, pre-enrolling in seminary—I had to get a bachelor's degree before I could formally attend—was another kind of start. It got me moving in a direction. Whether that would end up my final destination was uncertain. I was a Christian, of course, but whether I had a calling beyond devotion was still to be decided.

One of my anchors at TLC was again music. I sang in the choir. That brought me great joy and deepened my love of choral music as well as classical music. I majored in sociology and had a double major in history and Christianity. I also dabbled in radio. Seguin had one radio station, KWED 1580, down near the far right end of your radio dial. Stan McKenzie owned and operated the daytime-only station. He hired one, sometimes two, TLC students a year to work the weekends. I wanted one of those jobs, but for both my sophomore and junior years I didn't make the cut. Still, I hung around hoping to learn a few things and to show my dedication.

My junior year, Willie Staats was one of those chosen. He recently retired as chairman of the LSU economics department and is a huge SEC football fan. The other guy was Don Mischer. He eventually went on to work for ABC, producing Barbara Walters's specials and Howard Cosell's late-night variety show, ironically named "Saturday Night Live," and later the Oscars. I guess I shouldn't feel so bad about falling short in those first two years. Radio people have a thing about voices, of course, and I was disappointed my junior year not to meet or exceed Stan McKenzie's standards with what I was told was a lovely deep baritone. That year, I lost out to Larry Kramer, a guy whose basso profundo voice would have served him well in the Metropolitan Opera. It rattled rib cages and lampshades all over Seguin.

Finally, by my senior year, my perseverance paid off. I got the job, earning $1.05 an hour. At the beginning of the school year, my job consisted of showing up at the studio just before sunrise. I was shown what switches to throw and what dials to turn and what meters to monitor. Sounds more complicated than it was, but switching on a radio station gave me a thrill of power that's difficult to explain. Other aspects were even harder for me to understand, but I did them out of rote memory. Most of the weekend programming was remote— church services, primarily—and I had to unplug and plug in various cables. As I said, I didn't understand much of the technology, but I could follow relatively simple instructions. I sat there all alone in that studio from sunup to sundown, and it was like I was back in Everett. Instead of watching those guys at KRKO, I *was* one of those guys.

I got my first paid on-air experience at KWED doing station iden-tifications, saying no more than "This is KWED in Seguin." As far as I was concerned, I was relating Jesus's Sermon on the Mount. Even-tually, I got the opportunity to disc-jockey for three hours on Sunday afternoon. I went from switch boy to radio personality pretty darn quick and I was beyond thrilled. After I got word of my big chance, I told everyone on campus I knew—dorm mates, fraternity brothers, friends, classmates—to be sure to tune in the following Sunday.

I got to the station earlier than usual the day of my first show, *Play-house of Hits*. It was scheduled to go on from one to four. I wanted to get some practice in. I'd worked the turntables before. All the commercials we played were on vinyl, so I was used to counting cuts and setting the levels on the potentiometers (or "pots"). Still I was going to be host-ing, and I wanted to be sure that things went absolutely perfectly. All morning, while the church services played, I rehearsed. By the time one o'clock rolled around, my mouth was as dry as the Sonoran Desert and my heartbeat was presto. The theme or introduction music I chose was Percy Faith and his orchestra's "Brazilian Sleigh Bells." (If you don't know who Percy Faith is, do a quick Google search for top hits for a few years in the early to mid 1960s and his name will be all over those lists.)

I cued up the record, hand steady, and got it perfect. The sound started immediately. I let a ringing cascade of notes loose for a full ten seconds. I lowered the pot, bringing down the volume. I piped open my microphone and I said, using my best golden-throated tones, "Good afternoon and welcome to the *Playhouse of Shits*."

I felt my testicles retract and adrenaline rush through me. I recovered and kept up my patter. At the first commercial break, I knew what I had to do. Thankfully, my boss Stan McKenzie understood and he reassured me that something like that happened to everyone at one time or another—just usually not in the first ten seconds. Funny thing is, I remember those first ten seconds but very little of the remaining two hours and fifty minutes. I had a great group of friends and they didn't give me too much grief. The next morning, I went to class and the snickers and pointing weren't too bad—I heard "Playhouse of Shits" tossed at me and whispered in my ear the rest of the week. As tends to happen with things like this, some other campus mishap overtook mine in a week or two. I should make it clear that all the ribbing I took was of the good-natured, Lutheran variety.

Despite that faux pas ("faux pooh"?) I loved my time at TLC. Years later, in 2009, I was invited to sit on the board of regents of what became TLU, and the school holds a special place in my heart. I was too busy to ever attend a meeting in person until early 2018, and when I did, I was welcomed with open arms as a kind of prodigal son. I graduated in the class of 1962 before packing my bags and making another prodigal son move by heading to Rock Island, Illinois, to attend the Lutheran School of Theology, part of Augustana College, the same seminary my father had graduated from.

Unlike my father, I moved to the area of Illinois and Iowa at the start of the summer well before classes began. The Quad Cities consist of, ironically, five different municipalities. They are clustered on the east and west sides of the Mississippi in Illinois and Iowa. Rock Island is among the five. I'd worked my way through college, using monies I'd made doing a variety of jobs from the time I was thirteen—bagging groceries, operating a soda fountain, lifeguarding, laboring for a carpenter, along with my radio DJing. I decided that I needed a good summer job to help pay for my seminary tuition. I was fortunate to get a job at radio station KROS in Clinton, Iowa, about thirty-five miles north of the Quad Cities. My experience at KWED ultimately ended up serving me well.

I was hired on for the summer to serve as an announcer at this nice little local radio station that signed on the airwaves at sunup and signed off at midnight. I took up residence on the second floor of the Clinton YMCA, just across the street from the studio. For $8.50 a week, I got a tiny room, a single cot, and a mini-refrigerator. In there I kept cans of Spam, jars of peanut butter and jelly, and Ritz crackers. From June to the end of August I kept myself fed on sandwiches and little else. Given my cramped quarters and the small table I sat at, and the even smaller chair I sat on, I felt a bit like one of the giants that Lemuel Gulliver encountered in Brobdingnag.

I wasn't full of myself, but my chest definitely expanded a bit. I was working full-time. I was away from home. I was no longer living in a dormitory, where most of my needs were taken care of by others. I was working in radio. Sure, I played a minor role in a minor-minor market, but I was learning about station operations and engineering and getting a few minutes of airtime as well as doing station identifications and the like. You would have thought that my stroll across the street to the F. W. Woolworth building and my climb up to the second floor of that structure was the same as me crossing Fifth Avenue in Manhattan to get to Rockefeller Center. This was the excitement I'd been looking for. I worked the four-to-midnight shift, and as I left the studio each night, the quiet, darkened streets of downtown Clinton smelled of promise.

I knew that my time at KROS would end in August, so I kept applying for other radio jobs in and around the Quad Cities. Even though I was going to start seminary for the fall term, I still wanted, and needed, to work. With five small cities, each with its own radio stations, my chances seemed good. Just before Labor Day, the station manager at WOC in Davenport, Iowa, a man named Bob Gifford, called to invite me down for a lunch interview. Over soup and sandwiches Bob told me he wanted to hire me to work the nine-to-midnight shift as a disc jockey. Without thinking much, and not negotiating terms at all, I accepted. I don't recall my exact wages but they weren't much, probably no more than fifty dollars a week. That wasn't nearly enough to put a dent in my expenses. In order to make up for any shortfall, I got a second job, working in the kitchen at the theological school. I'd get home from DJing music to make out by, grab a few hours of sleep, get up before sunup to get to the cafeteria's kitchen, and then hustle off to my eight o'clock class in classical Greek.

By mid-September 1962, one thing had emerged from the fog of my sleep deprivation and the steam rising from the industrial sinks: I didn't have the calling that it took to complete theology school. The siren song of disc jockeying was an alluring one, but my decision to leave seminary was based on an honest realization that I really didn't feel a true call to be of service in the way my father had. The discussion with my parents about my decision was, all things considered, easy. My father understood that I couldn't lead a congregation if I had doubts about my ability or my faith. I knew that it hurt him to know the latter. He was unshakable in his beliefs and I wasn't. He faced that with other congregants and he never took anyone's crisis in faith as a sign of any failing on his part. He took his role seriously but knew that matters of faith and fidelity to that faith were personal choices. He could lead but he couldn't coerce.

For my part, I felt as if I was letting him down, but I wasn't racked with guilt, mostly because of how he handled my revelation. I'm firmly convinced that even if my life hadn't turned out the way it did, my father would have still supported me and my choice. He was that wonderful, and that wise, a man. I had made a commitment to attend seminary for a year and I honored that, keeping both of my jobs as well.

As I pulled out of Rock Island in the spring of 1963, I left one other thing behind besides a potential career—my "La."

Let me explain.

The evening before I went on air at WOC in Davenport, Bob Gifford and I had a brief meeting.

"LaVerne." He looked as if he'd just bitten into something disagreeable.

He went on, "Take a seat."

I did.

"LaVerne," he said again, drawing my name out. A look that was half smile, half grimace spread across his face. He shook his head slowly.

I feared the worst.

"I just don't see it. I don't hear it."

He looked me square in the eye and said, "I can't put you on the air."

My heart fell and my mind raced.

An eternity lapsed.

" 'LaVerne' just won't cut it. You go on tonight as Verne. You understand?"

I nodded and left the room breathing easy for the first time in minutes.

I've been Verne ever since.

I suppose I've put this off long enough. As much as I wondered why I was burdened with such a mouthful of a moniker as Merton LaVerne, I felt doubly burdened by the fact that my parents named my siblings David, Dan, Tom, and Sharon. I've consciously not referenced them by their names before waiting for this moment when my name was the equal of theirs. While I'm at it, I also recognized that I should (and do) count my blessings.

Despite my name change, my mother continued to call me La-Verne for the rest of her life. Both my parents loved the name and I loved them for understanding what I'd done and for keeping true to what they felt. Best of both worlds.

ON MY RETURN TO AUSTIN, I moved back in with the family. I didn't feel great about that but necessity won out. Even before I left Rock Island, I'd started searching for job opportunities. I wrote to the program director at KTBC in Austin and asked for a summer job. I was hired as an FM disc jockey as a replacement for regulars out on vacation. I wasn't earning enough to afford a place of my own. Toward the end of that summer, the veteran sports director for the TV station, Dan Love, decided to move on. I saw my opportunity and decided to toss my hat in the ring. I loved sports, and though I hadn't covered it in any of my previous radio jobs, I thought I could manage it. With nothing to lose, I went to the office of the station's program director, Cactus Pryor, and offered up my services. Cactus looked me over and said, "We hired you for the summer. Aren't you going back to school?"

Once I cleared that matter up he said he was willing to see what I could do. I was given two hours to prepare a three-minute sports segment. I would then have to perform that live in front of Cactus and the station's president J. C. Kellam. I went after that task like my life depended on it. At the appointed time, I sat in the studio with those two men in a viewing room one floor above and delivered the best rendition of the copy I'd written to a single camera. I imagined them as they sat there stone-faced. I nodded and thanked them for the opportunity and went back to doing my regular job, which that day meant running the board for other on-air talent.

Toward the end of my shift, I got word that Cactus wanted to speak with me. He told me that I'd done well—real well consider-ing it was a first effort. Not quite good enough, though. They had another guy in mind and wound up hiring him to do the weekly TV broadcasts. Cactus offered me the weekend shift. I took it. Gladly. Between that and them retaining me to continue to do a five-to-nine shift as a disc jockey, I was going to earn a living wage.

Barely.

Come March 1964, I was hired to do the sports director job full-time. The other fellow hadn't worked out. I was going to earn a living wage.

Barely.

That's how, at the age of twenty-three, I was at the station on the afternoon of November 22, 1963. I was working the control board at KTBC-AM-FM-TV in Austin, the radio-television station owned by Vice President Lyndon Johnson and his wife, Lady Bird. The station was officially in Mrs. Johnson's name, but the vice president had a big impact there and was pretty hands-on, from what I remember.

I had a number of roles at the station: I was the weekend sportscaster on television, and management also had me working as a disc jockey ("Catch *The Verne Lundquist Show* from five to nine P.M.!"). I also occasionally ran the radio board. On that particular afternoon I was running the control board for our radio news block, making sure the sound levels were adjusted accordingly and the microphones were on. I remember we were airing the agricultural report, which was on tape, when I got a phone call from my boss's daughter, Nita Louise Kellam, who was also a high school classmate of mine. She was calling to tell me that her father had given me the night off and that they were going to let somebody take my place as the DJ that night so I could be her escort to go hear President Kennedy speak. We weren't dating; it was simply a chance to go hear President Kennedy speak. As I was on the phone with Nita Louise talking about our plans that night, Hal Nelson, who was one of our newsmen, came barging into the control room. It was shortly after 12:30 P.M.

"Put me on the air immediately—the president has been shot!" shouted Hal.

I did as I was told. I was twenty-three years old.

The rest of the day became one of the most memorable events of my life. The station was located in a five-story building in Austin at Tenth Street and Brazos Street, and within thirty minutes, we had Secret Service agents combing the building. I saw them at every elevator door on every floor, because at the time, no one knew if this was some sort of coup. In the newsroom, on the second floor of the building, we switched to CBS News. I was watching Walter Cronkite when he took his glasses off with a tear in his eye and announced, at 1:38 P.M. Central Time, that the president had been declared dead.

We were all pressed into service that day in some way, and here I was, just a disc jockey and a weekend sports anchor. But I went back into the newsroom and said, "Is there any way I can help?" KTBC was a CBS affiliate, and CBS Television was flying in a secondary White House crew that had not been traveling with President Kennedy in Dallas. The correspondent they sent was a man named David Schoumacher, who had a photographer and an audio guy with him. I was assigned as their driver that night. The four of us got into the car and we drove to Johnson City.

I remember we didn't leave Austin till 7:30 P.M. or so. The drive to Johnson City was about sixty miles. What they were searching for was backup material, because who knew how long Cronkite would be on the air? We got to Johnson City around 9 P.M. and all of us were obviously in a state of shock. Schoumacher and his group had a list of contacts they wanted to find. There were people who were high school classmates of Vice President Johnson that we contacted, but the one I really remember was A. W. Moursund, who served two terms in the Texas legislature and was a member of Johnson's inner circle. We were in his home for an hour. People were in mourning, but Schoumacher and his staff were very gracious and accommodating. We were welcomed by strangers and there would be coffee or iced tea waiting for us. It took time to set up the camera gear and sometimes it felt like an eternity. Then Schoumacher sat down across from LBJ's people and interviewed them. I listened very carefully to how he went about asking the questions and how the conversations would evolve. The questions were intended to elicit some sense of the character of LBJ, what he had been like when he lived in Johnson City, and these were people who had grown up with him. The purpose of the trip was to flesh out who this guy was and to do so through the words of people who knew him well. Back then, we did not know our vice presidents the way we do today. Keep in mind these were primitive days of television: there were no satellites, no color television. We spent the night traveling from home to home, and David would interview anybody and everybody who could tell him anecdotes or background stories on the man who was suddenly the president of the United States.

Here I was at the time, a twenty-three-year-old sports anchor and part-time disc jockey. To say that I did on-the-ground reporting would overstate my role. I was a chauffeur—and willing to do it. We drove back to Austin around 4 A.M. and I took the CBS newsmen back to their hotel, which was within a block of our TV station.

It was my first foray into a broadcast with national reach.

THE REST, AS THEY SAY, took forever.

Not quite forever, but at times it sure felt as if I would never move up in the world of broadcasting.

I enjoyed being around Cactus. He was a regional legend as a comic. I got a chance to go to one of the corporate gigs he did to perform at a national sales meeting. Before the main dinner, they held a cocktail reception hour. Cactus attended that in the guise of a Danish diplomat—he was a wonderful mimic and his accent could have fooled anyone. He circulated among the attendees and gathered a few facts about those people. Later, as the entertainment for the evening, he got up and spoke. Not dropping his faux persona, he told jokes and worked in facts about those he'd "interviewed" earlier. I laughed along with the rest of them. I've done my fair share of personal appearances since then, and I love to regale an audience, but my shtick pales in comparison to Cactus's.

I liked being in Austin but it was a small market. I enjoyed getting to know the coaches of the various UT teams and spending time at that beautiful campus, going out into the field to shoot my own film, covering high school football in all its Texas Friday night lights glory. To this day, I'm still amazed by the size of those crowds and the quality of the stadiums. While in high school, I was invited by Lou Maysel, the sports editor at the *Austin American-Statesman,* to assist him at the sports desk on those Friday nights. I manned a phone and took calls from coaches or someone else affiliated with the high school football team. They'd let me know the scores and I'd write up a brief summary of the Hutto Hippos beating the Taylor Ducks 17–14 in a real barnburner decided by a last-minute field goal that squeezed just inside the right upright. That experience helped hone my writing skills and fired my imagination.

But my main beat was the UT men's teams. Darrell Royal was the football coach then, and I would immediately idolize the man. At first I wasn't allowed much access to him. He did a Thursday night show for us during the season, but Cactus handled that on-air assignment. Instead I was on baseball. One of the first baseball interviews I did was with head coach Bibb Falk. Maybe Bibb should have worn a bib. He was a tobacco-chomping, expectorating machine. He looked and spoke as if he hadn't woken up on the wrong side of the bed, but with the bed on top of him and with a large man jumping on it. I was still a young pup, and I decided to offer up an easy question to lubricate the process.

"Coach Falk, what do you think of your team's prospects for this year?"

Bibb Falk didn't bat an eye. He shifted his chaw from one cheek to another. Looking out from the dugout to some distant point beyond the outfield fence he said, "I'll tell you one thing, you can't make chicken salad out of chicken shit."

That didn't make it on-air.

I was undeterred by that early stumble and kept my nose to the grindstone. I had a long-term relationship with UT that I cherished then and now. It went all the way back to when I was in seventh and eighth grade. I spent home football game Saturdays walking up and down the steep steps of Memorial Stadium lugging a tray of sodas while working concessions. I'll always associate Longhorn football and the fervid nature of its fans with the sensation of a crowd's roar working its way up from my sneakered feet to my spine. Those lovely afternoons were workdays, but they felt more like play days for me, adventures. I'd cast a glance at the field now and then, and the green grass against that backdrop of mostly white shirts was stark and beautiful. The 1952 season, the Longhorns came out of the gate strong, but after going 2-0, back-to-back losses to Notre Dame and Oklahoma made things look bleak as the team dropped out of the national rankings entirely. That Notre Dame game was the first college football game I saw in person. The 14–3 loss to the Fighting Irish reduced the raucous throng to a silent procession filing out of the stadium. Fortunately the 49–20 shellacking they suffered the following week against hated Oklahoma took place in Dallas and so I wasn't there to witness it. Fans always took losses hard, and I remember someone at school muttering that week that the bronze statue of Democracy atop the north end of the stadium had leaked a few tears. Can't say I blamed her. The team recovered, winning its next seven, including a shutout of Tennessee in the Cotton Bowl. They wound up ranked tenth in the nation. Good but not great.

By the time I came on board at KTBC in the summer of 1963, UT football fans were about to celebrate a national championship—

their first. That 1963 team went undefeated and capped the season with a titanic matchup of number one (Texas) versus number two (Navy) in the Cotton Bowl. I have to admit that the sentimental side of me wouldn't let me have ill feelings toward Navy. After all, the Cotton Bowl in Dallas that year was held a few weeks after President Kennedy, a naval veteran himself, had been shot in that same city. The games go on, as they should, but at least in my mind, some of the joy of the 28–6 victory over Roger Staubach and the rest of the Midshipmen diminished a touch.

Later on, Roger and I would have a long association; eventually the two of us talked about that game. I'd watched it on TV with the great Lindsey Nelson doing the play-by-play. I can't remember the name of the fellow who did the pregame show, but he had both coaches on before kickoff. Navy's Wayne Hardin got the first question and he rambled on and on, clearly relishing having a national TV audience. The poor interviewer kept looking into the camera and back at Coach Hardin. Darrell Royal was in the shot also, and he stood there politely, though his arms-folded posture suggested he wanted no part of the deal. When he was asked for his comment, instead of addressing his remarks to the man with the microphone, he faced the camera head-on and said, "We're ready!" He trotted out of shot and I truly appreciated his brevity.

Roger Staubach wasn't crushed by that defeat and the loss of a possible national championship. He felt that Texas was the better team and deserved its victory. He was more disappointed by an earlier loss that season to SMU. He felt the Midshipmen had underperformed against an inferior opponent. He could accept losing, but a loss resulting from underpreparedness was unacceptable. I'm sure that many players who haven't attended a military academy feel the same way. Knowing Roger, and seeing how he prepared and performed later on, I think that there is a special flavor of work ethic that military guys cook up. They seem a breed apart, imbued with an ethical sense of duty that I can relate to.

Darrell Royal was cut from the same cloth. As much as I admired him instantly, he gave me a reason *not* to very early in my career at KTBC. One evening, three of his players went to the Villa Capri hotel in Austin. That hotel, now closed, looms large in UT football lore. It was the site of a weekly postgame gathering for the media, fans, and staff. Somehow these three guys got it into their drunken minds that it would be fun to go to the Villa Capri and run along the hallway knocking on doors well into the night. One poor hotel guest opened up his door and got smashed in the face with a punch or punches and was fairly seriously injured. The players were arrested and charged with assault. The story was headline news.

The day after the incident, I was instructed to run the story at the top of the broadcast. I did what I was told to do. After that six o'clock show, I went home. I was living with my family then. The phone rang and my mother picked it up and told me the call was for me. I got on the line and a woman asked me if I was Verne Lundquist. I replied affirmatively.

"Hold on, please. Coach would like to speak with you."

What followed was Darrell Royal engaging in a five-minute harangue in which my suitability as a journalist was questioned. I also came under attack for undermining the coach's program, sullying its reputation, and rumormongering. I may have even been accused of anti-American activities and communist leanings. I was still very much a young pup in the business but I wasn't going to back down, especially after Coach Royal said that the story wasn't newsworthy. I told him that I disagreed strongly. I did. That kind of assault may not have led the news if it were Joe Schmoe who'd done the attacking, but these were three UT Longhorns. If you were in a prominent position in that town, you were going to get treated a bit different from so-called nobodies. That's just how it was. If you wanted the fame and the glory and the notoriety, you had to accept some of the downside of that.

A slammed phone was the only reply I received.

Fast-forward to the off-season, following that Cotton Bowl victory. The three alleged assaulters had a pretrial hearing of some sort. We dutifully reported on that. The show ended; I went back home. The phone rang. Mother answered. I got on the line when informed that the call was for me. The same woman's voice that I vaguely recognized from before. Coach Royal spoke, his tone even. He told me that he'd been wrong the first time we'd spoken. He owed me an apology and he made good on that debt. I don't think it was winning the national championship that softened him. He was a good man at heart and it was inevitable that his sensible and caring nature would even poke its head up through the cracked earth of a stressful incident and season. I thanked him and in later years developed a nice friendship with him. In fact, he would eventually become one of the dozens and dozens of broadcast partners I'd have.

The Longhorns entered the 1964 season ranked number four in the nation. Ole Miss earned the top honors but by week one they'd dropped out of the polls and Texas had climbed to number one. Then came a heartbreaking 14–13 loss in a rivalry game that had national championship repercussions. Those border war games are always intriguing. Though Texas dominated the series between the two, the interstate rivalry gives it an added dimension. Arkansas was the only team outside of the state of Texas in the Southwest Conference. They used that outsider status to their advantage as a motivational tool. Texas was uppity. Arkansas got no respect.

The 1964 game was a classic. Led by head coach Frank Broyles, the Razorbacks beat the Longhorns in Austin. Arkansas fans remember Ken Hatfield's long punt returns. I was in the press box for them, and like a lot of Texas fans, I remember a two-point conversion failure that was the difference in the 14–13 game. Many say that victory was the turning point in Arkansas's football program. I don't know about that, but it still boggles my mind that following that epic win, Arkansas did not allow another *point* the remainder of the season—five straight shutouts! Under their brilliant coach, Frank Broyles, Arkansas finished the regular season undefeated. So did Alabama, thanks to the exploits of its quarterback Joe Namath. Texas rebounded from that loss to the Razorbacks and faced Alabama in the Orange Bowl. Most fans remember that game because of Tommy Nobis's stop of a Joe Namath fourth-and-inches run near the goal line with the team holding on to a 21–17 lead. Some Texas fans say, and I agree, that that tackle was the greatest in the history of the Texas program. Others will debate that, and that's part of the fun of being a fan. I also know this: sports fans love to have these kinds of arguments and make these kinds of proclamations. They also love trivia. Can you guess two prominent figures in Dallas Cowboys history who were on that Arkansas squad? Future owner Jerry Jones and future coach Jimmy Johnson.

That being the case, the 1964 season was a veritable feeding frenzy. With its loss, Alabama was no longer undefeated. Arkansas went on to win the Cotton Bowl 10–7 over Nebraska to stay undefeated. The final polls were a jumble. The Associated Press named Alabama number one based on its regular season results. The Football Writers Association of America, voting after the bowl games, gave their Grantland Rice Trophy to Arkansas. The National Football Foundation named a 9–1 Notre Dame team, which did not allow its teams to participate in bowl games from 1925 to 1968, its number one selection. Pick your poison, I suppose. For college football fans, this scenario will sound all too familiar and like too much fun.

For me, and for Texas Longhorn football, even better days were ahead, including back-to-back national championships and the kind of national notoriety every program longs for. Those were great times to be on the campus and covering those great teams.

Not even driving to work that awful day in 1966 and hearing gunshots ring out as Charles Whitman fired from atop the Main Building tower on campus could diminish my appreciation for what the UT offered.

But I had my ambitions beyond Austin. Some of my desire to move on to a bigger stage had to do with an experience I had in the summer of 1964. This was shortly before I got the full-time sports director job. Three former college roommates and I planned a road trip out east. J. C. Kellam, the general manager of the station, was okay with the trip. He even offered to make some calls to set us up for a few fun stops. I was earning enough money to afford a flashy white Chevrolet convertible with a red leather interior. We headed out of Austin with a plan to make a large loop taking us as far north as Niagara Falls.

One of our early stops, on June 21, 1964, was in Meridian, Mississippi. That same night, three young men who were helping the cause of civil rights and who had traveled south during what became known as the Freedom Summer were abducted. They were kidnapped and murdered after leaving Meridian to speak to congregants in nearby Longdale whose church had been burned. Three days after we pulled out of Meridian, the bodies were discovered in an earthen dam in Philadelphia, Mississippi. When we heard radio reports of their murders we grew somber. Still, we recognized how fortunate we were to have the opportunity we did, to enjoy the kind of freedom denied to so many others.

Because LBJ and Lady Bird Johnson owned the station, we were told we'd be given a private tour of the White House. LBJ's press secretary, a former UT student and KTBC radio guy, Bill Moyers, met us outside the West Wing to apologize. Neither the president nor he was going to be able to spend any real time with us. Instead, he turned us over to LBJ's trusted aide, Walter Jenkins. That same day, we toured FBI headquarters. J. Edgar Hoover still reigned over the office, but his number two man, Cartha Libby, led us around the facility. The real highlight of all of this was a complete surprise. I was given a number to call at CBS in New York City. I found a pay phone and dialed the number. At first I thought that the traffic noise and the general hubbub that is the streets of Manhattan were playing tricks with me. The female voice on the end of the line said, "Walter Cronkite's office, how may I help you?"

Well, you can start by picking my jaw up from the sidewalk.

Once I identified myself, she told me that he was expecting my call. A moment later that familiar voice nestled in my ear.

A few hours later, we all stood and watched as he strode out of his office, got his makeup done, and then sat behind his desk. An enormous black-and-white camera was wheeled out in front of him. We watched as he intoned, "And good evening, I'm Walter Cronkite."

The lead that evening was the story out of Meridian, Mississippi.

That trip pushed me once again to set my sights to bigger horizons. Hoping to make a real name for myself, I twice auditioned for a job at WFAA in Dallas, the ABC affiliate there. Both times I didn't get it. I was pleased that for the first time in my career, in 1966, someone came calling to offer me a job. WOAI, the NBC affiliate in San Antonio was looking for a newsman, someone to anchor the six and ten shows. I would also have to cohost an afternoon show called, somewhat oddly, *The Early Evening Report*. I looked forward to the challenge of making the transition from sports to hard news. It was also better money. Each year I'd been at KTBC I'd gotten $25 per month raises, but I knew that wasn't enough. I wasn't a great negotiator and had no agent, so I accepted what I was given. But at age twenty-six I had a kind of tunnel vision, imagining a parade of $25 a month raises until I was in my fifties.

In 1966, when I walked in to my boss's office to let him know that I was leaving for San Antonio, he nodded and asked me, "What are they paying you?"

"Seven hundred and fifty a month."

He pursed his lips and said blandly, "You're making the right move. No future in this business for a four-eyed sportscaster."

Yikes. That was my going-away party.

The highlight of my time in San Antonio, in retrospect, was interviewing a Texas state congressman by the name of George Herbert Walker Bush. The lowlights? Well, almost all the rest of it. WOAI was my first real exposure to the "if it bleeds it leads" style of reporting. Many evenings and nights we led with a story of a horrific car crash, complete with images from the scene. I didn't have the heart for it. Instead of images of higher ratings and burgeoning advertising dollars, my mind filled with visions of the broken bodies of the victims, their shattered families, hospital rooms, and tearful scenes at funeral parlors. Anyone who knows me well will tell you that I can get sentimental on occasion. That's true. Tears will well up in my eyes at the first sign of emotion. That was the case to a lesser extent when I was a younger man, but I've always had that vulnerability. I recognized even then that I ran the risk of hardening my heart. If that was the price of doing hard news instead of sports in order to advance my career, well, then that was a price I wasn't willing to pay.

Sure, I wanted to tell stories, but I always hoped that they would uplift people, not make them fearful or sad.

After a while, I thought if we led with one more car crash and horrific images from the scene, I was going to have to get out of there. And I did, eleven months into a twelve-month contract. I had learned a lot at WOAI about video production and writing and delivery. I was grateful for the opportunity to learn what I didn't want to do as well. I suppose that it was a case of being careful what you wish for but I also learned that you had to be true to yourself and who you are. That's been one of the guiding principles of my professional career. If you tried to fake it; if you tried to create a false image of who you weren't, then you were doomed to eventual failure if not as a television personality but certainly then as a person. I didn't know it then but later on I began to see that my ethos would serve me well at times and hold me back at others.

I was going to have to learn to be okay with that.

CHAPTER THREE

Cowboy Days

If you ask me, the old saw about the third time being the charm is true. I've been happily married to my third wife, Nancy, since 1982. The previous two marriages were far more brief and only checkered with good moments. Life with Nancy has been as wonderful as could be. I don't know about the expression "my better half," but the two of us form a whole that is pretty damn near unbeatably reliable and pleasurable. I had to pursue her pretty diligently, but I persevered, as you will eventually see.

Similarly, in 1966, the third time I applied to WFAA in Dallas, I punched my ticket to what I then defined as the big dance. Dave Lane, who'd beaten me out for the job six months earlier, had a change of mind and life circumstance. He and his wife, Jeannie, were expecting their first child. He wanted to move into sales with hopes of next stepping into management. He let me know about the opening and I got an audition after contacting the station's GM, Mike Shapiro. I drove to Dallas and stayed with a friend.

At the time, WFAA had a poor man's version of Dick Clark's *American Bandstand* that they broadcast every afternoon. They had a studio set up at one of the first shopping malls in the country, a place called North Park. The studio was nearly entirely glass-walled so that shoppers could watch the kids dancing to the latest rock-and-roll tunes. That was where they taped my audition. While I waited for the crew to finish their setup, I took in the scene. I felt a bit like a Scandinavian goldfish in a bowl. I tried my best to ignore the younger women strolling by in their Summer of Love miniskirts. Disapproving matronly types clicked past in high heels, noses high while flying the flag of Jackie Kennedy. Moms with kids in tow sailed by like dazzling camouflaged ships, tentatively toeing the psychedelic waters in bold splashes of paisley and other bold prints. I was in my broadcaster's uniform—a solid navy blazer, white shirt, and striped tie. Despite what J. C. Kellam had said about four eyes, I edged my wire-rimmed glasses back into place and began, "Good afternoon. I'm Verne Lundquist."

After we wrapped, I headed to the downtown office and studio to await my fate. I sat there anxious and fretting. I eyed the Lincoln Continentals and Cadillac Coup de Villes parked out in front of the building, gave in to driving daydreams. Finally, after an hour, I got summoned to Mike Shapiro's office. I sat down and Mike told me that they were offering me the job. I felt my cheeks give me a standing ovation as I raised my glasses in toast. A moment later, reality spilled across Mike's desk.

"You'll make one hundred fifty a week," he said.

He went on as I did some quick math. That was $150 a month less than what I'd been making in San Antonio. Visions of a Cadillac transformed into an Impala.

"And you'll also do a Sunday night sports show. We'll pay you another fifteen bucks per show for that."

I desperately wanted that job. But a pay cut? I thought that going from San Antonio to what was then the tenth-largest market in the country was going to mean hitting pay dirt. For the first time, I really thought about just what that expression meant and wondered why we said that some people were dirt poor.

Instinctively, I knew not to take on the larger subject of the weekly pay stub—that expression made sense in this case since I felt like I was being shorted. Instead, I tried to be logical, "Mr. Shapiro, typically when someone does extra work they receive time-and-a-half pay, not half time."

He eased back in his chair and smiled affably. "It's fifteen minutes. No big deal."

He had to know that fifteen minutes of airtime didn't translate into fifteen minutes of work. I'd have to be there all day doing preparation work.

Third time was the charm, all right, but I was under the spell of ambition. Dallas was better than San Antonio. Sports reporting was better than anchoring the news. I accepted the terms. I was pretty much in a take-it-or-leave-it position. Uncomfortable as that was, I'd finally gotten what I'd been striving for. Count your blessings, I told myself.

I walked out of the lobby and into the bright daylight. Both of the luxury cars were gone. I climbed into my Ford and drove home.

Rather quickly, the third time did turn out to be charming, thanks to a kind of fairy-tale godfather of a team who granted me a wish that I didn't even realize I had.

The very first week I was there, I got a call from Al Ward. He was then the number two guy behind Tex Schramm, the Cowboys' first general manager and president. (Ironically, Tex wasn't a Texan originally; he was born in California.) Having covered the Cowboys while working in Austin and in San Antonio, I was familiar with names of the major figures in the organization's management. In 1967, the team had been in existence for only eight years. They'd had some great success the previous year, advancing all the way to the NFL championship game. It was also nearly impossible to live in Texas and not be aware of the presence of the team's owner, Clint Murchison, Jr. He and his brother John had inherited an enormous oil-based fortune from their father, Clint Murchison, Sr.

The NFL approved of the franchise in Dallas to offset the influence of the American Football League's team in that city. Another oil baron, Lamar Hunt, the son of the oil tycoon H. L. Hunt, had established that league and was the owner of the AFL's Dallas Texans. Lamar Hunt founded the rival league because the NFL had rejected Hunt's overtures to put a team in Dallas. Clearly, we're talking about some big boys with big egos and even bigger stockpiles of cash that allowed them to play with big toys. To his credit though, I must say, Clint Murchison was the kind of owner every management team dreams of having. He did his homework, hired the right people, and then let them do their job with an absolute minimum of interference. Also, Lamar Hunt deservedly made the Pro Football Hall of Fame and I got to know him and work for him later on, when he helped professional soccer get a toehold on American soil. The man was a pioneer.

Al told me that the Cowboys normally didn't do this, but I was new to town and would be covering the team as part of my duties at WFAA. Would I like to join the team on its charter flight to Washington, D.C., for the game at what was then District of Columbia Stadium? (It was more famous in later years as RFK Stadium.)

Charter flight?

Me?

I eagerly accepted. I thought that nothing else in my life would ever top this experience. I sat up front on a Braniff jet with the rest of the team's management and guests while the players kept to the back of the plane. I'd been around athletes most of my life, so I can't say that I was in awe of them. But I sure appreciated the chance to see the game from the press box. As I would later come to know, my inclusion was part of Tex Schramm's handling of the media. I know that "handling" might have some negative connotations, but I don't intend any. Tex treated the media well, one way he and the rest of the organization grew a well-deserved reputation for being first-class. In these more cynical times, it's easy to think that if the Cowboys treated journalists and broadcasters well, those individuals would be less likely to be critical of the team.

I know it's hard to believe, and I don't think I'm being too Uncle Verne–ish here, but that wasn't the case at all. I never felt coerced or even influenced in any way to report on stories in a way that was favorable to the Cowboys. I also don't think that any one of my colleagues would sacrifice their journalistic integrity at the altar of pre- or postgame spread. I'll grant this: At first I was covering them as sportscaster on the afternoon and evening news. I eventually became a part of their radio team. I even covered them later on during my NFL play-by-play days. I wasn't an analyst or a critic or a call-in host who wanted to stir things up to get ratings. But, as far as I saw, no one ever came down on a reporter or broadcaster for speaking his mind. Maybe I'm naïve, but it seemed like the Cowboys were just doing what they could as best business practices, a kind of hospitality and respect reflective of the values of the ownership and management. Simple as that.

Simpler times.

I did face a dilemma on that first trip. Halfway through the outbound flight, Al came up to me with a proposition. Cowboy games were on KLIF radio, the main rock-and-roll station in Dallas at that time. They were able to bring their play-by-play guy, Bill Mercer, and their analyst, Blackie Sherrod. They didn't "travel" a pregame or a postgame host. Would I be interested in doing that for the upcoming Redskins game?

I was on the horns of a dilemma. I was being treated to this trip. I was an employee of WFAA television. In the back of my mind I saw this as an opportunity but also as a way to thank my hosts and do them a favor. Contractually, I wasn't in a good spot. Working for a competitor without permission was a clear no-no. No gray area there at all. But what about a possible future with the Cowboys in some capacity? Besides, what was the likelihood that anyone from WFAA would hear me on the radio?

I did the show, enjoyed it, and then relaxed on the flight while sipping a few adult beverages. When I arrived at work the next day, I got called in to speak with the assistant general manager, a guy named Jack Houser. He said, "Could I possibly have been mistaken or did I hear you doing the after-game show on KLIF yesterday while I was driving home?"

My knees buckled a bit and my mouth went dry. Since my knees were already bent, I decided to assume the full kneeling position (metaphorically speaking) to apologize for not having gotten permission in advance. Apology grudgingly accepted. It turned out that my instincts to take the gig to possibly develop a relationship with the Cowboys was a good one. The team's management, who were responsible for hiring the radio people, wanted me to be the permanent guy for pregame, halftime, and postgame. It took a lot of wrangling with my TV employer, but we worked it out. All that time on my knees took its toll on me, but at least I was there in Green Bay on the last day of 1967 for the legendary Ice Bowl to keep the swelling down.

We flew up on the Cowboy charter to Green Bay on a Thursday for a Sunday game and got there late Thursday afternoon. I had arranged with the Green Bay public relations director, a guy named Chuck Lane, to do an interview with Coach Vince Lombardi on film on Friday afternoon. That same day, the Packers held a press conference, which Lombardi attended. It was only for the members of the Dallas traveling press. About six print guys—columnists and beat writers—were there. I was the only television guy and I had a cameraman with me. I was allowed to bring him because I was going to do the radio program—one of the concessions to WFAA in our deal.

Before Lombardi's press conference, we set up to film the one-on-one interview down on the field after the writers met with him.

I sat in on that first go-round with the print journalists. Lombardi wore his familiar brow-line glasses. Because we were indoors, he was bareheaded, his familiar felt fedora likely stowed away somewhere in his office. (His signature look is still available for purchase online—glasses, tie, hat.) Coach was warm and downright jovial with the press that morning. He smiled frequently and laughed, revealing his tobacco-stained gapped teeth. His voice revealed his Brooklyn roots. I can still imagine him saying one of his classic lines, "Winners never quit and quitters never win."

At the end of the press conference I went up to Chuck Lane to remind him of what we'd agreed to. He walked over to the coach and whispered in his ear. Lombardi's jowly face darkened, his knitted brow closing like a gate. He shook his great leonine head vigorously. This was part of his legendary temperament; a switch was thrown and glib turned to glum. I could hear him above the murmuring of the print guys.

"No. I'm not going to do it."

He walked out of the room. My heart fell.

It was a small conference room. He had been very jovial.

I went to Chuck Lane and said, "Listen, I promised my bosses at the TV station that if they let me go for the weekend I'd have Lombardi on film."

He said, "Give me ten minutes." He went into Lombardi's office and came back out and said he was to tell me that Lombardi didn't do television without a coat and tie. He didn't have a coat and tie with him that day. This was a different, pre-Belichek era, and coaches' sartorial splendor was a real thing. Tom Landry had his coat, tie, and hat look. Alabama's legendary Paul "Bear" Bryant had his take on that same combination with a houndstooth hat to top it off. I wasn't sure if Lombardi's reason was legitimate and he was worried about his image or not. At the time, he was just becoming a bright star in the coaching universe. If he was that keenly aware of his public persona, I wanted to make him more comfortable and not show him up. I offered to take off my coat and tie. Chuck Lane laughed and asked me to wait five more minutes.

Sure enough, Lombardi came out and apologized for the inconvenience. We got in the elevator and went down to the field. It was below freezing but the temperature was expected to plunge by game time. We chatted for a bit about the team. His face lit up when we talked about the weather forecast. He explained about the new electric grid system the Packers had installed beneath the field's turf. The system had cost twenty-five thousand dollars, a princely sum at the time. It will never freeze, he told me, sounding like a proud owner of the first color TV set boasting about the vivid blues and greens and reds. I thanked him and shook his hand and off he went.

Off I went to the airport with our large canister of film. With no FedEx or UPS, it had to travel on a commercial flight back to Dallas to arrive the next morning, Saturday. The guys would "put it in the soup," as we called the processing and editing of it. They aired the interview on the ten o'clock news Saturday night, Lombardi telling me that the field would never freeze. The next morning, my wake-up call was "Good morning. It's seven thirty and thirteen below zero." That's when we knew what we were going to be in for. Well, not completely. I got out of the hotel and walked to the third of the coach buses the Cowboys provided. I sat next to Frank Luksa, a writer for the *Fort Worth Star-Telegram*. We were near to the front and every time that door hissed open a blast of arctic air chilled us. When we got to Lambeau Field and disembarked, Frank was ahead of me, clutching his portable typewriter to his chest. Next thing I knew, that case was flying in the air and Frank was on his back sliding down into a steep ditch. Fortunately, he wasn't hurt, but it took a kind of fireman's brigade to haul him back up the steep slope.

I'd done all of my pregame work at the hotel in the days preceding kickoff—player interviews at the hotel that sort of thing. As a result, I was able to watch the start of the game from the Cowboys' radio press box. Anyone who has seen old footage of the game will be familiar with the images I recall—puffs of cloud coming out of all the spectators' mouths like smoke signals. I had on an overcoat and gloves but the chill crept in through the slight opening in the glass—to allow in ambient sound to help color the broadcast. To keep warm, I walked around a bit. I wandered down to the CBS television booth. The industry was small at the time. Everyone knew everyone. I slipped into the booth and no one got upset at my being there. The great Jack Buck was the Cowboys' announcer and he worked with Frank Gifford as the color man. Ray Scott split calling the game as the play-by-play man—a common practice then—with Pat Summerall joining him as analyst. Gifford was still playing for the Giants at the time. (It is very rare today for a network to have active players in the booth, but in 2017 Fox had Carolina Panthers tight end Greg Olsen do it.)

I listened in. I was at the back of the booth, so I couldn't see much of what was going on. I looked to one side and saw the writers sitting beneath the TV guys, closest to the slightly opened window. Their papers flapped in the breeze and the clacking of their typewriters was like the sound of chattering teeth. Buck and Gifford did the first half, and I had to stifle a laugh as Frank reached for his Styrofoam coffee cup and found his beverage frozen. I was standing closest to the space heaters as they sent out line after line of warmish molecules to battle the frigid onslaught.

On the field, the action wasn't as limited as I had thought it might be. Lombardi's prediction hadn't come true, though. The warming grid hadn't been able to keep the field thawed. It had malfunctioned sometime overnight. The field was covered with a tarp, trapping some of the heat and the moisture it produced on the grass. Once the tarp was pulled off, the moisture froze. A lot of—pardon the Paul Simon reference—slip-sliding away went on. I learned later the game time temperature was minus fifteen degrees Fahrenheit. The wind chill made it feel like minus forty-eight. I felt bad for the players. Years later, I would work with former NFL quarterback Dan Fouts. He played in the 1981 AFC Championship Game in Cincinnati in what became known as the Freezer Bowl. His warm-weather San Diego Chargers team lost—both the game and the claim for the coldest air temperature for an NFL game. It was only minus seven, but a steady wind put the windchill in the minus fifties throughout the game. That was back at Riverfront Stadium on artificial turf and Dan said it was like playing in the parking lot.

It was a good thing I couldn't see much of the first few minutes of the game. Green Bay scored a pair of touchdowns on Bart Starr touchdown passes. Dallas's offense didn't make a first down in the entire second quarter but thanks to two Green Bay fumbles—one recovered and taken into the end zone and the other resulting in a chip-shot field goal—at halftime the score was 14–10. Longtime Cowboys fans will no doubt remember quarterback Don Meredith's third-quarter fumble inside the red zone that thwarted the only sustained drive to that point. Finally, Dan Reeves completed a 50-yard touchdown pass on a halfback option to Lance Rentzel. It was a thing of beauty, a great call from Tom Landry's sideline, and it had to warm the cockles of the hearts of those back in Dallas. If only they could have shipped some of that warmth via airline to Wisconsin.

I watched the end of the game back in the Cowboys' radio booth. Dallas was ahead 17–14, setting up what has gone down in NFL lore as the Drive and the Block. Never in my mind has an offensive lineman's role in a game garnered so much attention. Before that, though, the Packers had to move from their own 32-yard line. With the sun sinking lower and the wind picking up, the ice had also turned brutish and dangerous. The Drive began with Bart Starr completing what we called then a safety-valve pass to running back Donny Anderson. Then Vince Lombardi, sensing something maybe that none of us knew, inserted Chuck Mercein into the game. Mercein was out of Yale, and he was used sparingly during the regular season. Due to injuries to regulars, he was in the starting lineup that day. Somehow, maybe it was his fresh legs, maybe he was a hockey player in his youth, but he managed to do pretty well on that frozen field. Of the 68 yards that the Packers would travel to score the game-winning touchdown, Mercein accounted for 34 of them. That was nearly the total he had for the season to that point.

We always say that games are frequently won or lost due to some X factor—a little-known player stepping up, some other unforeseen or impossible-to-predict event or circumstance. We all liked to be surprised. Funny thing was, when the Packers got down inside the one-yard line with only sixteen seconds remaining and it being third down, Lombardi rolled the dice. Instead of kicking a field goal there, he decided to go for it. An incomplete pass would have stopped the clock, of course, and that's what Tom Landry later said he believed the Packers would do. He expected a rollout pass—get out of bounds, throw it away, or complete it.

As it turned out, Lombardi had another idea. Even though on the previous two attempts from the goal line his running back had gained neither traction nor yards, during a time-out he instructed Starr to call "Brown right, 31 Wedge." A handoff to Mercein with wedge blocking, a double team with Jerry Kramer and Ken Bowman taking on the great Cowboys defensive tackle Jethro Pugh. Well, Starr had a surprise for his teammates. Instead of handing off as the play called for, he ran a quarterback sneak and scored. Starr seldom, if ever, ran the ball. Later, in a postgame interview he'd say that he had told Lombardi he could make the run. Mercein claimed that he had no clue that Starr was going to keep it. The play called in the huddle was "Brown right, 31 wedge." He was the 3 in that 31—the fullback.

Much has been made of the block that Kramer put on Pugh. In my mind, it was the double team that really made the difference. In any case, Starr was in. Thirteen seconds remained. The Cowboys' Don Meredith threw two incompletions and the game was over. Later, in the locker room, I had the sense that I was in a small billeting area behind the trenches after a winter encounter at the Somme in World War I. I know the football-as-war analogy is tiresome, but in this case the glassy-eyed faces of the Cowboys—attributable to the loss, their tears, the extreme cold—the comparison seems apt. The blood had retreated from the surface of their skin and they all looked sallow at best—except for places where red splotches broke out like bruises. Three Cowboys—George Andrie, Willie Townes, and Dick Daniels—were frostbitten. Unfortunately for Andrie, that injury troubled him for the rest of his career.

Don Meredith was gracious and defiant in his postgame remarks—defending his teammates and the effort they put in. He didn't use the term "moral victory" but in his own unique fashion he conveyed that notion. In fact, Don's responses after the game to his friend Frank Gifford, at least according to Gifford, gave ABC producers a sense that he would be a great guy to have in the booth. Eventually they hired him for *Monday Night Football*. I know that I still retain memories of Bob Lilly churning his legs and flailing and failing on that frozen surface. It wasn't just the Cowboys who struggled with the footing, though. The eight sacks they had were a result of the Packers receivers not being able to get open and their linemen failing to hold their ground.

The other indelible memory I have of that game is the deathly quiet on the charter back to Dallas. Along with that, Tex Schramm hosted a New Year's Eve party at his home for the Cowboys' staff later that evening. A more somber "celebratory" affair I have not attended. "Auld Lange Syne" never seemed so dour.

In the end, the final note in my first year with the Cowboys organization was not a false one. I'd witnessed a part of what is now NFL history. Two legendary teams, two legendary coaches. Whenever I hear people talking about how they would like to have some moments in their life frozen in time, I smile wryly, appreciating the sentiment but also thinking, Be careful what you wish for.

Fortunately for me, eventually one of my wishes was granted and it turned out spectacularly well. Before I was hired to become the play-by-play voice of the Cowboys radio network in 1972, I played a couple other roles. I was the pre- and postgame host on KLIF and did the color analyst job for the 1970 and 1971 season. All the while I was still doing my TV sportscasting assignments as well. To show you how much things have changed in the NFL, during that 1970 season, when KLIF was the radio home of the Cowboys, they declined to do the radio for Super Bowl V. NFL rules prohibited them from using the full Cowboy network. They'd only be able to do the local broadcast and pay $5,000. I was already in Miami doing remotes and sending them back to Dallas to be played on TV. On the Wednesday before the game (I don't recall if we referred to that time leading up to the game as Super Bowl Week back then), Tex Schramm told me to expect a call from management at Dallas station KRLD. I was asked if I wanted to be the radio analyst for the broadcast. I was a bit confused, since KLIF had passed on doing the game. Eventually I learned that management at KLIF didn't want to pay the five-thousand-dollar rights fee. Can you imagine that today? Turning down the chance to get that many listeners at a relatively low price?

Anyway, just to show how improvisational my first coverage of the Super Bowl was, along with being hired three days before the game, my perch for that game was a platform quick-built on the roof of the Orange Bowl. KRLD got the rights so late that all the designated press spots had been filled. I didn't think much about it then, but now it all seems quaint and humbling—in a good way. Despite the Cowboys losing 16–13 to the Baltimore Colts, one of the real blessings of the weekend was that I got to work with Frank Glieber, who did the play-by-play. Frank doesn't get the credit he deserves as a truly wonderful and talented broadcaster. Maybe he's not recalled along with other giants of the profession, but I treasured my relationship with Frank. Maybe if he'd not died tragically young in 1985 at the age of fifty-one he'd have gotten more recognition than he did.

Frank was a product of Northwestern University and its fine school of communications. (Young people with an interest in broadcasting often ask me how they can advance their dream to become a sports broadcaster. I tell them that I had no formal training but that Northwestern, Syracuse, and the University of Missouri have produced a number of excellent sports journalists.) He migrated to the Dallas area, left briefly for Cleveland to work the Browns games, then back to Dallas as the sports director at KRLD. I'll spare you the details of Super Bowl V—well, not all of them. After so many years and so many games, they tend to blur a bit, but I do have a vivid memory of a helicopter flying over our aerie. Frank and I were up there along with our spotters. The wash from the rotor blades scattered my notes and I watched them drift down into the crowd.

Similarly, I watched the tiny figures of the Cowboys and Colts drift around the field. This was the first postmerger Super Bowl, the two competing leagues having agreed to combine. In a way, I missed the notion of the Super Bowl being a kind of Appalachian blood feud. The underdog, upstart, rebellious AFL versus the favored, established, conservative NFL always provided a nice entry point into storytelling. I don't know if I agree with the sentiment that had many people later refer to the game as "the Blunder Bowl." It's true the game was mistake filled. I don't know if this says a whole lot about the quality of play, but linebacker Chuck Howley of the Cowboys is the only Super Bowl MVP who was a member of the losing team. He was notable for making two interceptions. Colts 16, Cowboys 13. Maybe we should have known the game was going to be underwhelming. The Colts were led by Earl Morrall. He'd taken over for Johnny Unitas who was in the later stages of his illustrious career, and, a bit like Peyton Manning leading the Broncos to victory in 2016, he wasn't his best self that year. During the regular season, he threw more interceptions than touchdowns. His veteran leadership, his strengths as a field general, and the general sentiment that here was a guy who paid his dues and deserved one final hurrah made him a guy to root for. It was also an opportunity for him to redeem himself for the loss in historic Super Bowl III, when Joe Namath of the Jets famously predicted a victory in the face of long odds against them. Of course, with me being with the Cowboys, I wasn't pitching stories of that type.

For our part, the story line was that the Cowboys had to overcome a whole lot of trouble just to get to the final game, including injuries (running back Calvin Hill's season ender in particular), a quarterback controversy with Roger Staubach and Craig Morton both starting at various points, Bob "the World's Fastest Human" Hayes being benched for underwhelming play, and then wide receiver Lance Rentzel being arrested for indecent exposure deactivated late in the season. Though the nickname "Doomsday Defense" wasn't a result of all that, it might as well have been applied to the whole squad.

In particular, I never fully understood why Bob Hayes was in Landry's dog house that season. He was an amazing downfield threat. Hayes's story was compelling. A two-sport athlete (track and field and football) at Florida A&M, he had won Olympic Gold in Tokyo in 1964. He won the 100 meters in borrowed spikes and tied the world record while doing so. He won a second gold, anchoring the 4x100 relay. His come-from-behind effort in that race was thrilling, and his 8.8 time remains the fastest relay 100 ever run. Handheld and automated timing and rounding off times complicates this but the point is that Bob was *really* fast. Though he was considered to have "rough" football skills as a result of splitting his time between track and football, in his first two years in the NFL he led the league in receiving touchdowns. This was before the league's rules and offensive philosophies changed but his 12 and 13 would have put him at the top of the 2017 NFL charts.

For a variety of reasons Bob Hayes didn't mesh with Tom Landry. In 1978, after Bob retired, he came up to the radio booth to say hello and watch a part of the game from there. At one point, I caught him staring, not at the field of play, but at the recently installed ring of honor, first unveiled in 1975. When Bob scanned it, Bob Lilly, Don Meredith, Don Perkins, and Chuck Howley were the only honorees. He leaned near me and said wistfully, "I'd give anything if my name was included."

Super Bowl V truly was a tragedy of errors. On the Colts' second drive, Unitas threw a pass that linebacker Howley picked off. The Cowboys took over at the Colts' 46-yard line, but a holding call on third down—at this point in the NFL it was a spot-of-foul type penalty—resulted in a 25-yard loss. Fortunately, the Colts' Ron Gardin muffed the punt and the 'Boys recovered it on the six-yard line. They couldn't punch it in from there, typical of the day, and settled for a field goal. That sequence of blunders was typical of the afternoon.

Even the 75-yard touchdown pass that Unitas threw in the second quarter was tainted. He delivered the ball high and behind his intended receiver, Eddie Hinton. Mel Renfro of the Cowboys got his hand on it and deflected to Colts tight end John Mackey, who took it in for the score. Of course, the Cowboys blocked the extra-point attempt, keeping the score 6–6. Taking advantage of a Lee Roy Jordan quarterback sack and fumble, the Cowboys led 13–6. Unitas would take another brutal hit later on, injure his ribs, and not return to the game.

Two plays stick in my memory. In the fourth quarter, the Colts attempted a flea-flicker. Running back Sam Havrilak took the ball from

Earl Morrall. He ran right and turned to lateral the ball back to his quarterback. Jethro Pugh got between them. With the play busted, Havrilak looked downfield and tried to hit Mackey with a pass. Instead, the Colts' Hinton cut in front of him and took the pass. He sprinted toward the end zone, but the Cowboys' Cornell Green caught him from behind and stripped the ball at about the 11-yard line. From there, the pigskin became animated and ran around like a greased version of its former self, evading capture by both sides. How it stayed in bounds as it was kicked, slapped, and otherwise went unrecovered remains a mystery to this day. Eventually it got pushed out of the end zone, resulting in a touchback. The Cowboys took over at their own 20.

The other play was a heartbreaking officiating gaffe. Running back Duane Thomas was going in for a score from the one-yard line when the Colts' Mike Curtis, a legendarily fierce defender, punched the ball loose. The scramble for that loose ball prefigured that fourth-quarter melee. I always try to wait for things to come to an official conclusion before declaring possession. When Dallas's center, Dave Manders, emerged from the scrum holding the ball aloft, I called it as I saw it. Unfortunately, the officials saw it otherwise and line judge Jack Fette awarded the ball to the Colts. Ask any member of the 1970 Cowboys squad and they will tell you that that officiating error cost them the game.

There was more football to be played, and it really came down to a pair of Craig Morton interceptions in the fourth quarter. One led to a Colts touchdown knotting the score at 13–13, and the other to a famous Jim O'Brien field goal as the clock wound down to nine seconds. One lasting image I have of the game is Bob Lilly tossing his helmet in anger and frustration at the very end. His headgear traveled a perfect forty-yard parabola, probably the best-looking pass on a less-than-stellar day of football. Of course, no one caught it and it bounced on the turf before settling upside down and empty. That was how the whole organization felt.

The only consolation was the after-game party the team held at our hotel. Bedford Wynne was a minority owner of the club. He came through in a pinch when Clint Murchison realized at the last minute that he had not booked any kind of entertainment for the party. Wynne called in a favor. I showed up at the party at 11 P.M.— just as Willie Nelson began his first set. Before the affair shut down at five the next morning, Waylon Jennings and Jerry Jeff Walker had joined him.

So many of the names and personalities from that game were a big part of my time with the Cowboys. I became the team's play-by-play announcer in 1972 and stayed in that role until 1984. I was around these guys during one of the heyday periods in Cowboys history. Duane Thomas was a fascinating individual. A Dallas kid, he was an accomplished running back at Lincoln High, then went to start alongside the Miami Dolphins' Mercury Morris at West Texas State. That school might not bring up many memories for fans of NCAA football, but Thomas was good enough at fullback to become the Cowboys' number one draft pick in 1970. He was supremely gifted and performed well his rookie season. His career is probably most notable for what he didn't do than what he did do: for periods of time, he didn't speak.

His personal life was complicated. He went through a divorce; he had financial troubles and difficulties with the IRS; he believed that his efforts on the field weren't appreciated and he was underpaid. He also seemed to chafe under Tom Landry's style. He sometimes ignored teammates when they offered a hand to slap in congratulation for a great play. His approach, shutting out some teammates, and his lapses into silence earned him the nickname "the Sphinx." Rumors swirled around him and a few teammates—including Tony Dorsett, who eventually came on board in the backfield—have related odd interactions with him. I didn't witness those, but I did see Duane do some things possibly to alienate himself. On our charter flights, non-players sat in the front. The players sat in the rear—almost without exception seated in a window and an aisle seat with the middle seat vacant. Duane would board, settle into a middle seat, pull a knit cap over his eyes, and remain silent the entire trip.

In 1971, the Cowboys made it to the Super Bowl again. The game was against Miami, in New Orleans. Upset that the Cowboys had refused to renegotiate his contract, under financial pressure due to his life circumstances, Duane Thomas had gone silent for the entire season—not talking to the press and to the best of my knowledge not to any of the players. During pre–Super Bowl media day, he sat silently while the other Cowboys conducted interviews. (Before there was a Marshawn Lynch, there was Duane Thomas.) Thomas was under pressure to cooperate with the media. The Dallas PR guys got him to agree to speak after the game, but only if the Cowboys won.

However, before game day, Frank Luksa, who fell into the ditch in Green Bay, saw Duane siting on the seawall outside the Galt Ocean Hotel in Fort Lauderdale. He decided to approach him. As Frank related it, they were both seated there looking out over the Atlantic. Duane was staring intently, the waves lapping at the rocks. Frank asked him what he was looking at or for. Duane replied, "New Zealand."

Ever the journalist and interested in factual accuracy, Frank told Duane that he wasn't looking in the direction of New Zealand. He was looking east. A daring move given Duane's sullenness. Duane offered his own bit of logic.

"Maybe so, but it's out there somewhere."

The two continued speaking for a bit. At one point Duane asked, "If the Super Bowl is the ultimate game, why is it going to be played again next year?"

The man saw things his own way, and I've always loved that about him.

Given Duane's unique worldview, perhaps it wasn't surprising that he and Tom Landry didn't always see eye to eye; Duane even went so far as to call Tom a "Plastic Man" at a press conference in which he expressed displeasure with the Cowboys management. Tom had little room for idiosyncrasy on his team—right down to his own clothes. I've already mentioned Tom and his sartorial choices. Long past the time when most men were wearing hats, and when some coaches took to dressing less formally along the sidelines, Landry clung to his image. They represented the values that he professed. Landry was raised in faith, but it wasn't until his career took off and he felt less than fully satisfied by his success that his commitment to religious faith went deeper. More important in shaping him as a man and a coach was his experience in the military. Landry's brother Robert was killed in 1942 while piloting a U.S. Army Air Corps bomber. Tom enlisted after that, interrupting his engineering studies at UT, and eventually completed a combat tour of thirty missions.

Engineer.

Pilot.

Coach.

Defensive mastermind.

Even without that background information and armchair profiling, what I observed was this: Tom Landry was clearly a man who liked to be in control, who was meticulous in his preparation and had a laser focus for details and preparation. Those attributes served him well for a long time. Inevitably, as is the case with any coach or leader, there were those who bought in to the program and those who didn't. As much as Vince Lombardi could be jovial and inspirational and hard-nosed, Tom always struck me as a serious man. He was a great tactician, and the oft-repeated statement that Walt Garrison made likely says a lot more about his temperament than that. When asked if he'd ever seen Landry smile, Garrison said no, but he'd been there for only eight years. Don Meredith, when asked if Landry was a perfectionist, laughed a bit and said that if his coach married actress Raquel Welch, a "sex kitten" as she and other females were then "known" and labeled, he said that Landry would expect her to cook.

I can say this: Tom Landry did smile. In July 1969, during the preseason, the Cowboys rented a conference room at the Las Robles Country Club. Like most Americans, we were fixated on the upcoming moon landing. The press and other members of the organization gathered there after the workout. I was seated on a couch watching the coverage of the lunar module landing. Drinks and food were on offer as we waited for Neil Armstrong to take those historic first steps on the lunar surface. As I sat there, Landry walked in. He settled on the arm of the couch alongside me. When Armstrong stepped out and uttered those famous words, we broke into spontaneous applause. Tom joined us and I think that as a military man and a pilot he took special pride in the accomplishment. His grin was as wide as the brim of his fedora. Ironically, years later Tom and I also sat together during one of the country's lower moments. President Richard Nixon came on the television in August 1974 to announce his resignation. There was no applause. No smiling. Just a deep sadness at a moral failing we'd only just begun to understand. Tom's disappointment and disapproval were palpable.

As far as I could tell, Tom was impervious to criticism. That was true in the quarterback controversy when he shuffled Roger Staubach and Craig Morton in and out of the starting lineup. At one point, against the Bears in 1971, he had them in and out of the game on alternating *plays,* for gosh sakes! He was a results-oriented coach in a results-oriented league. How he managed personalities is subject to much speculation and interpretation. That aspect of coaching and how coaches were evaluated was evolving, but Tom Landry was never afraid to go his own way.

CHAPTER FOUR

California Dreaming, Dallas Realities

How many times in your life have you found yourself wondering about what might have been? I'm sure that those 1967 Cowboys did a bit of thinking about how the NFL championship game might have turned out if the playing conditions weren't so bad. I don't think that they knew about the malfunction of the heating elements under the turf. I know that we can drive ourselves crazy "what-if-ing" our way through life. I also know that sports fans engage in a special variety of "what-if-ing"—what if *(insert team or player name here)* had done _____ back in the _____, then they would have won. (Note the use of "they" in place of "we" in this losing situation.) Well, let me share a little what-if story that fills in some blanks about my career and how I very nearly missed out on having a Cowboy existence for more than a decade.

Right before the Cowboys' Super Bowl VI victory in New Orleans, I received a phone call from KNXT television in Los Angeles. They wanted to know if I was interested in coming out to the West Coast to become the sports director for that CBS affiliate. At the time, Los Angeles was the second-largest market in the United States. I told them, well, yes of course I would. This was shortly after the New Year, and by the time we finalized arrangements for me to go to Los Angeles to audition, I was in a bit of a scheduling jam. I was going to cover the game on radio for KRLD, and I was going to do my remotes for TV. The game was scheduled for January 16, 1972. My audition was the day before the Cowboys' charter flight would take the team and all other personnel to New Orleans. I was scheduled to return to Dallas in time to make that flight the following day. Obviously, any delays or cancellations and I'd be in a tough spot.

I decided it was worth the risk. The folks at KNXT did their best to woo me. They put me up at the Beverly Hills Hotel for two days. They took me to lunch at the Bel-Air Country Club, where I was sitting and eating my cheeseburger when I saw Jack Benny and George Burns dining together in the corner. I thought, Boy, this is something. Two of my early radio-days favorites sitting in the same restaurant as me. Boy, I could get used to this!

I did the audition and felt it went well. I figured I'd get the usual "we'll let you know" response, but to my surprise, before I left I had in hand a five-year contract at twice my WFAA salary. I agreed to accept those terms. Though I took the commercial jet back to Dallas, I barely needed it I was flying so high. I'd miss Dallas, and the opportunity to do the radio work for the Cowboys, but this was Los Angeles, the home of swimming pools and movie stars! Step aside, Uncle Jed; Uncle Verne is coming through!

It's funny the things you remember, but I recall touching down at Love Field and hustling from my arrival gate to B3, where the Cowboys' charter was loading. I made it just in time and settled into my seat. Once we were in the air, it hit me: this was going to be my last Cowboys game. I knew that I had to let them know. I found Tex Schramm seated a few rows in front of me. He'd been instrumental in my first working for the Cowboys five years earlier. Since then, I'd grown to appreciate his ways even more. I also knew that like certain gunslingers, he took verbal shots first and asked questions later. He spoke his mind and sometimes what was on his mind was not the most gracious sentiment in the world. Nonetheless, I had to let him know and I preferred to tell him face-to-face. After I'd let him know that I'd agreed to the Los Angeles deal, he pursed his lips and asked if I'd signed a contract. When I told him I hadn't, he asked me not to, or at least not until we got back to Dallas after the game. He wanted to have lunch with me; he had an idea, some plan, and he couldn't share that with me now.

A week or so after we got back to Dallas, Al Ward and Tex took me out to lunch and what turned out to be a four-hour business meeting. They offered me the Cowboys' play-by-play job. I was hesitant at first, mostly wondering what that meant for Bill Mercer, my partner in the booth. His lifelong dream had been to be a baseball play-by-play man. The Washington Senators had decided to relocate to Arlington, Texas, and, unbeknownst to me, Bill had accepted that radio job. They wanted to slide me over one seat and have me assume his responsibilities. From the time Tex asked me to wait before signing until this meeting, I'd only vaguely entertained the notion of sticking around. I'd verbally committed and considered myself a man of my word. Mostly out of respect for Tex and the rest of the Cowboys, I'd gone to lunch to hear them out. I told him as much.

Tex's middle name was Earnest and he embodied that word when he eyed me when he led me down the well-trod interview path by asking where I wanted to be in my career in ten years. I told him: network play-by-play announcer. He asked me what it was that KNXT had offered me. A six-and-eleven sportscast. Well, if any play-by-play jobs came up in LA, I'd be forty-seventh on the list of those considered for it. His blunt assessment of my chances of gaining traction in Los Angeles wasn't a ploy just to keep me in Dallas. His argument had some merit, especially when he backed it up with the following questions:

Have you heard of Chick Hearn?

Have you heard of Dick Enberg?

Have you heard of Vin Scully?

They've all got pretty good jobs and they're all pretty good at what they do? Where do you think you're going to fit in?

I don't recall humble pie and a reality chaser being on the menu, but Tex served them up and I gulped them down. The truth was, the Los Angeles market was populated by Hall of Fame–caliber play-by-play men, guys who were well on their way to becoming legends in the field. I trusted what Tex was saying because he was a football guy and knew what was going on around the league and the media that covered the game. He also was a UT guy, a journalism major, and he'd written for the *Austin American-Statesman* while at school. From 1947 to 1956 he'd worked for the Los Angeles Rams—he knew that market well.

Being with the Cowboys wasn't small potatoes, either. They had 119 stations along their radio network. The team was doing well and gaining exposure across the country. I'd never done play-by-play but Tex believed that I could do it. He had that kind of trust in me.

I asked about the compromise position. I go to Los Angeles and take the Cowboys' offer as well. Tex was smart. He wanted me in Dallas and on Channel 8 all week. He wanted me on his radio network on Sundays. He wanted me to be known as a Cowboy guy. In a sense, I was like free advertising for the team. I saw the wisdom of that approach for him and for me. I asked for four or five days to think about it. I faced a tough choice. I hate to make this about the money, but the fact was that I was earning $10,000 a year for my TV job. KNXT had offered me $35,000! Sense won out over dollars and cents. If I truly aspired to be a Big Three network play-by-play man, then I needed the Big Double-E—experience and exposure. I could get that in the Big D. I sent my regrets to Los Angeles and signed with the Cowboys. I never looked back. What if I hadn't listened to Tex's advice? I've had a few men in my life who I consider mentors and Tex is one of them. A more colorful guy I have not met.

Tex was passionate about the Cowboys, to put it mildly. He understood that he could occasionally pop off and say things an executive of a major sports franchise probably shouldn't say. Once, in the mid-1970s, Tex assumed his usual position in the second row of the writers' press box. Joe Bailey, executive vice president, or Doug Todd, head of the public relations staff, usually sat alongside him to keep the boss steady and his excitability level below overload. Tex had invited NFL commissioner Pete Rozelle to attend the game. Tex had hired Pete to work for the Rams back in the day and remained friends. Rozelle sat in Tex's suite, adjacent to the writers' box.

As the game went on, Tex believed the referees were blowing calls all over the field. He'd jump and shout and curse and turn red-faced. Doug was with him on this occasion and was doing his best to keep Tex from banging on the glass and whatnot. Tex's voice was booming and the writers were used to his antics, so no one paid him too much mind—that is, until at one point when the referees were huddling on the field discussing some call against the Cowboys. Tex was close to apoplectic. He jumped out of his seat and walked over to the soundproof glass partition separating the writers' box from his. The pounding got Rozelle's attention. Startled, he looked over at this loon of a man waving his arms and gesticulating wildly. Pete laughed. Tex wrapped his hands around his own throat in the universal choking gesture and Pete kept on laughing. That didn't quiet Tex for long. He stomped back to his seat and unleashed a tirade of trash talk that lasted until halftime.

Tex left the press box. While the writers sat there relaxing, Doug Todd commandeered the PA system that only went into the press boxes to announce in his most formally modulated voice, "According to General Manager Tex Schramm, the C———ers are leading the M————ers eight to seven."

I think I stopped my laughter and tears by the second-half kick-off. Barely.

No, sir, you can keep your LA dollars, my money is on Tex.

Speaking of gambling, after the last preseason game of the year, a group of us would get together and engage in a betting pool on who would make the final squad for the regular season. Tex and his wife, Marty, my wife, Nancy, broadcast partner Brad Sham and his current date, and Joe Bailey and Doug Todd and their wives would all enter. We jokingly accused Tex of having an insider's advantage. He swore he didn't and the proof is in the pudding. Tex never won the pot.

Before that, of course, I had to begin my rookie season as the Cowboys' play-by-play guy. As the defending Super Bowl champions, the Cowboys had the honor of playing the College All-Star squad at Soldier Field in Chicago to open the preseason in August 1972. I'd done some play-by-play for basketball and baseball when I was in Austin, but not a single minute of football. I was as nervous as heck, and what I mostly remember of that experience was when I wandered through Chicago's Grant Park and along Michigan Avenue well past midnight on the eve of the game, trying to walk off some of my anxiety. I was splitting the play-by-play duties with Frank Glieber. We flipped a coin to see which of us would do which part of the game. I wanted to listen to how Frank handled things. I was glad that I did. Frank was a real pro and I learned a lot in that first half.

I'd developed a love of classical music along the way, and later in life I would watch the movie *Amadeus*. When Mozart, a recognized genius, finished conducting one of his symphonies for Emperor Joseph II, Wolfgang asked for input from the ruler. Joseph II replied, "Too many notes." That was what I learned from Frank and what I tried to put in practice as much as possible in my career: the human ear can only take in so many notes. I wanted to keep to the facts—down, distance, time, and, periodically, score—mixed with concise descriptions of the action. That served me well in Chicago and from then on. I would learn when to add the occasional flourish to the formula but not that first night.

The 1972 season was a tough one for the Cowboys. Roger Staubach went down with a shoulder injury in the preseason. Duane Thomas was traded when management tired of his antics. The offense would have been expected to struggle a bit with Roger's absence, but thanks to Tom Landry's shuffling of quarterbacks Craig Morton was accustomed to starting and performed well. In fact, he set the Cowboys' passing yardage record that year. The Doomsday Defense was starting to feel Father Time catching up to them. Age and injuries are always a part of the game and it's tough to let go of the past. I felt privileged to see the great Bob Lilly have an All-Pro season despite a back injury and assorted leg injuries that hobbled him.

For the seventh straight season, the Cowboys reached the postseason, albeit as a wild card entrant. They faced the San Francisco 49ers in the first round of the playoffs. Earlier that year, back in November, the Dick Nolan–coached 49ers beat the Cowboys 31–10 on a blustery Thanksgiving Day in Dallas. At that point, the 49ers had former Heisman Trophy winner Steve Spurrier at quarterback. Their veteran signal caller, John Brodie, had gone down with an injury and Spurrier had stepped in. In the regular season, Spurrier had gone 6-2. leading the team to the Western Division crown. I'd get to know Steve later on, when he was the head coach at Florida and later at South Carolina.

Steve was highly regarded as a coach in many circles but not all. Some didn't like his approach to the game. He was as competitive as they come and didn't always take other folks' feelings into account. In 2000, I was covering the Kentucky–Florida game. Florida had a great football tradition, and, well, let's say that Kentucky had a great basketball program. UK had never beaten the Gators during Steve's time at the helm. As I recall, the Gators were putting a whipping on the Wildcats, 45–7, with less than a minute to play. Florida had the ball just their side of midfield. Most coaches would have just let the clock run out. Not Steve. He called in the play and Jesse Palmer (who later went on to become TV's Bachelor) dropped back and threw a perfect strike for a touchdown.

Final score, 52–7.

After the game, Steve was asked in a peevish tone by one of the writers why he'd called that last play. In so many words, Steve said that nobody had scored half a hundred on Kentucky and he wanted to be the first to do so. His grin was a lot louder than the silence that followed his utterance.

For years I traveled with my personal statistician Chuck Gardner. After the game, Chuck and I were standing waiting for the elevator to take us down from the press box to the stadium exits. Unbeknownst to Chuck, the Florida athletic director, Jeremy Foley, got on it with us. Speaking to me, Chuck asked why in the world would Spurrier have not just run out the clock.

Before I could answer or indicate that Chuck should pursue another line of questioning, Jeremy Foley spoke up and said that we had to admit that Steve was a perfectionist.

Without skipping a beat, Chuck said, "So was Hitler."

The elevator seemed to me to have slowed to a crawl; I scanned it for an escape hatch.

Truth is, Steve was a perfectionist and as I've said, anyone who achieves success has to have a strong sense of self. I know that Steve was humbled a bit by his brief excursion into the swamp that is Washington, D.C., and NFL football. His tenure with the Redskins wasn't anything like he'd hoped it would be. I saw him after he'd signed on to undertake the challenge of resuscitating South Carolina's program after it was put in a choke Holtz. We were at the National Football Foundation's banquet. I gave him a quick hug and whispered that I was glad to have him back home where he belonged.

I meant it.

I was fond of Steve because I was able to glimpse the other side of him. I liked how he kept things in perspective. As driven and perfectionistic as he was, he stuck to his Friday-before-game-day ritual—a haircut and nine holes of golf. One year, my partner Todd Blackledge and our sideline reporter Jill Arrington were in Gainesville before a game. We went to Steve's office. It was a virtual museum with memorabilia covering nearly every square inch of the place. Jill was relatively new to the team. Steve welcomed us all in and could see Jill scanning his office. He showed her a photo of one of his Duke University teams. This was obviously before he took over at Florida and attained so much success. That he was proud of the job he'd done at that school spoke volumes about him. He wasn't going to brag about himself or his better-known squads. He pointed out some of the players and what they'd gone on to do in other things besides playing in the NFL. His evident pride in them impressed me.

Even though the Cowboys had a better regular season record, that 1972 playoff game was held in Candlestick Park. I was grateful that it wasn't frigid up there on our rooftop perch overlooking the bay. Candlestick was a tough venue. The park was designed for baseball, so we had to deal with being at an odd angle to the field of play. With the cutouts for the infield diamond still there, yardage markers frequently got obscured, adding to the difficulties of perspective. The Cowboys had beaten the 49ers in the previous two NFC championship games, and the old third time's a charm was once again in play. It seemed as if the magic was in the home team's corner. Vic Washington fumbled but returned the opening kickoff for a 97-yard touchdown, and the nearly 60,000 in attendance were making enough noise to register on the Richter scale—not a good thing considering the city's seismic history. The Cowboys got a field goal from Toni Fritsch, but a pair of San Francisco touchdowns had them up 21–3 and things looked bleak for the Cowboys despite the bright Northern California sunshine. Two Craig Morton turnovers—a fumble and an interception—led to those scores. Fortunately, he threw a touchdown pass and then led the team on another drive that resulted in a field goal. At halftime the Niners were up 21–13.

It pains me to relive some of these Cowboy memories— particularly as it applies to Morton and other Cowboy quarterbacks. Seems as though all I'm recalling is Craig's failings on the field. That hurts me, not because the facts aren't accurate, but because I really like Craig Morton. I also really like and have built a lifelong friendship with Roger Staubach. Don Meredith was a great and lovable guy who left the game and earth far too soon at age seventy-two in 2010. Quarterback is never an easy position to play, and each of these three men provided Dallas fans with a lot of thrills and not a little anxiety in their careers.

Of the three, I think that Dandy Don, a nickname Meredith tried to disassociate himself from, was most sensitive to the criticism that he took from passionate Cowboys supporters. For all the ups and downs in his pro career and his remarkable run as a broadcaster on *Monday Night Football,* many people likely don't know how great an athlete he was. Don Meredith, before I got to Dallas, played at Mount Vernon High School in East Texas. He was a basketball and football player and his scoring record of 52 points in a Dr Pepper high school basketball tournament in Dallas stood for many years. I didn't witness that feat, but when I came to Dallas, folks were still talking about it.

What's interesting about Don's emotional response to his perceived (and often real) poor treatment by the fans was that he remained the loosest man I've ever known. He had a great sense of humor and seemed on the surface to be as carefree as could be. He'd remind his teammates to remember their ABCs—Always Be Cool— sang in the huddle, and called out names of fruits from behind center. He was also saddled with the burden of being a quarterback on an expansion franchise. The two years before he became the starter the club went 4-20-2. They won five games his first season as the starter in 1963. It wasn't until 1966 that the team had its first winning season, going 10-3. He bore the brunt of a less-than-stellar offensive line and the wrath of some fans.

As carefree as Don was, maybe he cared too much. He worried a lot about the success of the team and, like it or not, he played a position with more than a fair share of glory and blame. Don suffered the agonies of those defeats. One of my most vivid memories of him took place in Cleveland, at old Municipal Stadium, hard on the shore of Lake Erie. This was in 1968, and our radio booth was on top of the roof of that old monstrosity. We all shivered. Near the end of the game, Al Ward escorted me to the sidelines. Even if I had still been at that more distant locale, Don's pain would have been palpable. It was as hard as the pellet-like snow spitting down on all assembled.

As the game staggered on, the fog rolled in and the Browns were handing the Cowboys their collective ass as the saying goes. Down by a lot, Tom Landry pulled Don out of the game and inserted Craig Morton. Didn't matter who was in there because the Cowboys eventually lost, 42–10. For the day, his last on the playing field it would turn out, Don was 3 for 9, with three interceptions. One of those was a pick six, and the two others resulted in 10 points for the underdog Browns. The glorious 12-2 regular season came to an ignominious end. In 1966 and 1967 the Cowboys had ended their season with a loss to the Packers in the NFL Championship Game. This time, they fell short of that lousy mark. Don was only thirty years old. Though he was often injured and beaten up, he was still relatively young for a quarterback in the league.

I can see now that what I witnessed toward the end of the game had greater significance than just another frustrating playoff loss. With about five minutes left to be played, Don was stoically standing on the bench, a low-slung plank that ran from the 30 to 30 on one side of the field for use by both teams. He had a hooded cape on and was staring straight ahead. In the gloom he was a vision of forlorn failure. I was on the field making my way toward the locker room to do my postgame show. Tex Schramm passed me going the other way. I turned and watched as Tex approached Don. He wrapped his arms around his disconsolate quarterback. Don reached down and patted Tex on the back. That's the kind of guy Tex was. Later, we boarded the charter and Don took his customary seat in the last row. That season, his row mate was Pete Gent. Pete was a wide receiver and later the author of a bestselling tell-all novel, *North Dallas Forty*.

We took off and I didn't think much about it until we got to Dallas and everyone was wondering where Don was. The aircraft had two exits, and before we left Cleveland he and Pete had slipped out the rear one without anyone noticing. Later we learned that Don and Pete had booked another flight to New York City and were holed up in Frank Gifford's place. He contacted Tex and said that he was done; he was going to retire. Nineteen sixty-eight was going to be his last season. And what a season it was for him. He passed for exactly 2,500 yards and threw 21 touchdowns, earning All-Pro honors. Too many fans focused on his 12 interceptions.

My other vivid memory of Don is of him being nearly in tears following a Cowboy loss in the Cotton Bowl. I worked my way down to the locker room and his hangdog look and tone after the game was painful to witness. He'd been removed from the action and was lustily booed by a sellout crowd. He told me that he couldn't understand these people. Why were they booing him? Did they think he wasn't trying? He said that he was out there trying to do his best on every play. Did they think he wasn't out there putting in the effort? In fact, he was more than putting in the effort. He was laying it on the line. He famously threw a touchdown pass to future Denver head coach Dan Reeves one play after he'd had his ribs broken. His buddy Pete Gent recalled on Don's passing how he'd visited him in the hospital after that game. Don was in intensive care (and intense pain) having his collapsed lung reinflated.

Don's fun-loving side clearly rubbed the all-business, all-the-time Tom Landry the wrong way. That was a huge reason why Don walked away from the game at such a young age and while still being very productive. He enjoyed great success as a broadcaster and did some acting as well. Maybe he had a vision of what his life could be like beyond football, understood that life was meant to be lived larger than what the confines of the gridiron allowed for. No matter the case, he was a real treat to be around. I just wish he could have been around longer.

When Meredith struggled, Morton came on in relief after being drafted fifth overall in 1965. Another gifted athlete—he was pursued by several Major League Baseball teams as a pitcher—Craig enjoyed a standout collegiate career at the University of California, Berkeley. I also really enjoyed getting to know and become friends with Craig. He wasn't as famous as Don was for his sense of humor, but his laid-back Californian vibe made him a pleasure to be around. You have to keep in mind that I was around these young guys when I was a young man myself. We were contemporaries with the same interests. We were young, single, and pursuing an active social life. Also, back then, the athletes I knew weren't as guarded with the media as they are today. They didn't have to be wary of what we might report on social media or to friends who might repeat something told in confidence and have it find its way onto TMZ or some other scandal-mongering outlet.

Like Don, Craig suffered the slings and arrows of Cowboy fans and their high expectations. At this time, the Cowboys were on their way to becoming known as America's Team. Roger Staubach was Craig's foil. A graduate of the U.S. Naval Academy, he had to wait until completing his four years of active duty before joining the team at age twenty-seven. Roger's maturity and discipline stood in contrast to Craig's slightly more lax approach to life and to the game. Both were very, very talented. Both would have liked to have been Tom Landry's number one. It took a while, but eventually Roger won out.

And the beginning of the end for Craig was that 1972 divisional round playoff game against the Niners. With the Cowboys down 21–13 at the half, things were made worse by a Calvin Hill fumble inside his own five-yard line, which resulted in a San Francisco touchdown to push the lead to 28–13. Dallas wasn't moving the ball much on offense, and Craig was having an off day. Near the end of the third quarter, Landry decided to make a change. Craig's 8 out of 21 completions with an interception and a fumble just wasn't going to cut it with so much at stake. (I should note that the interception was on a pass that was right on target but went through the hands of the intended receiver.)

Roger's day began inauspiciously. His interception and fumble stalled the offense but a Bruce Gossett miss on a relatively easy 32-yard field goal kept the score unchanged. Roger and the offense got untracked and a Toni Fritsch field goal brought them within two touchdowns. The problem was the clock. The Cowboys got the ball back with just a little more than two minutes left and a huge hill to climb. A least the first step of that climb wasn't going to be too arduous.

A poor punt gave them the ball on the Niners' 45-yard line. I sat there amazed as, 32 seconds and four completions later, the Cowboys were in the end zone. Roger connected on a 20-yard toss to Billy Parks for the score with 1:20 left in the game. Exciting stuff, but we all knew that if the Cowboys had any hope of victory, then something special was going to have to occur. It did in the form of a Toni Fritsch onside kick. Toni was Austrian and had played a lot of European football in his day. Tex, ever the innovator, had his scouts checking out foreign soccer players. Much of that had to do with Tex hating the idea of "wasting" a draft choice on a kicker or punter.

Toni had great footwork and frequently practiced on his own unusual approaches to kicking the ball. That day in San Francisco, he lined up as if he were going to kick the ball to the left, but in a somewhat balletic move, wrapped his kicking leg behind his plant leg and kick-punched the ball to the right. The Cowboys recovered. Roger scrambled for 21 yards on the first play, niftily evading tacklers. He next hit Parks on a perfect sideline route to set up the winning score—a bullet of a pass to Ron Sellers from the 10.

That 15-point fourth-quarter rally got the Cowboys to the NFC Championship Game. It also became the foundation for the legend of Roger "Captain Comeback" Staubach. That nickname, along with "Roger the Dodger" and "Captain America," formed a wonderful trio. Unfortunately for Roger and the Cowboys, that magic didn't last. George Allen and his "Over the Hill Gang"—a Washington Redskins team composed of wily veterans—took out the Cowboys, 26–3. The Redskins had a quarterback controversy of their own with Billy Kilmer and Sonny Jurgenson swapping roles as starter and backup. It hardly mattered who was behind center. Allen was as defensive-minded as any head coach and despite having six starters older than thirty on that side of the ball, they had the stingiest defense in the league. The Cowboys managed fewer than 200 yards in total offense and just 8 first downs total. No repeat championship. No fourth-quarter heroics from Captain Nickname.

Another of those long, silent flights ensued. At least everyone on the team boarded and stayed on board.

Despite the loss, I know that I was truly blessed to be with the Cowboys during that amazing stretch in the 1970s when they went to the Super Bowl five times. I wasn't with the team professionally in the 1990s when they reestablished themselves as a major force in the league and truly became America's Team. Some people say that all good things must come to an end, but that doesn't mean they can't start over later. I don't want to turn this into a downer, but one of the other vivid memories I have of my time with the Cowboys was just before Super Bowl XIII in Miami.

I was still doing my nightly newscast, and that particular Wednesday, we did a remote from Fort Lauderdale with Jackie Smith as my guest. Jackie had come out of retirement to join the Cowboys after the fourth game of the season when starting tight end Jay Saldi fractured his arm. Jackie was a terrific player for the St. Louis Cardinals in his fifteen years with them. He was lightly regarded coming out of college. He was drafted in the tenth round but eventually became a Hall of Famer. His years with the St. Louis Cardinals were marked by his excellence and the Cardinals' mediocrity. From 1963 to 1977 the Cardinals only made the playoffs twice, losing both times in the divisional round.

Jackie came back believing that he'd have a shot at what every competitor truly wants—the ring, the championship. Jackie and his wife were on camera with me that night. It was clear that he was giving this one more shot and that, win or lose, this would be his final game. I asked him what he hoped for. He said that his fantasy would be to make a meaningful catch in a Cowboys victory. Jackie was a stand-up guy and I hoped that he'd see that vision brought to life.

Standing in the way were the Pittsburgh Steelers. And, man, those Cowboys–Steelers match-ups were a real hoot given their relative rarity and the consequences adjoined to each one. Not only was this a contest to determine the champion of that season, it was in large measure a test of football dominance. The Steelers had beaten the Cowboys 21–17 in Super Bowl X. Both teams had each won two Super Bowls in their history. The winner of this game would be the first to three victories in the ultimate game. The Cowboys had won in 1977, so they were seeking back-to-back league championships. The Cowboys had dominated Denver the previous year. Craig Morton versus Roger Staubach was one of the main story lines going into that game. The Cowboys' 27–10 victory capped off an amazing playoff run in which they beat their opponents by an aggregate score of 87 to 23 and humbled the Bears, the Vikings, and the Broncos.

For their part, the Steelers had won back-to-back titles in 1974 and 1975 and their roster was populated with names like Mean Joe Greene, Jack Lambert, Lynn Swann, Terry Bradshaw, Chuck Noll, and others who formed a who's who of NFL football. Any time two franchises with histories of great success square off, expectations are very high. The Cowboys entered the game with a record of 13-4 while the Steelers were 14-2. Clearly the two best teams in the league would be going at it. To top it off, this was going to be the last Super Bowl held in the historic Orange Bowl. According to many, this was the greatest matchup, on paper, to that point in Super Bowl history. In retrospect, it's easy to see why that was so. Nineteen participants in that game—players, coaches, owners, management—made it into the Hall of Fame.

One other sidelight. Thomas "Hollywood" Henderson was quite a character, as his nickname suggests. Born and raised in Austin, Thomas moved to Oklahoma to live with his grandmother since his home life in Austin was less than ideal. He wasn't a particularly good high school football player by NFL standards. He wasn't heavily recruited by NCAA Division I schools like most pro football players are. Instead he attended a small National Association of Intercollegiate Athletics school. He walked on at Langston University, a historically black college in Oklahoma. He was a standout at that small school and the Cowboys selected him with the eighteenth pick of the first round of the 1975 draft. He was a part of what some referred to as the Cowboys' Dirty Dozen—one of the twelve rookies who made the team from that draft. As for Thomas, how great of an underdog story is his?

And how is this for a great line? Prior to the Super Bowl, he said of the Steelers' Terry Bradshaw, "He couldn't spell 'cat' if I spotted him the *C* and the *T*."

The letter that most people expected to be prominent in the game was *D*. Both teams had the top defenses in their respective conferences. The game didn't go to plan in that regard for the Doomsday Defense or the Steel Curtain.

In the previous year's draft, the Cowboys had gambled on Tony Dorsett. They made a big trade in order to move up to the number two spot in the draft to select him out of Pitt. The day of the draft, before the trade was made, I was at my desk at Channel Eight when I got an anonymous tip. This individual reported that someone had been at one of Chuck Howley's dry cleaning establishments (Chuck was long-time linebacker for the Cowboys). Inside, someone was sewing the last "t" on a number 33 Cowboy jersey. I ignored the possibility and missed a big scoop. Tex laughed at me later when I confirmed the dry-cleaner story and never let me forget how I'd missed out on making a big news splash.

Some regarded Dorsett as too small, but he figured large in the Cowboys' plans. They also paid him large—he was the first Cowboy to top the $1 million per-season mark. Back-to-back 1,000-yard-plus seasons in his first two regular seasons demonstrated the Cowboys' scouts knew a thing or two about what it took to succeed in the league. Dorsett was something special, and his 99-yard touchdown run against the Vikings in a 1983 Monday Night Football contest ranks as one of the most memorable. He did it when the Cowboys only had ten men on the field.

Five years earlier, in the opening moments of Super Bowl XIII Dorsett showed why he was worth trading up for, gaining 38 yards on 3 carries. To mix things up a bit, instead of letting the league's leading passer, Roger Staubach, air one out, the Cowboys elected a bit of trickery. A wide-receiver reverse-pass play resulted in a Drew Pearson fumble. Tight end Billie Joe Dupree, the intended receiver, had broken free but the handoff went awry. The Cowboys had practiced that play for weeks in anticipation of needing it against a stout and aggressive defensive opponent. The moment was right but the execution wasn't. The Steelers took over near midfield and a few plays later, Terry Bradshaw connected with John Stallworth on a 28-yard touchdown pass. Similarly, the Cowboys capitalized on a Bradshaw fumble late in the first quarter to tie the score on a Staubach–Tony Hill pass. Taking advantage of an all-out blitz, Hill beat his man in single coverage and the Cowboys scored the only first-quarter touchdown the Steelers defense allowed that season. In my mind, that could have possibly been the only touchdown either side would surrender. The game might have come down to a battle of the kickers.

The second quarter opened with the Dallas D doing its thing. Mike Hegman and Hollywood Henderson blitzed. Bradshaw tried to evade them, and did initially, but he ran into his own Franco Harris. He dropped the ball but picked it up. Hegman and Henderson double-teamed him, with the former stripping the ball loose and running it into the end zone. The Cowboys were up 14–7 and the Steelers had turned the ball over on three straight possessions. That lead didn't last long. Three plays into the following possession John Stallworth turned a 10-yard completion into a 75-yard touchdown with a combination of breaking a tackle and patiently waiting for blockers to join him downfield. Just before halftime, and taking advantage of a Staubach interception, a Bradshaw to Rocky Bleier touchdown strike gave the Steelers the edge at 21–14.

Following the lengthy halftime show, both offenses struggled as the defenses asserted themselves. The most notable play came with about three minutes left in the third quarter. On third down from the Steelers' ten, Roger went back to pass. Jackie Smith broke free and was wide open in the end zone. From our vantage point, it looked like a sure touchdown. Roger threw the ball softly, Smith seemed to struggle to keep his feet beneath him, and the ball bounced off the veteran's hands. I flashed back to that earlier interview with him and his wish to contribute with a big play in a Cowboy victory. Instead, that dropped pass has gone down as one of the great gaffes in Super Bowl history. As Roger told me later, he didn't put a whole lot on the pass. Smith himself said that the ball was low but catchable. What really troubled Roger is that the play as called was designed to go five yards. When the call came in, he tried to get Landry to change the play selection. All Tom said was to run it. They did, and maybe that bit of confusion resulted in the drop. Difficult to say, but 9.9 times out of ten Roger delivers a strike and Smith makes the catch. One of those what-ifs, I guess.

I benefited from that dropped pass. I remember my call: "Bless his heart, he's got to be the sickest man in America." NFL Films used that bit of audio in their production, and it got me a fair bit of attention then and down the line. I suppose that it's true in so many sporting moments that we all treasure—one man's pleasure is another man's pain. How many of us remember who it was that Dwight Clark beat in the end zone to catch Joe Montana's pass against the Cowboys in 1982? Well, I do, but that's part of my job. It was Everson Walls, a rookie who made the Pro Bowl for an outstanding freshman campaign with 11 interceptions and one fumble recovery. He's forever immortalized for that year on the countless posters that were sold depicting "the Catch." Hardly seems fair, but so it goes.

Later on, after learning about the confusion about the play call, I'd wondered a bit about how that figured into a pattern with Tom Landry. A couple of times he was apparently unsure of down and distance and sent in plays that weren't right for the situation. I don't mean to speak ill of the man, but a lot of speculation swirled around him and whether or not he had begun to lose command as a head coach. I'm not trying to point fingers or assign blame, and just as that Jackie Smith drop was one of dozens of plays in that Super Bowl, it does take on exaggerated importance due to the circumstances. Jackie had played for so long and played so well. I immediately felt bad for him, but there was still plenty of time left in the game. I hoped that he'd get a chance to redeem himself.

As sometimes happens, a questionable officiating call helped determine the game's outcome. From his own 44, Bradshaw drifted back to pass and spotted Lynn Swann downfield. Benny Barnes was in coverage and it seemed to me, and to a lot of others, that Swann ran into him. The call should have been no call—incidental contact. Instead, Fred Swearingen—the referee during the Steelers' Immaculate Reception game—called pass interference on Barnes. Wrong call but it gave the Steelers a first down at the Cowboys' 23.

Two plays later, Hollywood Henderson got involved in a mix-up. On third-and-four from the 17, the whistle blew just before the snap. Most players stopped, but Hollywood didn't. He took down Bradshaw. He later claimed that he didn't hear the whistle. Franco Harris came to his quarterback's defense, and it looked like things could get ugly, but they didn't. Pittsburgh was assessed a five-yard penalty for delay of game, nullifying the 12-yard loss resulting from the Henderson nonsack. The weirdness went on. On the very next play, Bradshaw handed off to Harris, who went untouched from the 22 into the end zone. He was ably assisted by a "block" from Umpire Art Demmas, who got in the way of safety Charlie Waters. Things like that happen with the officials being in the middle of the action, but it was certainly frustrating.

A two-touchdown deficit in the fourth quarter was a lot to overcome. Things got even a bit more odd after that. Pittsburgh's kicker seemed to slip as he approached the ball on the ensuing kickoff. It traveled, bouncing and skidding to the Cowboys' 24, where lineman Randy White tried to corral it. Playing with a cast on his broken left hand, White failed to secure the ball. Tony Dungy was in on the hit that produced the fumble. The Steelers wasted no time in cashing in. Bradshaw hit Swann in the end zone. Thirty-five to seventeen Pittsburgh with seven minutes left.

My mind was spinning with so much going on in so short a time. That would continue. Down three touchdowns, it would have been easy for the Cowboys and Roger to wave the white flag. They didn't. With some of the Steelers' players celebrating on the sidelines, the Cowboys continued to work. Roger scrambled for a huge 18-yard gain on third-and-eleven; Dorsett ripped off a 29-yard run; Roger threw for seven yards to Billy Joe Dupree for a touchdown.

The 89-yard, eight-play drive took up a healthy chunk of time. I can still picture Roger in the backfield standing, waiting, drifting around as he waited for receivers to come open against the Steelers' prevent defense. One sideline ball to Dupree seemed to hang in the evening sky forever before it parachuted into the tight end's arms. I bet if the referee checked the ball he would have discovered burn marks from its reentry into the earth's atmosphere.

With 2:23 left, the Cowboys lined up for an onside kick. Everyone knew what was up. Rafael Septien did his job getting the ball to travel along the ground for the necessary ten yards. But that ball rolled along the ground like a weak grounder off the bat of a jammed hitter. It just didn't do a thing that you would expect of an oblong object. Number twenty-one of the Steelers bent down to field it like an infielder with plenty of time to spare. While the ball didn't go through his legs Bill Buckner–style, it did bounce through Tony Dungy's hands and into the arms of Cowboy rookie defensive back Dennis Thurman. He went down on his own 48-yard line.

A single second wound off the clock. A short time later, facing fourth and 18, Drew Pearson found an opening and Roger found him for a 25-yard gain. Eventually, Roger and Butch Johnson hooked up on a 4-yard touchdown with just 22 seconds left. The extra point cut the Steelers' lead to 35–31. Could the Cowboys count on another miracle and recover a second onside boot?

Hope springs eternal but it wasn't to be. Septien's second attempt was even more of a dribbler and the sure-handed Rocky Bleier—the

Vietnam War veteran turned running back—made the easy recovery. A valiant effort, as the saying goes, but it did fall short.

I've never been a fan of broadcasters talking about the betting line. I know that millions and millions of dollars are bet on Super Bowls and regular season games. Maybe I'm old-fashioned or naïve, but I never wanted that to be a part of the story line. Same here. The Cowboys fell short and those two late-game touchdowns provided a whole lot of excitement and kept hope alive deep in the heart of Texas and elsewhere.

There were enough what-if incidents to keep fans busy for years. Folks would be able to spin tales of what might have been. As I see it, that's a kind of victory, too. A lot of folks think that Terry Bradshaw had the last laugh on the Cowboys and Thomas "Hollywood" Henderson. He asked if Henderson knew how to spell *MVP*. Terry had been awarded that honor for his stellar performance in the game. That would put a neat bow around the story. But I kind of like this one; there's more to it than that.

Henderson didn't last long with the Cowboys. Eventually his descent into drug abuse, particularly crack cocaine, led to his arrest and time in prison. He eventually got clean and sober. He won the Texas lottery and used some of the funds to establish an antidrug foundation. Henderson still travels widely, speaking to young people about the perils of illicit drugs. His story illustrates the power of human beings to change and to make an impact in this life. That's a moral victory worth talking about. He's someone to cheer for.

And then there was Roger, who'd almost pulled off yet another improbable comeback. By the time he retired in March 1980, Roger had accumulated 15 fourth-quarter comeback victories and had led his team to 23 game-winning drives. (A game-winning drive is the offensive scoring drive in the fourth quarter or overtime that puts the winning team ahead for the last time.) One of my favorites of those fourth-quarter comebacks was his last. On December 16, 1979, the Redskins came to town. Among sports rivalries, for my money the Cowboys and Redskins battles back then were at the top of the list. Subsequent years and exposure to other games have me dropping it down a few pegs, but at the time, there was nothing like 'Skins versus the 'Boys.

That 1979 game was memorable because the stakes were somewhat high. A great comeback is a beauty to behold, but it doesn't climb to the top of my charts if the results aren't of any real consequence. The two teams came into the regular season finale with identical 10-5 records. The division title was on the line. That 1979 team got off to a great start, going 8-2 before a three-game November losing streak had everyone on edge and the phone lines buzzing with "What's-wrong-with-the-Cowboys" calls. The defense had suffered some losses due to retirement, injury, and Ed "Too Tall" Jones ignoring his nickname and deciding he could be a professional boxer.

Perhaps fittingly, that December 16 game in front of a packed and raucous house in Irving, a suburb of Dallas, had the qualities of a championship boxing match. The Cowboys climbed up off the canvas a couple of times. The Redskins were led by future broadcaster and then quarterback Joe Theisman and the punishing running back John Riggins. The Cowboys decided to play Santa Claus in the early going. Rookie running back Ron Springs and the fireplug Robert Newhouse both fumbled. The Redskins converted both turnovers into points and led early, 10–0. A second-quarter Theisman pass had them down 17–0. As we always say in those situations, because it's true, there was still a lot of time left and no need to panic. A pair of long second-quarter drives pulled the Cowboys within three at halftime. The second of those was culminated by an amazing Preston Pearson sliding catch in the end zone. That drive was vintage Roger and the Cowboys' offense that year. Taking possession with just 1:48 to go before halftime and 85 yards to the end zone, he ran the two-minute offense to perfection.

The third quarter belonged to the Cowboys. Newhouse punched one in from the two-yard line and the defense punched holes in the Redskins' offensive line. The Cowboys went into the fourth quarter up 21–17. Seemingly in no time, the Redskins rattled off 17 straight points. The backbreaker seemed to be Riggins rumbling 66 yards with just under seven minutes to play, which had the visitors up 34–21. As usual, turnovers were key. Roger threw an interception that led to the first of those fourth-quarter touchdowns. Turnabout is fair play and Randy White recovered a Redskins fumble.

Roger went to work. From his own 41 and with about four minutes left, he completed a 14-yarder to Butch Johnson, a 19-yarder to Tony Hill, and then a 26-yard scoring pass to Ron Springs. The touchdown had as much to do with tenacity as talent. Springs caught the ball at the five and dragged the defender into the end zone. Not only did he provide points; he saved precious time on the clock.

Despite giving up 34 points, the defense deserves a lot of credit for the win. Larry Cole threw John Riggins to the turf on a third-down run that set the stage for Roger's heroics. Taking over at their own 25 and with less than two minutes to go, they got big chunks of the 75 yards needed on the first two plays—completions to Hill for 20 and Preston Pearson for 22. With 1:01 left, Roger hit Pearson for another 25-yarder, putting the team in great position at the Washington eight. On second down from there, Washington chose to blitz. The offensive line picked it up and Roger saw it. He lofted a pass to the deep right corner of the end zone for Tony Hill. It climbed and climbed then settled into the veteran wide receiver's hands after he beat single coverage.

For the day, Roger completed 24 of 42 passes for 336 yards and 3 touchdowns. Not stellar completion numbers but the results were then. When he really needed to be on target and unflappable, he was. That was Roger. As Tom Landry later pointed out, Roger had pulled them out of the fire before and that contributed greatly to his and the team's confidence he would do it again. Much later, in speaking to an interviewer from NFL Films, Landry characterized Roger's performance as his best ever. In my estimation, the 1972 and 1979 efforts are equal.

I wish that I could have witnessed the 1979 comeback in person. I was in Japan on assignment with ABC. My body was in Tokyo but my mind was back home. Brad Sham and Charlie Waters took over for me. I relied on my brother Tom, who was also in the booth, to keep me posted. We were on the phone for that final drive, and when the touchdown came, Tom dropped the phone to scream and jump around. He forgot to tell me who caught the pass, a significant detail. He should have been flagged for a delay of game. It took several minutes before I got the details of the victory.

Greatness comes in many forms and what Roger said after the game demonstrates how great his character was: "They deserve a better fate than to be knocked out of the playoffs," he said, knowing that because the Bears wiped out the Cardinals the 'Skins lost the wild card due to point differential. "They're a fine team and played well. It's a shame that someone had to lose. Both teams played with a lot of emotion." A cynic might say that Roger resorted to tried-and-true clichés in victory. I know him very well and his words of praise were genuine. Many thought that the Cardinals, with no shot at the playoffs, maybe phoned it in against the Bears. The Redskins seemed a sure bet, win or lose that game, but they went home empty-handed. Well, not completely so; there was another turnover. An anonymous fan had sent a funeral wreath to the Cowboys locker room. After that crushing defeat, Harvey Martin paid his respects by taking that floral arrangement to the Redskins' locker room. He opened the door and tossed it in. Adding injury to insult, the wreath hit Redskins kicker Mark Moseley in the knee, opening up a small cut. Small cut or large gash didn't matter; the hurt was the same.

I wish I could tell you that the Cowboys went on to play in their sixth Super Bowl of the 1970s following that rousing victory. I wish I could tell you that Roger rallied the team from behind in their divisional round game against the Los Angeles Rams. I am glad I can report that Roger Staubach, despite not producing a fourth-quarter comeback in that 21–19 loss, has continued to live happily ever after. In light of what we know now about the effects of concussions on the brains of athletes and others, I'm not going to speculate on what might have been as it pertains to Roger's decision to end his playing career following that season. Roger told me that he'd made up his mind to retire.

One of my lasting memories of that loss to Los Angeles is of Roger taking a serious hit and wobbling to the sidelines. Backup quarterback Danny White immediately began throwing. He didn't enter the game, but it was clear to me that the punishing hit Roger took limited his effectiveness. Like Don Meredith's last game, Roger's was anticlimactic. Roger was hit as he threw his final pass of his career. The ball was deflected and hit his own lineman, Herb Scott, in the rear end. So few athletes retire on top with a glorious and unforgettable play enshrined in our memories. As fans or observers it's hard to let go of our heroes. Imagine how hard it is for the players to let go of the game they love.

Just days after he retired, Roger confided in me. He said that he was concerned about his health and the effect his concussions might have on him down the line. He'd likely suffered as many as seven of them. He played when tape an aspirin to your forehead was the league's concussion protocol. We'd talked a bit about them, but Roger had never sounded so concerned before.

He told Tex of his decision to hang them up. A few weeks later, Tex called him and said that he understood about Roger's worries. (Keep in mind that this was decades before the medical evidence about CTE we take for granted today was available.) Tex wanted him to reconsider. Not everyone within the organization believed that

Danny would be effective as a starting quarterback in the league. Tex offered Roger a substantial raise if he came back for another go.

Roger considered the offer and eventually told Tex that if Landry wanted him back and called him to tell him as much, he'd return. Roger is still waiting for that call. I'm no mind reader and no psychologist, but it seems to me that Tom was constitutionally incapable of making that kind of request of a player. I've also wondered if Roger knew that as well. Tom wasn't one to kowtow to any player. I'm sure he thought that he was a strong enough coach that he could lead the team back to the playoffs and the team's accustomed perch atop the league.

In hindsight, I'm glad that Tom didn't reach out to Roger. I'm sad for the team, for the game, but seeing Roger enjoying his retirement free of any effects of chronic traumatic encephalopathy is a real blessing. I'm sorry that so many players have suffered from pursuing their passion. It pains me to know that some individuals put profit and winning ahead of player safety. Whether that was willful or benign neglect doesn't really matter as far as treatment, prevention, and restitution go. I was fortunate to make a great living and to enjoy the heck out of covering a great sport. That a shadow has been cast over the sport deeply troubles me. I hope that minds greater than mine are at work on ways to mitigate the problems. I don't like thinking of a sports world without the game of football in it.

CHAPTER FIVE

New Horizons

In 1992 I was at my first Olympics in Albertville, France, working with Scotty Hamilton. This assignment for me was at least as big as getting the Cowboy radio job. We were at practice one afternoon and Scott looked up in the corner of the auditorium, the ice rink. He pointed toward Paul Wiley, Nancy Kerrigan, and Kristi Yamaguchi of the U.S. team. He wanted to go up and say hello to them. He wondered if I knew any of them and I told him I didn't. Scott made the introduction to the two women first. Nancy would go on to finish third and Kristi won the gold medal. Paul, a real underdog, wound up earning silver in the men's competition. (That's still one of my favorite Olympic moments ever.)

By way of introduction Scott said, "Paul, I don't think you know Verne."

Paul shook his head and smiled. "Oh," he said, "I know Verne. He just doesn't know me."

I looked at Paul and was puzzled for a moment trying to figure out a possible connection between us.

He went on: "I grew up in Dallas. I grew up watching him on *Bowling for Dollars*."

I groaned inside.

Well, the girls went crazy. What the hell was that all about? And we laughed and had a giggle about it.

I've always referred to myself as an accidental sportscaster. As you've seen, from childhood on, I had an interest in radio. That eventually evolved into an interest in television but I didn't grow up fantasizing about becoming a nationally known sports guy. In some respects, then, it's fitting that while I became a television and radio personality in and around Dallas, I'm probably best known among a segment of the population for hosting that franchised game show—sports program called *Bowling for Dollars*. I can't tell you the number of times, and often under the oddest of circumstances, that someone I've met has recalled my hosting that show. Those occasions are humbling, gratifying, mystifying, rewarding, and a bit frustrating.

I was an inadvertent (and reluctant) host of it. In 1974, a few years into my play-by-play radio duties, my television general manager, Mike Shapiro, called me into his office at WFAA. He informed me that the station had acquired the rights to a franchised show. A group out of Baltimore named Claster Productions sold the rights to *Bowling for Dollars* and the children's educational program *Romper Room*. Entire generations of kids started to learn as part of that television classroom; entire generations of adults hoped they'd get a chance to earn cash and prizes on the bowling show. I was vaguely aware of *Bowling for Dollars*—trivial stuff like the fact that in Boston it was known as *Candlepins for Cash*—but I had no real interest in hosting it.

I told him that I wasn't interested.

He asked me if I was his employee.

I told him I understood.

He said that he figured I would be resistant to the idea. He gave me a number to call. I spoke to Chick Hearn, the Los Angeles Lakers legendary broadcaster. He did the program in LA and assured me that it was a ratings winner. They were up against Walter Cronkite's evening news and were slaying him in the seven P.M. time slot. I hesitated a bit. I told him I was a bit worried about my reputation. I'd just gotten the Cowboys gig and I worried about being associated with a show of that type. He laughed and said not to worry. The people who listened to him doing the Lakers games had no idea that *Bowling for Dollars* existed. His advice was to do the show, save up the money from it to build a pool in the backyard, and enjoy myself. Very LA of him.

I told Mike I'd do it.

Before the first taping, I got a briefing on the format and procedures from the producer. Each show consisted of six contestants (I was told in no uncertain terms to always refer to them as "contestants" and not as "competitors") coming on to roll two balls. They wrote into the station and were selected. Viewers could also opt to participate by becoming a Pin Pal. The on-air bowler would be playing for someone at home who'd also receive the prizes awarded. Depending on how well they did, they'd earn a cash prize of a dollar per pin. If they got two strikes they earned the jackpot. It was a combination of a cash prize that accumulated each week by ten dollars until someone won it. They also won an all-expense-paid three-day trip to Acapulco with deluxe accommodations at the Regency hotel, right on the beach. (I ended up hosting 511 of those shows and that bit of patter is indelibly etched in my cortex.)

When I showed up that first Monday at nine thirty, I went into the makeshift dressing room they'd set up for me. A makeup person gave me a quick going-over and then I was shown my wardrobe. I nearly lost my breakfast. In fact, the shirt I was instructed to wear looked like it was splattered with someone's upchucked omelet. This was the mid-1970s and bold patterns and prints were just coming into fashion for younger men.

A bit red-faced and anxious—we did no pre-interviews so I was meeting the contestants for the first time with the cameras rolling—I had ninety seconds to get the lowdown on their lives. I had a cheat sheet that helped me with names and pronunciations but I was basically flying blind. They'd roll their two balls and another contestant would be spit out of the machine, then step out from behind the sliding doors. I'd ask them the same questions as they stood bug-eyed in front of the cameras and the live audience. Six of those per show, six shows in a day, six new shirts and sport coats that defied (not defined) the style of the day.

I was in a kind of bizarre Rube Goldberg machine, but I learned over time to really enjoy it. Even though the people on the show were mostly cut from the same cloth and provided many of the same machine-punched answers—I like hunting and fishing—every now and then a bit of humanity shone through that made me glad I was a part of it. I even got used to the clothes. Folks at the station told me that many viewers of the program took pleasure in wondering what in darnation that Verne fellow was going to show up wearing next! I didn't have to worry about being associated with *Bowling for Dollars* and having that overlap with my radio and sportscaster roles. People thought of Verne the *Bowling for Dollars* guy as a character I played.

Forty-three years later and at least once a month someone will approach me and ask if I'm Verne Lundquist from Dallas and didn't I once do that bowling show. I went from fear of embarrassment to being proud of my participation in it. It filled a gap in people's lives, gave them a chance to do something that I sometimes took for granted.

At just about the same time I was settling in to my spot on *BFD*, I got my first chance to do a nationwide television broadcast for one of the major networks in November 1975. September 18, 1974, I walked into work at one o'clock to find a pink message slip the receptionist had left for me. It said to call Chuck Howard at ABC Sports in New York. He was the senior vice president of production, which meant that he did all the hiring.

As it turned out, this call from Chuck Howard had been set in motion by a chance meeting I'd had with ABC's Jim McKay a couple of years earlier. In 1973, McKay had written a book about his role in the Munich Olympic games. He came into town to promote it and was booked on our television station. My boss suggested that I do the interview with him rather than either of the news guys. I jumped at the chance. For a lot of reasons, I had long admired Jim. After we did the on-air interview, Jim and I spent some time chatting. I took a chance and showed him a human interest piece that I'd been working on. He liked it and told me I should send it to Chuck in New York. I did as Jim suggested and now the pink slip I held in my hand—a bit ironic, as it would eventually turn out—felt like a ticket to the big time.

When I called Chuck, he told me that ABC wanted to use me on a couple of the fall telecasts. The caveat was that they were simultaneously going to use a guy from New York City named Sal Marciano—essentially, it was a tryout for the fourth team on their college football broadcasts.

And so my first game for ABC was Ohio University at Kent State and Sal's first game was Air Force at Oregon. I so wanted to do this right and I so wanted to be prepared, which meant doing a bit of research. To give you an idea of how primitive things were, I got on a long-distance phone call with the sports information director (SID) at Kent State, who gave me the team's depth chart. I spent a good hour on the phone in my little cubicle of an office with a yellow legal tablet writing down numbers 1 through 88 along with the name, height, weight, and position of every player. I recorded the hometown of every player on the roster. I did the same thing with the depth chart.

The production team all stayed at the Holiday Inn in Kent, Ohio. The billboard out front said HOLIDAY INN WELCOMES ABC SPORTS TO KENT. I thought, Boy, is that something. I'm part of this crew. And we had a broadcast associate—an entry-level position for people who want to become producers and directors. I still remember her name was Barbara Roche and there was no such thing as a Chyron machine or a graphics machine. You used a menu board. I couldn't sleep so I went out and walked around the parking lot two or three times at two in the morning. And I happened to walk by Barbara's room, which was down in almost a different wing from mine. We were all ground level and she was sitting on the bed with a menu board in front of her, taking the small plastic letters you'd usually see in a cafeteria saying MAC AND CHEESE SPECIAL $0.69 THIS WEEK to spell out players' names for the on-screen graphics. The starting quarterback for Kent State was named Greg Kokal. I still remember that.

The next week we switched. Sal did Holy Cross–Harvard and I had North Carolina–Maryland. At the end of the two weeks we both waited by the phone and I got a phone call from Chuck saying "You're the guy." My next game was Brigham Young at Arizona and I worked with a variety of different analysts all that year, no steady partner. But I did do the entire season.

And then as a reward, at the end of it, I was assigned to the Division III championships, the Amos Alonzo Stagg Bowl in Phenix City, Alabama. I wound up doing three of those over the years. I was working hard those football seasons—five nights a week in Dallas, *Bowling for Dollars* on Monday, a college game on Saturday, and a Cowboys game on Sunday. The more I did it, the more I wanted to do more of it. More didn't necessarily mean more games.

On Thanksgiving Day 1975, Texas was facing Texas A&M down in College Station. This was a game with huge regional interest as well as a match-up of two top-five teams—with one defeat Texas was at number five while the undefeated Aggies were ranked number two behind the Woody Hayes–coached Ohio State Buckeyes. Never mind the turkey and say farewell to the pie. I was going to take a Thursday road trip. I brought along my best buddy and spotter, the guy in the booth who helped me identify who, what, when, and where: Joe Cash. The analyst would be none other than Frank Broyles of Arkansas. Frank would go on to fame following his tremendous coaching career, partnering with Keith Jackson for ABC telecasts as the number one team.

My situation couldn't have been better. I was going to be calling a game between two teams I knew incredibly well, I'd have a great analyst by my side, and a nation at holiday leisure would be tuning in. Don Ohlmeyer, who would become one of the more famous sports producers in TV, filled that role and Roger Goodman, who produced all of ABC's news shows, was the director. Trust me, that's a who's who of TV production at work in the truck. That year, Texas had the great Earl Campbell in the backfield. A bulldozer of a man-child, Earl went on to enjoy an outstanding NFL career with the Oilers and gained entry into both the college and pro football halls of fame. In 1975 he would earn All-American honors at fullback, lead the Southwest Conference in rushing with more than 1,000 yards, and establish himself as the legendary "Human Wrecking Ball." Only thing is, A&M's defense would have none of him in their 20–10 victory. Texas was held to a paltry six first downs and 179 yards of total offense. Campbell carried the ball 15 times for 40 yards.

I don't mind telling you that I was feeling like I was a BFD after that first taste of the fruits of national television. I kept on my gold-yellow-drab ABC sport coat as Joe drove us back toward Dallas, our waiting wives, and a Thanksgiving dinner for conquering heroes. Joe egged me on, asking me to imagine all those folks from Port-land, Oregon, to Portland, Maine, who sat there drumstick struck as I wove my stories of the action. About a third of the way into the drive we pulled into a filling station in Fairfield, Texas. The pump attendant came out; Joe went in to use the restroom. The young man checked the tires, popped the hood, all the while eyeballing me surreptitiously. When he got to washing the windshield, I thought that he recognized me.

I sensed that he was going to say something about the game that he'd just watched, congratulate me on a good job on national television. He took a rag out of his back pocket and went to work on a stubborn insect stain, eyes narrowed and brow furrowed. Suddenly he straightened up and said to his pal in the filling station, "Rudy! Rudy! God almighty, get out here. It's that *Bowling for Dollars* dude on the TV!"

Still, I'd worked hard at my craft. I use that word with neither a sense of shame nor an inflated sense of self. I'm certainly no artist and I'm proud to be a craftsman—a furniture maker or cabinetmaker comes to mind, someone who makes an object. Though what I did produced something less tangible, less permanent, I still kept that notion in mind. I worked with tools—my voice and words—to produce an image. For my own use, I did create lasting objects of my work. During my early days doing play-by-play with the Cowboys, I always carried a small reel-to-reel recorder. I'd tape its microphone to the broadcast one. I'd review those tapes to listen for redundancies, overuse of adjectives, and tempo. Being studious about the work before and after the games taught me a lot. I could gauge my own improvement and so that call from ABC to do the Thanksgiving Day game was a real boost in confidence.

That game fanned a young but already growing flame. As my years at WFAA went on, I was gratified by the work I was doing. But I wasn't by any means satisfied. I'd gotten the national exposure I'd wanted, just as Tex Schramm had predicted back when he convinced me not to take the job in Los Angeles. He's just one among many whom I thank for helping me move my career down the field.

As my star was rising, another was setting. The Cowboys would continue to be one of the top teams in the NFL but after that 1978 season they wouldn't return to the Super Bowl until 1992, when Jimmie

Johnson came aboard and helped revitalize the franchise. Famously, the new owner, Jerry Jones, brought him on. The former Arkansas teammates made the Cowboys into America's Team once again. I was no longer doing the radio broadcasts by then, but as an outside observer, I wasn't pleased by how that regime began. Admittedly, Tom Landry had lost his touch as a coach. A 3-13 record in his final year to cap three sub-.500 finishes and no playoff appearances had fans howling. I'm a very loyal person, so to have a front-page photo of Jerry and Jimmy dining together before the purchase agreement fully went into effect didn't sit well with me. It was obvious what Jerry was going to do, but Landry was still under contract. Tom was twisting in the wind to begin with and though he didn't stay up there long, he'd been with the Cowboys organization long enough to deserve better. Firings are hard, I know, but they can be handled with class and Tom's wasn't. When Clint Murchison owned the team, when Tex Schramm was running things for them, the Cowboys were the epitome of class and character. Bum Bright's brief tenure as owner took some of the shine off that fancy finish.

Under Jerry Jones—and this may be true of all franchises as the game grew in popularity and their value increased greatly—the game became a "product." The bottom line became profitability and not people. I suppose it's a case of reality setting in. I'm not naïve. I witnessed a similar kind of thing in so-called amateur athletics with the NCAA and its ongoing issues with college football and basketball. It's sad to see the NCAA and FBI mentioned in the same headlines instead of in different sections of the same newspaper. Greater minds than mine will have to sort all of that out. I know that ignoring those issues won't make them go away, but as I've eased into semiretirement, I prefer to think about the moments of joy and pleasure and not the pain.

Well, sometimes a little bit of pain was the result of too much pleasure seeking. As I've mentioned, Tex treated the press so well. In

1976, we were in Philadelphia. The club had made arrangements, as they usually did, for a private room at a restaurant. All the media, the coaching staff, and front office personnel who'd made the trip were invited to dine and drink on the Cowboys' dime. Even the flight crew and flight attendants from the charter were in attendance. Tex, Joe Bailey, and Al Ward represented the front-office people and they were marvelous hosts.

On this particular trip, we were at Bookbinders in Philly, a famous seafood joint. Before we ordered dinner, we were offered cocktails. Tex was famous for his love of J&B and the rest of us were familiar with various kinds of libations. Also, the Cowboys always hosted a hospitality room with an open bar at whatever hotel we stayed at on the road. Tom Dillard was the head of the photo department for the *Dallas Morning News*. He normally didn't make the trip to help organize and supervise his team of photographers. This time his underling was under the weather so he made his rookie debut. He enjoyed the hospitality on offer at the hotel and staggered onto the bus chartered to take us to the restaurant. He looked a bit lost in the dining room at Bookbinders, unsure of the protocol or unclear of vision I can't be certain.

In any case, he waited for a long time before taking a seat. Instead of joining his fellow members of the fourth estate, he staked a claim at the coaches' table. He plopped himself down in a chair between Alicia Landry, Tom's wife, and Ernie Stautner, the defensive line coach and a Hall of Famer to boot. Tom was to his wife's left. At our table, we noticed this but didn't make a move to redirect him.

The first course was turtle soup and things proceeded normally for a while. Mid-course, we noticed a commotion. We looked over to where Alicia Landry sat looking slightly aghast. Tom Dillard had passed out facefirst in his soup. Stautner grabbed him by the nape of the neck and kept him from drowning. Mrs. Landry, the very definition of genteel, uttered a slightly disapproving "Oh, my."

Dinner went on. Tom Dillard was hauled up and loaded into a cab to take him back to the hotel.

Collectively, we media guys decided to award Dillard the Soup Nose Award for his drunken display. Eventually we named a weekly winner of the award and kept a point tally to crown a season champion of making a drunken ass of himself. I only earned the coveted (?) title twice. I still claim innocence on the first of the pair.

We were in Chicago staying at the Executive Inn Hotel, in the Loop. The hospitality room was on the thirty-second floor. Glass doors on one wall led to a patio balcony. A few of us stepped outside to take in the night air and the lovely view. I had been with the Cowboys only for about three years at this point. Jokingly I spread my arms out wide and said, "Someday, this will all be mine," indicating the Sears Tower, the John Hancock Center, and the rest of the city shouldered up against the lake. I turned dramatically and ran straight into the glass doors and fell on my ass. The rest of the media crew swore that I was both inebriated and serious in making that proclamation. I will admit to having had a few but I was not serious.

We did have some sense of decorum. Though Tex was eligible for the award and could have earned it on a few occasions (I'm being conservative in my estimates here), we never voted for him. No Cowboy would look a gift horse in the mouth. We all got a kind of schoolboy thrill of pleasure in voting for the winner on the plane and even more so in making the presentation the following Monday at the weekly Landry's Luncheon. We'd always do that before Tom came into the room. We'd sit there like innocent little angels after that with Tom none the wiser.

That said, I have no idea how Tom Landry would have felt about another little scheme I had going for a while. Ermal Allen was a former University of Kentucky quarterback. He served as Tom's head of research and development. In that capacity, he had access to the scouting report of the opposition. I didn't receive the Cowboys' game plan, but Ermal did slip me a copy of that assessment document. To be honest, much of it was technical jargon and gibberish. There were a few valuable nuggets in it that I mined for use on the broadcast. Mostly, though, I relied on Ermal, who sat in the coaches' booth adjacent to the radio booth to signal me what play would be run next. We'd developed a code to silently transfer that information. We didn't utilize it too often, but every now and then I'd get on a roll of successfully "predicting" what the Cowboys were going to do.

Once, in San Diego against the Chargers in Duane Thomas's first game against his former teammates, I decided to implement the system. Good time for play action. Right on the money. Screen pass would be effective here. Bam. Cowboys were driving the length of the field and my partner Brad Sham was giving me the stink-eye and wondering what was up with me. Finally, in the red zone, Ermal let me know that Roger was going to throw a slant pass to tight end Mike Ditka. I suggested as much over the air, but Roger audibled and handed the ball off to Walt Garrison for the score. I *think* I managed to muster up the proper level of enthusiasm, but a bit of confusion and frustration at having my streak ended may have crept into my tone. I looked over at Ermal and he shrugged. I guess that's what makes sports so great—the unpredictability of it all.

Unfortunately, I wasn't able to predict how things would go for me at ABC. That Texas–Texas A&M game in 1975 had set my sights pretty high. I figured that getting that assignment meant that I would no longer be the fourth play-by-play guy for the network. The same year I was hired, ABC also brought Jim Lampley on board. Management had undertaken what they called a talent search and plucked him out of graduate school at the University of North Carolina. At twenty-six he was eight years younger than me, youthful looking, and the network hoped that he'd attract a younger audience to its college football telecasts. Back then, collegiate games got nowhere near the ratings that they do now. Also, because of NCAA restrictions, far fewer games were available and so ABC essentially had the only game in town during the regular season. Bowl games weren't under the NCAA's control so both NBC and CBS broadcast them. That meant that there weren't a whole lot of jobs for broadcasters.

Keith Jackson was the network's number one guy and was widely thought of as the voice of college football. I've no problem with that assessment. Keith was a truly great play-by-play man and any fan of college football can probably still hear him saying things like "big uglies" and "Whoa, Nellie," and "He's a biggun!" Chris Schenkel was number two, and another young up-and-comer by the name of Al Michaels was in the number three slot. Talk about a Murderer's Row of on-air talent. I was in good company, but still I believed that I had the skills to be at the top of that heap. I aspired to be at the top and worked hard to get there, but I never felt like Chuck Howard was in my corner, even though he had picked me, or that I was "his" guy. It wasn't as if I were sitting on the bench, so to speak; I was out there, but in basketball terms I wasn't the go-to guy, the scorer everyone counted on. That was made very evident. I never got to go to the Olympics when ABC had the rights to them.

That stung.

A lot.

I *really* wanted to do those broadcasts. Just as athletes in many sports pointed to the games as the pinnacle of their careers, so did most broadcasters I knew. Why? For one thing to be a part of a worldwide phenomenon. Casual sports fans, non–sports fans, and dyed-in-the-wool sports fanatics all tuned in. The Olympics provided broadcasters with opportunities to cover sports that normally didn't get a lot of recognition and offered you a chance to do some wonderful human interest pieces. Getting the assignment was a kind of pat-on-the-back validation that you were doing a good job and the company valued your contributions.

I also felt like I'd demonstrated my loyalty to the company and

had demonstrated my versatility and willingness to do what it took to
get the job done. I'd rearranged schedules, asked for and received fa-
vors from Tex Schramm and others to accommodate ABC's requests.
Sometimes those things were recognized, but more often they were
overlooked. And through it all the implication was clear: I was ex-
pendable and I should be grateful for what I had. I didn't like hearing
that, but what could I say? If you want to succeed you sometimes have
to swallow a lot of stuff. I suppose that's the lesson to be learned—
though I wouldn't be doing this book if I took those words too literally: don't hang on to regrets for too long. I also know this: everybody
has them.

Perhaps this is true even for those who got to call the Olympics
for ABC. One of my favorite stories about Keith Jackson is set in
Memphis, Tennessee, in December 1979. I was working sidelines at
the Liberty Bowl between Penn State and Tulane University. Keith
was doing the play-by-play along with his longtime partner and former Notre Dame head coach Ara Parseghian. We were at another
Holiday Inn—the glamour of those stays had worn off since I first
saw that welcome sign in Ohio back in 1975—and a few of us had
gathered in Keith's suite. (He had a couch in his room and none of
us others did.) We were gathered together having a few drinks and
talking. With the 1980 Winter Olympic games approaching in Lake
Placid, New York, talk naturally turned to that. Ara asked Keith if
he was going to do ice hockey—one of the signature events of the
games given the participation of the Soviet Union, renowned as masters on ice.

Keith narrowed his gaze and shook his head, his bulldog jowls
wagging slightly. "Oh no, sir," he said in that wonderful voice of his.
"There's a young man out of West Allis, Wisconsin, by the name of
Eric Heiden. A speed skater. A marvel on ice. Has a chance to win
five gold medals and I believe he will do it. He's going to become the
most decorated speed skater in the history of the sport. Let somebody

else do ice hockey. I'm going to be there to describe every stroke of those speed skating races!"

Now, I'm not saying that Keith was even considered or offered the ice hockey announcing. All I know is that Al Michaels's "Do you believe in miracles?" call has gone down in the history books as one of the most iconic utterances in sports broadcasting. Both of those men went on to do pretty well for themselves. Eric Heiden did win those five gold medals. Funny that in most circles he's far less known than the other two. He's still the only skater to win all five events—sprints to long distance—at a single games, let alone in an Olympic career.

In the end, my Olympic moment was still to come, and when it did for the first time in 1992, Paul Wylie, bless his heart, paid me a real tribute in Albertville. After the conclusion of the competitive portion of the event, the skaters received their medals. They take two laps of the ice surface in the Skate of Champions. Kristi Yamaguchi was up in the booth with Scott and me. The first lap, Paul looked up at us and waved. The second time around, we caught one another's eye. As he skated toward us, he lifted his silver medal over his head and bunched up its ribbon in his fist. He then executed a perfect bowling motion with the medal.

CHAPTER SIX

Beyond Borders

If my desire to reach the top ranking of ABC's college football play-by-play men went unmet, then I at least earned a consolation prize that topped what *Bowling for Dollars* offered: I got to travel internationally to cover sporting events for the network. Ever since I was a young boy and heard those voices over the radio bringing stories to me from the far reaches of the United States and beyond, I had dreamed of traveling to see other countries and cultures.

In the fall of 1979, I received a call from Chuck Howard. ABC was going to televise a portion of the World Junior Boxing Championship from Yokohama, Japan. I was told that I was to go there to commentate. I was over the moon to have this first opportunity to travel overseas to do a broadcast. Even better, this international event would be featured as a segment on ABC Sports' award-winning *Wide World of Sports*. In my mind, if any show occupied the top ranking of sports programming year to year in this country, it was *Wide World*. In its run from 1961 to 1988, the show won eleven Emmy Awards, a prestigious Peabody Award, and was named by *Time* magazine as one of the one hundred most influential shows in television.

Its original host, Jim McKay, was the best storyteller on television. He won two Emmy Awards—one for sports and the other for news coverage. The two intersected in 1972 at the Munich Olympics when terrorists took eleven Israeli athletes as hostages. Jim was there to cover the gymnastic events but was pressed into greater service when the events unfolded. Roone Arledge at ABC quickly realized he needed someone with the right qualities to be on the ground to cover the incident. Chris Schenkel was hosting the Games but didn't possess the storytelling chops to cover what was now a very serious international news story.

Jim was lounging by the pool when the call came. He hustled over to the studio, put on his pants and jacket, and stayed on the air for the next fourteen hours straight. When the crisis came to an end with the execution of all eleven of the athletes, Jim uttered words that went down in history: "When I was a kid my father used to say 'Our greatest hopes and our worst fears are seldom realized.' Our worst fears have been realized tonight. They have now said there were eleven hostages; two were killed in their rooms this morn—yesterday morning; nine were killed at the airport tonight. They're all gone."

An anthology show, *Wide World* was conceived on the premise that many sports from around the world didn't get airtime in the States. Some of what it first broadcast became staples of sports programming—the Indianapolis 500, Formula One racing, the British Open golf tournament, among them. Others were more obscure—Irish hurling (a lacrosse–field hockey hybrid), curling, jai-alai, wrist wrestling, logrolling, and a host of others. I loved the show and its wide range of subjects; the intellectual curiosity reflected my own and many others' about the rest of the world.

As it turned out, the boxing assignment didn't turn out to be a very big deal, but in January 1980, a Cold War battle was going to be waged. The United States was sending a team of amateur boxers to the Soviet Union to take on their squad. A four-person team went over, including me. Terry Jastrow was there, as well as a young production assistant by the name of David Dinkins, Jr. His father would eventually become mayor of New York. Our technical work was farmed out to a crew from Sweden. The most fascinating member of our entourage was a young man named Igor Rostov. Igor's perfect English, good looks, and ease with us foreigners had me convinced he was a KGB agent. He swore to us that he'd never been out of the motherland, but that didn't add up.

We stayed at the Metropole Hotel, just off Red Square. I understood why that famous place was named for the color. It was holding its breath: the foul odors that emanated from the Metropole stank of long-ignored laundry and cabbage. Come to think of it, that's what the food tasted like as well. It became clear to me that the Russians were as paranoid about us as we were about them. Everywhere I turned, I saw Soviet security personnel; every time I came back to the hotel I had to present my passport at the front desk before being issued a card to allow me on the elevator. Once when I was at the elevator a babushka woman checked my card and passport before allowing me on board as she presented me with an enormous metal key. It would have been impossible to hide the key in a pocket, and it took some effort just to put it in the lock to my sparse room.

Even more involved was the method by which I could make a call home. I had asked upon checking in if such a thing was possible. Easy, I was told. The front desk would call the phone service company requesting an overseas call. When the call was approved, the phone service would call the front desk and state what time and date the call could be made. I was checking in on a Sunday. The clerk dialed the number and a lengthy conversation ensued. Many minutes and consonants later, I was told the soonest time available was Wednesday between 4 P.M. and 8 P.M. I took it. Again, the whole passport check ensued but eventually I got a chance to speak with Dick Hitt, a columnist for the *Dallas Times Herald*. I'm sure the KGB loved every second of our conversation, especially the parts about the Cowboys.

Once again, politics and sports intertwined. While I was there, I had a lengthy lunch with the producer Terry Jastrow and Igor Rostov. We sat at a large window watching an icy parade of overcoat-clad Russians scuttling past, burrowed in their furs. As Terry and I shared memories of a Texas upbringing, Igor, reminding us again that he was born in Russia and had never been outside its borders, chimed in from time to time in perfectly colloquial English. He was convinced that the United States was going to invade the Soviet Union. "I'd bet my life on it," he said, employing the euphemism perfectly and seemingly without irony. We tried to convince him that the United States had no such intentions. We just wanted to live in peace. We invited him to visit America to see for himself how we all lived. He declined, feverishly. What could he find in the United States that his homeland couldn't provide? He also added, nodding at the pedestrians outside, that every one of those people lost someone in World War II. Most Americans had not. They knew about sacrifice. We did not.

I thought of all the long lines I'd seen for provisions but didn't say anything. It somehow felt un-American to agree with any part of Igor's assessment.

The next day, our world changed. President Carter announced that the United States would not participate in the Moscow Olympics due to the Soviet invasion of Afghanistan. Suddenly, our little band of twelve boxers became the focus of the news/sports world. ABC had a very substantial news presence in Moscow but because this was a story about the fallout of the president's decision, they asked me to step in. I was to interview these twelve young men. They all happened to be African American and shared similar stories of coming from economically disadvantaged backgrounds; each dreamed of Olympic glory and what it might have meant as a means to improve their future prospects.

When I told them that it appeared as if those dreams would be left unrealized, that all the hard work they'd put in might ultimately be for naught, they looked alternately confused, crestfallen, and angry. I couldn't blame them; I thought that President Carter had made an awful decision. Why use these athletes as pawns? Why dash the hopes and dreams of hundreds of other athletes?

We were still going to cover the bouts. Terry asked me if I would like to comment on the recent out-of-the-ring developments. I told him I would and worked feverishly that week to develop an essay that I delivered on camera to be included at the conclusion of our broadcast. I said much of what I stated above—wrong choice, ill-advised denial of opportunity, and wrongheaded mixing of politics and sports.

A few weeks after it aired, I got a call from one of our ABC vice presidents—we had more than a few. I was eager to hear what he had to say; maybe I'd made my mark this time. I had, but as it turned out it was more like I'd been doglike in marking my territory. The vice president told me that he'd gotten a call from someone at the White House. The man had expressed in no uncertain terms his displeasure with my remarks. As it was relayed to me, the White House staffer said it was as if I "had been pissing in the face of the president."

There was no fallout from that call, but the message was delivered. I was dismayed. I consoled myself with this thought: at least I wasn't an Olympic athlete who would have to wait four more years for, or perhaps never get, a chance to be in the spotlight.

I only had to wait two months before being in the spotlight; again, not a place that worked to my advantage. Boxing was on the menu again—the U.S. team versus the East Germans in a small city north of Berlin. ABC promoted the heck out of it—the first sporting event ever televised live from East Germany to the United States. The American public seemed to have an insatiable appetite for these story lines about communist bad guys versus democratic good guys. It was good theater, and with the recent decision to forgo the Olympics, a new narrative thread was emerging: let's take a closer look at life behind the Iron Curtain; let's give viewers a chance to see what they won't be able to in Moscow.

For years, in covering events all over Europe, ABC had used a man named Kurt Fuchs as an interpreter and driver. He greeted me at the Berlin airport and was as gregarious and charming as I'd been told he would be. He carried both an Austrian and a West German passport, and used whichever one was best in a given situation. He took us through Checkpoint Charlie, the gap in the wall dividing East and West Germany, with little difficulty—an hourlong process. We began our car trip to Schwerin, an hour's drive north. Now, I'd lived in Texas for quite a while and traveled through a variety of no-man's-lands covering sports there and across the country, but that ride was memorable for being so unremarkable. The road was arrow straight, the scenery flat and endless farmland without any sign of life—animal or human. It was mind-numbing. My stay in the Hotel Stadtschwerin would numb the rest of me. The tiny bed wouldn't accommodate my five-nine frame and I slept with one leg dangling off it.

Didn't matter. I was excited to have my third overseas assignment in ten weeks. My colleagues had another take, wondering who they had pissed off to get sent to this godforsaken place. I had my rose-colored glasses on but wisely kept my views to myself. The broadcast went flawlessly. I was excited by the fact that this wasn't going into the can to be diced up later as TV spam. The matches were on Sunday night and they were going to be shown that same day back in the United States, in the afternoon due to the time zone differences. By 10 P.M. we were on the road back to Berlin and then on to the comforts of home. Kurt drove and Radio Luxembourg provided the sound track, the best of 1950s to '70s rock and roll—almost like I was back in Austin in my early days of DJing.

That's when the house of shits reestablished itself. We got to Checkpoint Charlie at three in the morning. A shroud of fog and mist hung over the lights illuminating our entry point into normal civilization. Through panes of glass dripping with moisture, I watched as Kurt spoke to the guards outside the car. German was always harsh-sounding, but there was an even more bitter tone to it. Kurt's voice rose—he was an avowed critic of the East German communists. From out of the dim lights near an outbuilding men came toward the car. The Vopos, the East German police, charged at us. They surrounded the car, yanked open the back door of the sedan, and ordered us out.

Once again, I had to produce my passport along with my visa. Another group of policemen searched the vehicle. One officer with a mirror attached to a long pole examined the car's chassis looking for a stowaway. The trunk slammed shut, putting an exclamation point to their fruitless search.

Kurt grew more irksome and shouted angrily. I walked toward him, hands up in surrender and to soothe our friend. All we wanted to do was get out of East Germany and then back home. I'd been accused of pissing in the face of an American president. Imagine what might happen if my bosses got wind of involvement in some international incident at the Berlin Wall?

A tense ten to twenty minutes passed. Our driver had seemed bent on breaking something. Fortunately, no irreparable damage was done. Once back on the Kurfürstendamm, the main artery through East and West Berlin, I remained tense. Even after we passed through Checkpoint Charlie and into the West, my jaw remained clenched. Just as the first lights of dawn were leaking across the edge of the horizon, we got to the Kempinski Hotel. At that hour, the city was ablaze in light, a warm glow against the winter chill. I exited the car and turned back toward the Wall and the dark expanse beyond it. I sighed deeply, grateful that the only smell on the predawn breeze was of freedom.

I suppose that in terms of my own career prospects at ABC, I should have read the writing on the wall. To an extent, I did, but my eyesight has never been the best. I wanted to keep myself in ABC's good graces. So I agreed to take on any assignment they "offered." I'd learned my lesson from that encounter I'd had with Chuck Howard when he pulled the plug on my PGA Tournament debut. I'd protested long and loud, ignoring advice not to, and felt like I was on Chuck's shit list as a result. I was learning that sometimes you have to go along to get along. So, now I can at least say that I've covered twenty sports in my time in broadcasting. Sometimes those sports came in bunches, as they did at a sports festival in Syracuse, New York, when Chuck told me to get my butt up there. I did weight lifting, short-track speed skating (with Eric Heiden as analyst), and archery (solo). I can tell you that a person can barely hear the sound of a string humming the breeze above the sound of the collective snoring back home. I also did post-event interviews with track-and-field participants.

I say that in jest about archery. I did learn a lot about different sports and applying those Glieber rules for Success paid dividends. I don't think I ever sounded completely out of my depth. Frank's other bit of advice, Don't ever say no to a request, tried my patience. Sometimes my ventures into other sports surprised me in ways I couldn't have imagined. In 1986 I was "invited" to do the Show Jumping World Cup in Aachen, Germany. I watched every bit of video I could find on the sport, and then sat in awe in a stadium crowded with sixty thousand fans watching those beautiful animals run and leap. Princess Anne was there, an accomplished equestrian herself. I had a first-time analyst named Robert Ridland in the booth with me, and despite being a complete television novice, he was an expert rider himself. He was the captain of the U.S. equestrian team at the 1984 Los Angeles Olympics. All I had to do was get the names of the horse and rider correct, the country they were representing, and Robert did the rest. Some of my best research material on Charlemagne the Magnificent—he was born in Aachen—went unused.

I enjoyed the travel and my colleagues, but the lack of high-profile assignments got to me. Like a lot of people, I thought that my employers didn't appreciate everything I brought to the table as a broadcaster. Versatility can be its own kind of curse—you don't get known for doing any one thing especially well. There's a fine line in some people's minds between being a professional and being a hack. I don't think that the folks at ABC ever considered me the latter, but when I asked Chuck Howard where I stood with him, he was honest. He said that I was a square peg that didn't fit into the proverbial round hole. He honestly wasn't sure what he could do with me. He had tried to figure out what I excelled at but hadn't been able to. I appreciated knowing exactly where I stood. You have to have a bit of an ego to succeed at anything; a man without pride isn't much of a man.

Funnily, Don Drysdale, the Hall of Fame Dodgers pitcher turned baseball broadcaster, said this to me when I was covering spring training for the Rangers. Don was known for his fearsome disposition on the mound and his willingness to hit or low-bridge hitters or back them off the plate just with his stare. We were talking about the business we both found ourselves involved in. "Verne," he said, "at the end of the day they're in charge and we ain't nothing but talking dogs."

If Don felt that way some of the time, then imagine what this little mutt often felt.

LIKE I SAID, I SHOULD have seen the writing on the wall, and to an extent I did, but I was also under contract. I was going to fulfill my obligations and see what I could do about improving my lot at ABC. I wasn't simply going to roll over and phone it in—given what happened in Moscow I'd begun to think that phoning it in was a lot more difficult than most folks thought. I was going to demonstrate my worth, rough off the square edges, and fit in that round hole.

I was attending the John R. Wooden Award ceremony in Los Angeles.

I received a call from Chet Forte at ABC in New York. (He had earned wide acclaim as the first director of *Monday Night Football*.) ABC had just signed a two-year deal to televise the North American Soccer League starting in 1979. They would do nine regular season games plus the playoffs that culminated in the Soccer Bowl championship game. The league had been in operation since 1964. I was aware of its existence because of the role that Lamar Hunt—the AFL's principal founder—had played in its formation. Lamar was an impressive proselytizer for the world's game. Because of his influence, I'd gone to the World Cup in 1970, 1974, and 1978 and enjoyed the passion and the pageantry of the game. Being on the streets of Buenos Aires in 1978, joining millions of fans celebrating the home country's victory, is among my all-time thrills in sports. I'll spare you the details of Uncle Verne the man of international intrigue and his involvement with Saudi princes, women of questionable virtue, and Henry Kissinger.

In spite of my admiration for the game, I wasn't sold on the idea of soccer doing particularly well in the United States. However, the owners of the league and of the New York Cosmos figured that if there was a problem, then throw some money at it. In this case, they threw money at some of the most prominent names in the game at that time—Pelé, Franz Beckenbauer, and a few others. Attendance and ratings rose through the mid-1970s, though many called into question the quality of the game play. ABC jumped in at what seemed an opportune time. I was going to report from the sidelines while Jim McKay handled the play-by-play. Networks seemed to have a rule of thumb back then. You needed an Englishman for games that originated overseas. ABC brought in Paul Gardner as the analyst. Gardner had been covering a variety of American sports for British publications for years.

The morning of the first broadcast, Jim McKay drove us to the Sombrero, the stadium in Tampa that was the home of the Tampa Bay Rowdies and the NFL's Buccaneers. The Rowdies were going to square off against the Cosmos. I was happy to see Jim again and to work with him directly was going to be a real treat. As we made our way to the game, Jim was effusive in his praise for this venture. He compared how he felt on the cusp of this game to 1961, when *Wide World of Sports* kicked off its first season with amateur track and field events, the Drake and the Penn Relays. Laughing, he said that we are all going to be off and running after this, chasing a great success. He felt that we had a tiny little secret and we were about to spring it on an unsuspecting and ultimately grateful nation. He had me convinced. When I was down on the field and looking up at the forty-five thousand fans in the stands, I knew this wasn't exactly Wembley Stadium, but it was something to see and feel.

The buzz in my stomach lasted until the first goal of the game. We missed it. We didn't show it live. None of us had a lot of knowledge about the game, and the confusion for the signal for a goal kick and a corner kick kicked our butts. With a goal kick the player takes the ball in hand and boots it down the field, similar to a punt. That would be a safe time to go to commercial. Thinking that was what had been signaled, the producer made the call to take a break. As it turned out, the officials had signaled for a corner kick—one of the more exciting plays and one that offers a prime opportunity for a goal. In this case, that opportunity got cashed in while we were making some cash through advertising dollars. Having to come back from commercials to say, essentially, here's what you missed while we were away, wasn't the best of starts to our coverage.

I can't say that things would have turned out different if we'd not made that opening blunder. For many reasons, our broadcasts only brought in about half the number of viewers projected. As with much of my time at ABC, I thought the NASL was going to open doors that even Chuck Howard could see. And it never did.

The only door that Chuck could see for me was the exit. To put it in polite terms, my contract was not renewed. I was informed of this before the actual date it would lapse. I was angry and a bit panicked. I was forty-one years old. What prospects did I have in a business that was seeing an influx of young talent? My agents were at International Management Group, the enormously influential sports marketing agency that Mark McCormack founded in 1960. It grew to prominence representing Arnold Palmer, Jack Nicklaus, and Gary Player. My representative assured me that I had no need to panic. Still, the clock was ticking on my ambitions.

I was enormously fortunate that prior to this period of professional unease, I'd been enormously blessed to find a partner to share my life with, a woman who made all these career disappointments bearable. God knows what might have become of me if it weren't for Nancy Miller coming into my life. I've witnessed some memorable sporting events, but for me, meeting her tops all of them and merits some play-by-play.

When I did that East German boxing telecast in Schwerin, my life was at low ebb. I was three months removed from my second divorce. I knew that if I went straight back home to Dallas, I would have been prowling around the house surrounded by little more than bad memories and mementoes of my failure. So, I went on a ten-day Scandinavian excursion, hoping that doing the tourist bit would get me out of a rut. Maybe some ancestral pull was at work as well.

This was the first week of March 1980, and I don't have access to all the weather data from Stockholm, but the three days I spent in that rain-soaked world capital were about as dank and miserable as any I can remember. To show you that my thinking wasn't particularly clear, I had a great thought. Why not go to Norway? The weather in Oslo will certainly have to be better than it is here. Oslo is a lovely city but at that time of year the weather in Scandinavia is hardly balmy and bright. I remember standing on a street corner of the busy thoroughfare that ran along one entrance to the Vigeland Sculpture Park. The morning snow had begun to melt and I stood there looking into a frothy puddle of slush and ice. A city bus screeched to a stop inches before it would have showered me. Later that day, I went to the SAS office and booked a flight to Copenhagen.

After ten days on the road visiting my ancestral homelands, I returned to Dallas in mid-March. Still feeling a bit haunted, I finished the ten o'clock newscast and decided to go out, hoping to meet someone. I went to the Greenville Avenue neighborhood in my beat-up Chevy. Greenville was one of the hot spots back then and I went into a disco called DaVinci's. I edged my way past the *Saturday Night Fever*-esque dancers, squinted through the pulsing lights, sat down at the bar, and ordered a drink.

Fortunately for me, a young man recognized me and saw I was very much a fish out of water at that spot. He suggested kindly that I might be better off going to a place called Arthur's. A steakhouse with a nice bar, people more my age tended to be there. The following week, I took the young guy's advice. Man, I'm glad that I did. On March 18, 1980, my life changed. Local notoriety paid off for me that night as well.

The restaurant had closed, but the bar was hopping. And it was an upscale bar. They had a trio playing over on the dance floor in the corner. A very attractive woman was sitting on a bar stool. Two guys were standing with her.

One of the men, the taller of the two, recognized me and said, "Verne, come on over here."

I did.

He told me that his name was Raymond Willey and he owned the Coors beer distributorship in Dallas.

He then added, "This is my date, Nancy Miller."

"And this is my friend Paul, who's a stockbroker, Paul Bass." The two of us shook hands.

"Let me buy you a drink," Raymond offered.

I barely heard him. All I could think about was the woman he was with.

Nancy was sitting down. She had the prettiest smile I'd ever seen in my life, and she still does, thirty-eight years later.

Raymond broke the spell. He sidled over to me and said, "I know you're single now, and I'd like to introduce you to a friend of mine. Maybe we could double date."

Meanwhile, I was looking at Nancy, thinking, Boy, is she pretty.

Nancy was keeping pretty quiet. Raymond was a talker. Given his business interests he was used to entertaining clients. Nancy didn't look enthralled at all.

"Listen," Raymond said, "I've got a schoolteacher who's obviously single. Her name is Janet Fulton. She's thirty-five. Let's double date."

He looked down at Nancy and said, "What are you doing Thursday night?"

And she said, "Nothing."

He said, "Good. You and I will have a date and we'll double date with Verne and Janet Fulton, and I will call her tomorrow and we'll set this thing up."

I thought, Great, but I kept looking at Nancy.

A while later, Raymond went to the men's room and I asked Nancy if she would dance with me. I'm not a dancer. I never do that. But I thought, Well, the door's open here for maybe two minutes.

We got on the dance floor and I said, "I don't mean to intrude, but how involved are you with Raymond Willey?"

Nancy shrugged a bit. "Well, this is our first date. We had a blind date."

A doctor, a surgeon who had both of them as patients, had suggested they get together. They had gone to see Ella Fitzgerald at the Venetian Room at the Fairmont Hotel and they were just having a nightcap.

Just to be certain I said, "So your first date, right?" And she said, "Yeah."

I said, "Well, in that case, let's forget about what he's suggesting on Thursday night. What are you doing on Saturday night?" Nancy got this grin that I will never, ever forget and kind of looked up at me: "I think whatever you're doing."

I asked for her number and she gave her work number. Turned out she worked as a radio and television spokesperson. She supplemented her income as a receptionist at a recording studio. I didn't have a pen or paper on me, but thirty-eight years later I can still recite it.

361-9189.

I can do that because that night Nancy said, "Imagine a dial tone, a push-button telephone, and it makes a certain tone." Her lovely voice went up and down singsong fashion as she repeated those digits. She rose at the end, hitting a high note and lifting my spirits. We spent a good twenty minutes out on the dance floor. I'm no dancer, but the longer I kept her away from Raymond and in my arms and in my sight the better.

By the time we rejoined the two other men, Raymond suggested that he and Nancy should be on their way.

I hoped that what I saw in Nancy's eyes was regret. I *know* that I saw the two of them getting into Raymond's Rolls-Royce. I had a formidable opponent to face, but I was undaunted by the challenge.

Well, I couldn't wait to get home and go to bed and call her the next morning, and she was out on an audition. I left a message; she never called back. I called again about one o'clock, and she didn't return the call. I called again at three o'clock, and they said, "Well, she just got back from her assignment. She's in her office, but she's got the door closed." And I said, "Well, please get a message to her that I've called three times and have her call me at Channel Eight."

And finally, about five o'clock, I called back again and she took the call. And she said, "Listen, I've been thinking all day about this. I'd love to go out with you on Saturday night, but I don't want to break up a friendship."

I said, "We're not friends. I've never met Raymond Willey in my life."

And she said, "Well, he greeted you like an old friend."

And I said, "Well, Nance, that's the phenomenon of local television. People assume, if you're a guest in their living rooms or their bedrooms every night and they know who you are, then conversely, you must know who they are," and it's a phenomenon that still exists. "And Raymond just . . . he knew who I was."

She said, "Well, you got along so well."

I said, "Well, he seemed like a nice guy."

She said, "Well, I still don't think it's a good idea."

And I said, "I promise you it's a good idea." So we did, she agreed, and that Saturday night, we went to a restaurant called Farfallo's.

When we did get married two years later, the bartender and the young woman who was our waitress that night both came to our wedding. Nancy and I enjoyed that special night and she's been my constant companion ever since. At every possible opportunity, she's joined me on the road. Back then, neither of us had a full sense of just where those roads would lead, but it didn't matter as long as we were together. I feel the same way today.

CHAPTER 7

Yes, Sir: A New Home
at the Masters

What in blue blazers are you talking about?

I didn't say those words back in January 1982 but I wish that I had. Knowing that my time with ABC was nearly over, I'd contacted my agent to see if I was going to have to resign myself to doing local news and the Cowboys radio exclusively. I didn't want to give up the dream, but sometimes in life reality intrudes. So, when Barry Frank told me that I had a shot at a job with CBS, I was thrilled. He said that they were getting back into broadcasting college football. They'd also acquired the rights to the NCAA basketball tournament and wanted to see how I could do at that as well.

Barry had done some negotiations on my behalf and he agreed that I would go to Columbia, South Carolina, the first week of March to do a Gamecocks contest against University of Nevada–Las Vegas (UNLV). This was a limited regional broadcast through six affiliates—four in South Carolina and one in Reno and one in Vegas. He sounded very pleased with himself.

My guts roiled. "But I'm still at ABC. My contract with them doesn't end until after that game is long gone and in the history books. Now you want me to put on a blue blazer and do a basketball game?"

I had visions of angry phone calls, lawsuits, men in suits, depositions, interrogations, Watergate-like hearings questioning who knew what and when.

Barry brought me back to Realityville. "Verne, do you really think that ABC gives a shit? They're not renewing your contract. Obviously you have no value to them."

Still, I was worried about what my boss at my ABC affiliate in Dallas would think of me being on a competing network.

Barry took the line that it is better to ask forgiveness than it is permission. Don't tell them. How in the world would they even know what was on CBS in South Carolina or Nevada?

Six stations.

Six stations.

What are the chances of this getting out?

I decided to do as Barry said.

Before that March date, I had another one lined up.

At a whorehouse. Not just any whorehouse but the "Best Little Whorehouse in Texas." I had to be on a soundstage in Hollywood to play myself in that film. Lee Grosscup and I were hired to play ourselves covering a Texas–Texas A&M football game. Nancy went to Los Angeles with me, and she warned me that this was Hollywood and she'd done a few films herself. Things always take longer than you can imagine so be prepared to do a lot of sitting and waiting. Of course, Nancy was right and we had to hustle to the airport to get to Dallas. I drove her home, packed a different bag, and was out the door to fly to South Carolina for the game. Rushing was both a blessing and a curse. While sitting there waiting to do my on-camera bit for the movie, I had too much time to think about what was at stake with the basketball game.

I arrived a day before the game and went with great apprehension out to the CBS trucks. The first person I ran into was Patty Tuitte, whom I'd worked with recently on an ABC broadcast. Patty said, "You know, I want to tell you something. I always thought you'd look better in blue than yellow." I had to agree with that sartorial assessment.

I introduced myself to Rick Sharpe, the lead producer for CBS college basketball telecasts. I also met Bob Fishman, who in 2018 directed his thirtieth Final Four telecast. I was in good hands, and I hoped that I'd prove to the powers to be that I was worth hiring. As it turned out, I was very fortunate. The game was close throughout. That UNLV team was coached by Jerry "the Shark" Tarkanian. What a roster they had: Sidney Green and Larry Anderson at forward were a potent pair for the Runnin' Rebels.

I was working with Irv Brown, a referee as well as analyst, and things were going very well. I'd done radio play-by-play for basketball before, and I loved the game so much, I fell into a nice rhythm immediately.

The other game being broadcast that afternoon was Louisville versus Memphis. The season was winding down and we were on the brink of Selection Sunday. That game was a blowout and was ending earlier than expected. The powers that be in New York decided they were going to switch over to our game. I heard the news over my headset.

Six cities.

Sick to my stomach.

I turned to Irv Brown and asked him not to use my name during the rest of the telecast. He looked puzzled but read my panic and agreed.

Then I heard the voice of my friend Frank Glieber over the headsets. He was doing the Louisville-Memphis game. I thought I detected a bit of surprise in his voice when he said, "That's a final, ninety to seventy-eight, and we're going to move you now to a game that's under way in the South. It's UNLV and South Carolina and for the play-by-play let's take you to Verne Lundquist?"

I may have imagined that question mark, but Frank had no idea I had this tryout with CBS because I hadn't said a word about it to anyone but Nancy.

Irv managed to avoid calling me by name, but we also had to do a bit of fill work to get to the top of the hour. UNLV was on the tournament bubble, so I went down to their locker room to talk to Jerry Tarkanian. Maybe the folks back in Dallas whom I didn't want to know about my venture could have tuned in and not really recognized my voice. But they were sure as heck going to recognize my face and the pained expression on it as I spoke with the coach.

After we wrapped, all I could do was laugh. My cover was blown. We'd have to wait to see what the result would be.

As it turned out, it wasn't as bad as I'd feared. I was able to convince Dave Lane, my ABC station's general manager, to let me take this as a short-term assignment on the first- and second-round games. Dave was always in my corner and I owe him a lot for how he helped me reach my goals. I had a fair amount to do to catch up on the 1981–82 NCAA basketball season. For longtime fans of the game, the preseason top five in that campaign were familiar names North Carolina, UCLA, Kentucky, Louisville, and Georgetown. Each of those received votes for the top spot going into the season.

I got to do games in the first two rounds of the Midwest regional in Tulsa, Oklahoma, with Houston, Alcorn State, Marquette, and Missouri squaring off. Dale Brown, head coach at LSU, was at my side. Alcorn State was the champion of the South West Athletic Conference, earning an automatic bid for that small school. Marquette's Hank Raymond relied heavily on his wonderful guard Doc Rivers. Doc and I would eventually be paired at TBS doing NBA games.

In the end, though, Houston emerged from that part of the bracket and advanced all the way to the Final Four. That season was the first for Phi Slamma Jamma. Clyde Drexler, Rob Williams, Michael Young, and Larry Micheaux led the team. Hakeem Olajuwon was a freshman but already showed his brilliance. Famously, one year later they lost by two to Jim Valvanos's North Carolina State squad, playing a part in one of the great moments in NCAA history with Jimmy V's delirious dash. Olajuwon was named Most Outstanding Player in a losing cause, and he's the only one to have earned that distinction without cutting down the cords.

Even though I was only in it for the first two rounds, I really enjoyed doing those games. The tournament atmosphere was always fun, and as the field expanded from 48 teams in 1982 to its present 64-plus, the intensity and pleasure of the tournament continued to climb. Oh, and another bit of trivia about that tournament. Some guy named Jordan helped Dean Smith's Tar Heels win the championship over Georgetown. I'm not sure I know what became of that youngster. In fact, that championship game featured three players who would eventually be named as among the NBA's fifty greatest players—Jordan, James Worthy, and Patrick Ewing. Guess what Patrick is doing these day? Coaching his alma mater at Georgetown, of course.

I understand now that the staff at CBS had other things on their mind during the tournament than the fate of one Verne Lundquist, but still I was on tenterhooks wondering what my fate was to be. As it turned out, there had been a bit of an exodus at ABC, and one of those who crossed the waters to CBS was a brilliant young man named Ric LaCivita. I'm not impressed by pedigrees, and I don't know how much him having graduated from Harvard played in his savvy, but he was a young hot shot and CBS sought him out to be their coordinating producer for all their college football games. He reached me to tell me that he had contacted Kevin O'Malley, Executive Producer of College Sports for CBS, and he believed that if I was interested, he could get Kevin to agree to hire me.

Finally, about the time the elite eight was being settled, I got my own not-so-elite eight offer. Kevin did want to hire me, but for six NCAA football games and two NCAA basketball games. I told Kevin that was only 8 out of 52 weeks. I couldn't live on that. He told me that was the best he could do. I asked for some time to think about it. He agreed.

I spoke with Nancy and Dave Lane. I felt I was in a pretty good position to negotiate with Dave. I was a part of a really good team at WFAA. We had a lineup that included Paula Zahn, Scott Pelley, Peter Van Sant (now part of *48 Hours*' reporting staff) and most significantly, we battled Bill O'Reilly for a very short time. We won. If I could figure out a way to turn that 6 + 2 into a 52-weeks-a-year gig with CBS and my local ABC affiliate, I'd be able to make a go of things financially.

With the wisdom of Solomon, Dave devised a solution. I would no longer be under contract as an employee of an ABC affiliate. I'd be an independent contractor. I'd be paid only for the time I worked doing the local broadcasts. That would free me up to sign, and avoid a noncompete clause, with a rival network to do national broadcasts. He also got the people at CBS, who wanted me to do the NCAA tournament that week, to agree that whatever game I was doing wouldn't be shown in the Dallas market. This all took more time and anxiety and waiting and wondering than I've presented here, but bottom line is that I began my CBS career shortly after that tryout. My days of doing national broadcasts with ABC were over. Contractually, and in my heart, I was a CBS guy. Goodbye, bile yellow and hello blue.

For about another two years I did WFAA Monday through Thursday or Monday through Wednesday during the football season. I did the college games on Saturday and then I did the Cowboys on Sunday. Eventually, as my responsibilities at CBS increased, I couldn't keep those local commitments. My last sportscast for WFAA came in 1983. One year later I reluctantly relinquished my role as the Cowboys' radio guy. I knew that Brad Sham would do a great job when he slid over from the analyst's spot to play-by-play man.

Wearing those three hats for that span required some logistical expertise getting from one place to the other. At first CBS assured me that if there was a game in the Southwest, I'd be assigned to it. Also, I'd work with the same partner. Steve Davis, with whom I'd worked at ABC regularly, had also come over to CBS and we were to be paired. All that sounded great—in theory. The first weekend when the assignments came through, I ended up in Kansas. Sadly, I was paired with a rookie broadcaster I'd covered when he was a star quarterback in high school and later in college. I don't think the Wizard of Oz could have helped him much. He seemed fine in our pregame meetings, but his jaw got as rusty as the Tin Man's and he could barely stutter out any commentary that day. It was the last game he ever did, as far as I know. Tough game on the field and above it as well.

Fortunately for me, I'd done enough games that I could cover for his Oh-Shit-I'm-on-television moment. Funny thing is, it was another oh-shit scenario that changed the course of my career forever. After a bit of a rough start, when I was calling games that were being broadcast on only three affiliates and such, I got a break and was assigned to a Big Ten Illinois versus Wisconsin game. I had the highly regarded Rick Sharpe to thank for that. He put in a call on my behalf and I got my biggest gig to that point, a regional game.

I went up to work with Dennis Franklin in Camp Randall Stadium in Madison, one of the great college venues in America. It's always filled. It's located in a beautiful city, a great campus. And we had an amazing afternoon that Saturday. The Illinois quarterback was Tony Eason. He was part of one of the greatest trivia questions ever—name all six of the quarterbacks who were taken in the first round of the 1983 NFL draft. Tony was one of them. The Wisconsin quarterback was Randy Wright. He was not quite that gifted, but the old Big Ten brand of football, three yards and a cloud of dust, wasn't on display.

Dennis and I arrived on Friday. I watched Wisconsin practice a trick play. I made a mental note of it. You never know what might come up and it pays to be prepared.

So, sure enough, you talk about the stars aligning, game day arrives. Wisconsin and Illinois are battling it out. Across the CBS network, Arkansas–Houston ends early. So they pull that audience into us because we've got a very competitive game. Tennessee–Vanderbilt ends early. They pull that audience into us. Grambling–Jackson State ends early. We get that market. All of a sudden with about five minutes to go in our game we have the complete national audience. Seemed like every few seconds I heard Rick Sharpe telling me through my headset to standby and welcome those who had watched blank versus blank. I was like an anxious high school kid watching as invitees actually came to my little party.

By the time everyone was on board, Wisconsin had the ball at their own 48-yard line and they were trailing in the game. Randy Wright took the snap from center, bounced it off the turf once. Al Toon, who went on to play for the New York Jets, picked it up. The linemen all stood up and said, "Oh shit!" and threw their hands in the air in dismay and disgust. Illinois's defensive players froze. Al Toon threw the pass to the tight end, 52 yards, touchdown, almost untouched. Wisconsin went on top.

That was the trick play I'd seen. The instant the ball hit the ground I said, "This is a valid play. This is no forward pass." Thinking quickly, I switched things up and said that it was the "Oh, My!" play.

Afterward, during the replay, I told everyone that in 1965 I was at the Texas A&M–Texas game. I saw A&M run the exact same play against Texas, and it turned out to be the winning touchdown. The sad irony for Wisconsin is that Illinois put together one heck of a comeback, kicking a 48-yard field goal with ten seconds left on the clock to win the game.

The following afternoon, Nancy and I were watching Pat Summerall, John Madden, and Pat O'Brien do a Baldwin Wallace–Wittenberg game. Because of the NFL players' strike, CBS had their NFL number one team doing that small college game. That was the first time I'd ever seen Pat O'Brien and he was really terrific as the sideline guy. To their credit, Pat and John treated the game like they would any NFL game. As I was watching, I got a phone call from Rick. He asked if I had heard from anybody in New York yet. I said, no, I hadn't. And he said, well, you will. When your phone rings, don't ignore it.

About a half hour later Kevin O'Malley was on the line. He was really impressed that I knew the "Oh, My!" was a legal play and that I'd said so before they even tried to pass. He didn't know how many other announcers he had on our roster who would've known that play was legal. He just wanted to call to tell me how impactful my call was in his perception of me. He wanted to thank me and that I should plan on doing more games that year.

Do you believe in miracles?

Okay, that's a bit overstated, but isn't it funny how life can turn on such moments? You just never know—that's why they play the games.

Clichés like that possess essential truths. I'd stuck with it and believed in myself, had some great people in my corner, and a big break comes from an arcane Oh Shit! play that I'd seen back in the day. As I've said before, a lot of young people ask me how to make it in this business. Well, I don't know if this kind of thing is in the syllabus of any mass media or communications course, but sometimes things just go your way. Don't overthink it. Be grateful and remember that very often the difference between great success and disappointment isn't a matter of talent or work. Sometimes the ball just bounces your way. I can't thank Dave Lane enough for all he did for me. If it weren't for his willingness to compromise, I wouldn't have been there in Madison.

We talk about momentum in sports, and I'll leave that debate about its importance to others. I will say this: once Kevin O'Malley made that call, the proverbial worm seemed to turn. On December 1, 1982, Nancy and I were home in the afternoon relaxing when I got a call from CBS Sports, wanting to know if I'd ever done TV coverage for a golf tournament. I had covered several for ABC. It turned out that Frank Chirkinian, who was in charge of golf and tennis for CBS liked my work. They wanted me to cover five golf telecasts in 1983—the Bing Crosby Pro-Am at Pebble Beach, Jack Nicklaus's Memorial, the Colonial in Forth Worth, the Byron Nelson in Dallas, and the Masters in Augusta, Georgia.

I swallowed hard. I could scarcely believe what I was being told. Further, they didn't want me to go in cold for the Bing Crosby. Given the pro-am format and the early season appeal to those in the snow belt, ratings were always very high for that event. To help me get to know the rest of the broadcast team, they asked me to go to the Phoenix Open and join the group at the 16th hole. I hung up the phone and told Nancy what I'd just been offered. She stood up without saying a word and left the room. A moment or two later, she came back with a bottle of wine and two glasses. I felt sure that CBS wanting me to do golf boded well for my future in all areas. I could hardly imagine them sticking to the two basketball games a year that I'd originally agreed to. My sense was that I'd be wearing a blue blazer with far greater frequency than that.

What can I say about Frank Chirkinian? Well, we called him "the Ayatollah." He was about five four at best, with a big brush of gray hair, impeccably dressed every day, always with a cashmere sport coat, handkerchief in the pocket, Gucci loafers, the whole thing. And he was the most profane man I have ever known. I mean, he was a terrific producer and director, but God almighty, could Frank Chirkinian dress down people.

Frank was in charge of golf at CBS Sports. He did other things, including the Winter Olympics, the U.S. Open, college football, and horse racing's Triple Crown, but golf is what he was known for in the business. I recall entering the CBS Sports compound at the Old Phoenix Country Club for my debut assignment. There was a little room partitioned off in the back where Frank was. I told the secretary that I was there to see him. He heard me. I could hear him bellow, "Come back here!"

I walked into his little cubicle.

I said, "Frank, I'm Verne Lundquist."

He said, "I know who you are. Who do you think fucking hired you?"

So that was the way our relationship started.

He then sat me down and told me, "I have three rules. If you follow them, you're going to get along fine with us."

I had actually met Frank once when I was living in Dallas–Fort Worth. CBS had the Colonial and we had briefly talked. So I at least knew of Frank, but I had never sat across from him. He was intimidating for a short man.

Frank continued.

"Rule number one," he told me. "You never say your own name on television. Nobody gives a shit who you are."

Fine by me, I thought.

"Here's the way this works," Frank continued. "You're going to be at [hole] Sixteen. At the appropriate time, when we first come to you, Pat Summerall will say, 'Here's the newest member of our golf team, Verne Lundquist.' I don't want you to respond, okay?"

Again, no problem here.

"Rule number two: Don't talk over a shot, ever."

I can do that, I thought.

Of course Frank wasn't done.

"Whatever brilliant addition you have to make to the editorial content of this production, I want you to complete the sentence or the paragraph before the golfer ever takes his club back. Don't fucking talk over the shot. And don't predict where it's going unless you're absolutely sure. Just wait until the ball lands. Guys have been fucking wrong all the time!"

Frank paused to take a breath.

"Rule number three: Never state the fucking obvious. We have sixty-five technicians here. We have microphones and cameras all over the course. We've got videotape machines in the truck in case we have to use them. I don't want you to state the obvious. If a guy makes a two-foot putt, don't you dare ever say, 'He made it.' That's pretty fucking obvious."

I made my CBS Sports golf debut on a Saturday at the 1983 Phoenix Open. I was assigned to No. 16 and Nancy was with me in the tower. I recall the director took a two-shot of us, with Pat Summerall rather warmly welcoming us both to the CBS golf family. It was very unusual that Frank would allow that. Somewhere in my house I have a five-by-seven photo of Nancy and me that was taken off the monitor the moment Pat introduced us.

So as the newest member of our golf team, I said, "Here is Rex Crawford in the middle of the fairway, seven-iron, one hundred and fifty yards, the hole is cut back right." Then I shut up. Crawford hit it. I didn't say anything until the ball landed. It did, and wound up twenty feet away from the hole.

"He's going to have a swerving left-to-right putt for birdie," I said. So far, so good. I thought.

Summerall eventually brought it back to 16. Caldwell was twenty feet from the hole, currently three off the lead. If he makes this, he's going to be two off the lead. I shut up. He putts and leaves it about three feet short. I say, "Well, he's still got that chance for par," and we go away.

Pat brought it back to me again.

"Here is Rex Caldwell—this is going to break a little left to right. If he makes it he'll stay three off the lead."

Caldwell strokes the ball, never comes close to hitting the hole.

"He missed it!" I scream.

Oh, shit.

Frank pushed what we call the "All Key" button so that every announcer could hear him. This was obviously not on the air—just in our headsets.

"You stupid Scandinavian son of a bitch!" he screamed at me. "If I tell you not to tell me that he made it, can you not deduce on your own to never tell me that he missed it?"

Well, the guys zinged me for the rest of the day. It was kind of an initiation rite. I never did it again. I've never done it again in all the years. So the lesson was learned. Don't break Frank's rules.

When thinking about Frank, it's impossible not to mention the Masters. I remember the first time I saw the course. I flew in on a Tuesday in April 1983. Nancy and I drove over to the complex. Nancy didn't end up enjoying the Masters. It was really a boys' club, and Frank reacted somewhat angrily when I told him I was bringing my wife. He said, "You are bringing your wife to Augusta?" It just happened to coincide with the date of our wedding anniversary, April 8. She returned the next year and decided she didn't really enjoy it. More than a decade later, she came back at the invitation of then CBS Sports president Peter Lund and his wife, Teresa. We have celebrated our wedding anniversary together only three times since we were married.

My first time there I was just floating on air. We got in from Dallas on Tuesday and on Wednesday I walked into the office to say hello to Frank. At the Masters we had a permanent office structure for CBS and two production trucks. Today you walk into the CBS compound and there are forty-three production trucks. But it's the same old office. By now I had done Phoenix and Pebble. We had not yet done Memorial, Byron Nelson, or Colonial. So the 1983 Masters would have been the third telecast for me with the CBS crew.

Our director was Bob Dailey. He was an older gentleman. In fact, before he got into sports, Bob had directed the old Edward R. Murrow show *Person to Person*. He had also taken occasional turns at directing *The Ed Sullivan Show*. I mean, he was an established director. Bob was tall, stately. I think he was in his sixties when I met him. He was Irish with a little bit of a brogue, American-born but I guess he had grown up in an Irish family, so he spoke with just a little bit of an accent. He looked at me and he said, "Laddy, I know you think you've seen the golf course because you've seen it on television, but let me show you the golf course. Climb in."

So I got into a golf cart with Bob and we went down this long dirt road. To a degree, I still do this same drive today. Bob and I entered the golf course midway down the fairway at the eleventh hole. Nobody was on the tee. Nobody was on the green. We traversed the eleventh, then took a left. That year I was assigned to the thirteenth hole, which is a pretty damn impressive way to start Augusta.

In 1983, there had been no winter frost, no freeze, so the dogwood and azaleas were just incredible. My first view of Augusta was driving down the eleventh, and right in front of me was the beautiful and challenging par-three twelfth. You go up a hill and take a left and the golf cart road becomes a dirt road and you end up midway down the eleventh hole. Bob eventually took me to No. 13, which was my hole for the tournament. He and I parked the cart, walked across a little bridge, and went up into the thirteenth's tower, which is fairly low compared to the height of all the other towers on the back nine. It's just one of the great views in all of golf around the world. I'm sitting there in that tower, standing in the tower with Bob. He said, "Well, lad, this is your office for the next four days."

It was truly overwhelming.

We got back in the cart, and he drove me around the entire back nine. I didn't see the front nine until the next day. We went up to the main clubhouse. They don't want carts up in that area at all, so we shimmied over to the side and got out of the sight lines of the members, then went back down the hill, up a hill, and back to the concourse.

That was my first view of the course, that first Wednesday in April 1983. I did No. 13 for two years and moved to No. 14 in 1985. Then, on May 1, 1985, right after the Masters, Frank Glieber, my role model and dear, dear friend, died of a heart attack. Frank had done No. 17 from 1968 to 1985. He lived and worked in Dallas. I'd grown up listening to him. He was fifty-one when he died, only six years older than I was. When Frank died, Nancy and I were on vacation in Hawaii. I got a call that I had to go replace him on an NBA broadcast for CBS. We went straight from Honolulu to Portland, where the Lakers were playing the Trailblazers. My partner that day was James Brown, whom you can watch on *The NFL Today*. I can remember to this day sitting with Nancy and Pat Riley in the hotel lounge the night before the game. We all had a drink together. Riley was, of course, coaching the Lakers at the time. We shared fond memories of Frank and hoisted a glass or two in his honor.

Chirkinian called me when it was appropriate, long after Frank's death but three months before the Masters. He said, "We're going to reassign you, and you're going to be at Seventeen." So my first year doing No. 17 was 1986. It was very emotional. Frank was one of the first mentors I had. He taught me a lot about how to get along in this business. To lose him at that age, to have felt as connected to him as I did, and then to be chosen by Frank Chirkinian to move to 17, well, it was an emotional week for me. Perhaps that's partially why it was so fitting that the 1986 tournament would go down as one of the greatest in Masters history.

Jack Nicklaus was forty-six years old in 1986. He had not won a tournament in two years. Quite famously, a columnist named Tom McCollister, who has since passed away, had written a column for the *Atlanta Journal-Constitution* on the Tuesday of Masters week in 1986, ranking the ninety or so competitors. He didn't put Jack dead last, but he was in the bottom quadrant. Most people did not think Jack had a shot.

Jack Grout, one of Jack Nicklaus's golf teachers, who was either staying with the family or was visiting the Nicklaus home that week, saw the column, cut it out, and put it on the refrigerator door. Jack saw it every day. He never took it down.

So here he was, at forty-six, and he was not a factor in anybody's coverage. I mean, we put him on the air because he was Jack Nicklaus. But he was not in any kind of a featured group. No one, to my recollection, was writing sidebars about him. It was just like, okay, the five-time winner of Augusta is in the field. Billy Kratzert had the lead after thirty-six holes of the tournament. With a big smile Billy will say today, "I don't get it, nobody ever mentions me." On that Sunday, no one had Jack in their sights. Nobody. He was four back at the start of Sunday's round.

When we got to that Sunday, there were a couple of famous exchanges in the truck and on the air. The third round ended with Greg Norman leading, Seve Ballesteros one back, with Bernard Langer and Jack four back of the lead. There were ten or so golfers ahead of Jack. Keep in mind, back then Augusta National did not allow us to cover the first nine live on CBS. We had to fight for that for years. My first year was 1983 and Ballesteros won it. He eagled both 2 and 8. At least I know he eagled 8. We had no coverage of it because we couldn't get a minicam out there fast enough. It was early enough in the final round. Anyway, it's lost to history.

But on this day in 1986 for the final round, we had stationary cameras on No. 9. That meant we could cover everybody who came through on that hole. Lance Barrow, who is now the executive producer of golf, was the associate director of the Masters. He was in the truck with Frank Chirkinian. Again, you're talking about the most profane man I've ever worked with in my life (I say that with affection, of course). So Jack was having a mundane round. In the meantime, Ballesteros had taken the lead. Then Jack birdied No. 9, and Seve would have been on No. 6 at the time.

Lance in the truck looked at Frank and said, "Frank, we've got Jack Nicklaus with a birdie on No. 9."

"Buddha," Frank replied—he called Lance "Buddha" because Lance is a man of large girth—"you need to learn how to tell a story. Jack Nicklaus is no part of this story. Now don't bother me with him again."

Okay.

Well, Jack then birdied 10. So Lance said to Frank, "Frank, I don't mean to be persistent here, but Nicklaus just had his second birdie in a row."

Frank looked at him, *glared* at him, and said, "All right, we'll play it back on tape."

From that moment on, after he birdied 10, we showed 9 and 10 on videotape and stayed with Jack after that. Here is Jack Nicklaus within hailing distance of the lead of the Masters. We covered him on 11, 12, and 13, where he went birdie, bogey, birdie. Then he made a par on 14, with Seve kind of plugging along. So Jack went birdie, birdie, birdie, bogey, birdie, par starting with the ninth hole. Then at 15, that's when the drama really started to build. He was standing in the fairway with Jackie (Jack Nicklaus, Jr.), his son. He looked at Jackie and pulled out whatever club he had, a four-iron, I think.

Jack looked at his son and said, "Let's see how far a three [iron] would go here."

Jackie responded, "Dad, it's too much club."

Jack said, "No, I'm talking about an eagle."

Jack put it fifteen feet away. Ben Wright was on the hole, and Ben still gets angry about this part. When Jack made the eagle—"made eagle" is the proper way to say it in golf parlance. But Ben just exclaimed, "Yes, sir."

For years I didn't know that. Then one year David Feherty, Peter Kostis, and I were roommates at the Masters and Peter told me that Ben had actually said, "Yes, sir," on air first. Well, when I got home that year, I went back and looked at the VHS tape, and Ben Wright certainly did say, "Yes, sir," for the made eagle.

Jim Nantz was on 16. Par three. Jack hit a five-iron. Never looked up. Jackie said, "Be good." Without looking at the green, Jack said, "It is." The ball rolled across the cup—he almost got an ace. So now he had an eagle and a birdie.

They came to 17. He would have been two back at that time. Jack hit a very poor tee shot. He hooked it left over near the seventh green. So here is a little tidbit about our coverage: No one has ever seen that tee shot. We had a camera operator on a tower behind the green, but he lost it in the setting sun. You never see it. We go away. When we come back, Jack is standing 120 yards away to the left near the 7th green. We never saw the tee shot.

As he was standing over his ball, Seve back at 15 had hooked it into the water, and wound up taking a double bogey. So Jack was over this tee shot 120 yards out. If he could birdie 17, he'd have a chance to take the lead.

He hit his nine-iron shot, and I've never seen galleries respond like they did that day. From the time Jack got into the chase until he won the tournament I experienced the most electric feeling I've gotten from any group of fans anywhere. It was just magnificent. Jack hit it twelve feet from the hole. Seve had now double bogeyed. They were tied. If Jack made the putt, he'd have the lead.

The platform then on 17 was directly behind the green. We had two levels on it. I was on the top one probably twenty feet up in the air. My thought process: Just get out of the way. We bounced around the course, and when we came back, Jack was about to line up for the putt and I thought: Don't screw this up. So I said, "This is for sole possession of the lead."

He stood over it for quite a while. He finally stepped up. It had a very subtle double break. He hit the putt, and with the ball about a foot and a half away I said, "Maybe." Then it dropped in and I hollered, "Yes, sir!" I've probably seen it five thousand times over the years.

What I think made it work so well was the simplicity. If you watch the replay as I'm saying, "Yes, sir," Jack is pumping his arms almost in synchronicity with my words. It's like he's punching the air to underline the emphasis on "Yes, sir." It's perfect. He was giving an orchestra a downbeat.

A short aside: On Wednesday of that week before the tournament had started, we held a Calcutta with just the announcers, the production crew, the guys in the truck. I don't tell the story of the Calcutta often because if you are not a golfer, you would not know what the hell a Calcutta is. Essentially it is a gambling game, a betting game. It was always held on a Wednesday night before the start of the Masters and a sportswriter named Bob Drum was the emcee of the evening. Bob, who has since passed on, was one of the guys given credit for popularizing Arnold Palmer back in the 1950s while working as a sportswriter for a Pittsburgh newspaper. Later he came to work for us. In the early 1980s he did a feature called "The Drummer's Beat." He ran as a regular feature on most of our golf telecasts.

So Bob conducted the Calcuttas. We did it in the home that was shared by Pat Summerall and Ben Wright. This thing got real rowdy.

With Pat and Ben, it was almost guaranteed to get rowdy, especially the later into the evening it got. There are several permutations of the Calcutta, but Bob would announce a golfer's name in the tournament and the bidding for that golfer then started. There were usually thirty people involved. I'm not a gambler so I didn't participate, but I enjoyed the entertainment. I went in just one year, with my CBS Sports colleague Jim Nantz, but I don't remember who we bid on. The payoff was 85 percent of the pot to the winner, 10 percent to second place, and 5 percent to third. Everyone else was out of luck. I can tell you this no longer happens. Back then they were afraid word would get out that CBS guys were gambling. The brutal fact of the matter is that Augusta members also had their own Calcutta.

The subplot to this whole story is that Summerall couldn't stand Brent Musburger. Brent had pushed his way into hosting the Masters because he had the clout. He was down at the Butler Cabin while Pat was at 18. The two did not like each other at all. It went back twenty-five years. Brent was accused, and I think probably correctly, of listening in on the rehearsal that Pat and John Madden would do (or before that, Pat and Tom Brookshier would do). He would steal anything they had of relevance, and come on the air with it for *The NFL Today*. Something like, "Well, late news that Dexter Coakley is out with a knee injury that occurred in warm-ups this morning. Now let's go out to Pat and John." Of course, they were going to mention the injury.

Anyway, that was the background between those two guys. Both men could afford to be in the Calcutta, but Pat knew golf and Brent didn't. So Pat and three or four guys would artificially bid some golfers up knowing they had no chance but that Musburger would bite.

During this particular Calcutta in 1986, Musburger bid $7,700 for Raymond Floyd, who famously shot 77 in the second round and missed the cut. Pat put the all key down after that round and said,

"Mr. Musburger, I believe you spent one hundred dollars for every stroke Raymond took today."

Late in the evening during the Calcutta, Tom Brookshier came in as a guest of Charlie Brakefield, who was the owner of the CBS affiliate in Memphis at the time. Drum saw him walk in. Drum was infamous for his gravelly voice, and just then, Jack Nicklaus's name came up. Booming, Drum announced Jack's name, and nobody raised a finger. He said, "C'mon, you guys, this is Jack Fucking Nicklaus. Somebody has to bid something."

Crickets.

"Have you no decent sense of history? The greatest golfer in the history of the sport?" Drum said. "Somebody give me something for Jack Fucking Nicklaus."

Well, nobody did.

Drummer looked back and pointed at Brookshier. He said, "Mr. Brookshier, it is your lucky night. You have just bid on Jack Nicklaus for four hundred bucks." So Tom went along with it, and paid the money.

Fast-forward to Sunday afternoon. Jack makes the putt, takes the lead. I'm at the very top of the tower, and CBS Sports president Neal Pilson is up there with me. That was his spot to watch every year as the president of the division. I stood up as Jack was walking over to 18, I looked at Neal, and took the headset off and laid it down. I looked over at Brookshier, who had his back to the green on the platform below. He was looking at me and jumping up and down. I looked down at Tommy and said, "Wasn't that the greatest thing you've ever seen?"

He never stopped to take a breath. He said, "I've got him in the Calcutta!!!"

Brookshier would make seventeen grand on the day. I don't think any of our guys have ever shared that with Jack until now.

The other thing is, remember, the lead wasn't secure. Jack had a one-shot lead and he had to par 18. Two guys had the chance to tie him, Greg Norman and Tom Kite. After birdying 17, Greg pushed his four-iron up on the hill to the right. Later Kite had a ten-footer to tie, a birdie attempt at 18. His putt broke left and never touched the hole. Jack had won.

It's funny, but ever since I started covering Augusta, 1986 is the only time I've seen the finish of the tournament. I stayed in the tower for 1986 because Jack only had a one-shot lead. Ninety percent of the time when they come through 16, where I am now—and this is especially true when I did No. 11 and No. 12 for five years—the minute they're through my hole, I am out of there. I'm racing to the Atlanta airport to catch the last flight to Denver to get to Steamboat. I would listen on radio, especially once we had satellite radio, to the finish of the tournament. But on that occasion in 1986, I stayed and watched the end of the telecast in the tower at No. 17. I probably saw the replay within twenty minutes after the tournament proper ended.

Watching it then, I believed that my call was appropriate to the moment. I can also remember thinking to myself as we were in commercial before we came back for his putt, and I've seen it so many times and use it in speeches, I think I sensed the moment right away. I can remember saying to myself, not out loud obviously, but thinking to myself, "Get out of the way quickly and don't screw this up," because I knew how significant the moment was.

I'm proud of the fact that I'm not analyzing what Nicklaus has to do. Everybody knows what he's got to do. You've got to make the putt. And I would leave it to someone far more expert than me to explain that it's got to double break, and it did. But I didn't know. I'm not qualified to make that judgment twenty feet up in the air, so I just shut up. I've seen it so much, I can see the double break in my mind now.

I can also see Frank Chirkinian approaching me in the compound, a man who was not by nature a warm and fuzzy human being, and without a word wrapping me in his arms and kissing me on the cheek.

I find it intriguing that thirty years later, Jack and I have never discussed it. I've not seen him often, but do periodically. He's a most gracious man. I can remember doing a Miami Heat game once and Jack and Barbara were there. I was working with Doc Rivers, and Jack and Barbara came across the court from their seats at halftime just to say hi.

He's never said to me, "That was a really terrific call." And I've never said to him, "Thanks for helping me be a part of your history." That is, until 2014, when CBS did a documentary on me and they tracked Jack down. In the documentary he says, "Yes, sir, Verne Lundquist, we're linked forever because I made the putt and he made the call. That's always going to be a part of my story, him saying, 'Yes, sir.'" I was floored, because we never talked about it face-to-face. If I had the opportunity to talk to him about that day, I would be more curious about the whole back nine, the whole day, and not just that specific, famous moment.

The back nine at Augusta that Sunday in 1986 remains the single most thrilling sporting event I have ever witnessed. I still can't find the right adjectives to describe how intense that afternoon was. I remember saying to myself when he walked toward the green, "If he makes this putt, he is going to have the lead at Augusta at the age of forty-six." Nancy and I are good friends with a fellow named Tom Bennison. He works for ClubCorps (a course acquisition company) in Dallas and he's a good friend of Jack, too. Tom asked me on the twentieth anniversary of the 1986 win, in 2006, if I had any memorabilia from that moment. I said, "No, I don't." He said, "You need to go online and get a photograph and make it an appropriate one."

So I found a golf historian somewhere and ordered a 20x30 photograph of Jack, with his tongue sticking out and the putter straight up in the air, as the ball is about to drop in. Thanks to Tom, I sent it to

Jack's personal secretary. It came back about a month later. In a silver Sharpie in the lower left-hand corner, like he's done this before so you could read it, he signed it on a part of the green that's really outlined:

To Verne, Yes, sir!!! with three exclamation points and then a happy face. Your friend, Jack Nicklaus.

Needless to say, it's hanging right now on my office wall.

It was to be Jack's last green jacket; I'd wear my blue blazer for a lot of years after that. Funny how the colors of those magical moments in 1986 have never faded.

CHAPTER 8

Let's Invent Us a Football Player

The one constant in my professional life was the pleasure I took in working for the Cowboys. No matter whether I was working for ABC or CBS, being a part of the Cowboys was always a thrill. They were always entertaining, win or lose. They did a lot of the former and many episodes of the latter were as memorable as they were heartbreaking for Cowboys fans. I've been fortunate to witness many memorable moments in sports, and I was there doing the radio broadcast back to those along the Cowboy radio network for the 1981 NFC Championship Game. The Cowboys came into the game with high hopes following a playoff victory over the Falcons the week before. Pat Summerall wasn't doing the game for CBS, but he was there and kindly hung out in our booth and served as our runner, getting us beverages.

Pat wasn't doing the Niners–Cowboys game, either. Our booth was next to CBS's, with Vin Scully doing the play-by-play. I had arranged for a special treat for our listeners: Rudy Gatlin of the Gatlin Brothers musical group would be in the booth with us. If the game was in the Cowboys' hands late, he was going to sing, à la Don Meredith, "Turn off the lights, the party's over." The tense back-and-forth nature of the game kept Rudy on the sidelines. As much as "the Catch" was memorable for Dwight Clark's amazing athleticism, the drive leading up to it began in a surprising fashion. San Francisco used Lenvil Elliott left and Lenvil Elliott right as they got beyond the shadow of their own goalposts starting at the eleven. After that, Joe Montana was as good as it gets. Finally, from the six-yard line, he lofted a ball into the end zone. To this day, I believe that he intended to throw the ball out of the end zone. I know that Clark denied this, as did Joe, but I side with those who believe Joe was hoping for another shot.

I'm also still amazed that Ed "Too Tall" Jones and/or Larry Bethea didn't bring him down for a sack. Like many Cowboy fans, I'm sorry that Danny White's pass after the Niners score didn't go all the way. Drew Pearson caught it and only a superb ankle tackle from San Francisco's Eric Wright kept "the Catch" from becoming a footnote in one of the Cowboys' greatest come-from-behind victories. Regardless, I was still enjoying my time with the team, no matter how rigorous my schedule was proving to be.

That 1983 team opened the regular season on the road in Washington, D.C., against the vaunted Redskins. It was a Monday night game and that always added a festive note to the affair. The Redskins came in as defending Super Bowl champions, having claimed the crown in the strike-shortened 1982 season. The league used a revised playoff scheme to compensate for the short season and the Redskins finished the regular season with an 8-1 mark before beating the Dolphins at the Rose Bowl to end the foreshortened year. For their part the Cowboys finished 6-3, second best in the league, but lost in the NFC championship to their division rivals.

The match-up that Monday night was going to be one of the highlights of the season, an unofficially designated Kickoff Classic. Even though our radio broadcast was only going out to the Cowboy network, I still felt a real sense of anticipation. This was going to start the new season, it was between two bitter division rivals, and it was the only football game that night. When ABC's *Monday Night Football* circus rolled into town, you had to get caught up in the excitement. I knew each of the members of the broadcast team. It was no secret that Howard Cosell was a provocateur who loved attention almost as much as he loved the vodka his assistant poured him throughout the broadcast. Don Meredith agreed to play the country bumpkin role while Frank Gifford, a player I admired, did a yeoman's job as the straight man. I can see now that those guys prefigured the later trend of sports guys as entertainers, as focus seekers, as highly skilled circus clowns who kept the audience amused when the action was slow—and sometimes when it wasn't slow. That night, with this premier match-up of two talented teams, I didn't think that anyone would find it necessary to engage in any hijinks.

Joe Gibbs coached the Redskins and Joe Theisman was behind the center. John Riggins was still thundering out of the backfield while the speedy wide-outs Alvin Garrett and Charlie Brown caused grief for any secondary. Danny White had taken over at quarterback, and with Tony Dorsett handling much of the offensive load, White was tasked with playing the role we eventually came to call a "game manager." All those doubts about Danny's ability to lead and to inspire his teammates seemed to get answered in the first half of that game. He went 1 for 9. The Cowboys only generated 75 yards of offense at halftime. Tony Dorsett had broken loose for a glorious 77-yard scamper. Even that offensive display was overshadowed by the Redskins. Their defensive back Darryl Green, then in his rookie season, put his speed on display and hauled Tony down from behind.

At the half, the Redskins were up 23–3, and as Don Meredith might have sung, it appeared the party was over. White would later say that he was fuming in the clubhouse during the halftime break. He was embarrassed, angry, and his helmet throwing display probably had a few of his teammates wondering why he could complete those tosses and none on the field. No fat lady had sung, so the Cowboys went back out.

The start of the third quarter was a completely different story. In the first 8:25 of that period, Danny and Tony Hill hooked up on a couple of long touchdown passes. The second of those was a circus catch, with Tony stretching out to one hand the ball. As the fourth quarter began, the Cowboys were down by six. A one-yard Danny White keeper and a one-yard TD pass to tight end Doug Cosbie had the Cowboys in the lead at the 13:11 mark of that period. Twenty-eight straight points was something to behold. The Redskins scored a late touchdown to bring them within one, but a Ron Fellows interception with seconds to play sealed the deal.

We all enjoyed a happy flight home and for the first two months of the season, those happy trails led to six more victories. A real tense one in that string occurred against the Saints. Down 20–13 in the fourth quarter, the Cowboys went into the end zone. Rafael Septien's extra-point attempt was blocked and the Cowboys still trailed. The Cowboys got the ball back with a few minutes to go. Danny led them down the field and threw an interception at the one-yard line. Linebacker Anthony Dickerson saved the day by sacking Ken Stabler—yes, the Snake had been relocated to New Orleans from Oakland—in the end zone. The two points were enough to send Saints coach Bum Phillips and his son Wade home in defeat.

I can't really say what the troubles were that plagued the Cowboys at the end of the season. They entered December 11-2 and then beat the Seahawks to get to 12-2. The next week, a showdown with the Redskins in Dallas loomed. Both teams were 12-2, tied for the division lead, and both had the best records in the league. What more could you ask for? A division title, a first-round bye in the playoffs; bragging rights; Cowboys and Redskins; a fourth straight trip to the NFC championship; America's Team.

How fun was this one going to be?

Much was later made of the Redskins players going out that week and buying military fatigues that they wore on the plane and from the bus to the hotel. They were "invading" Dallas, as they put it. They wanted to get inside the Cowboys' players' heads. (As stunts go, I approve of this one much more than I do the Boston Bruins' Brad Marchand licking opponents' faces out on the ice.) To what degree they were effective in psyching out the Cowboys is hard to say. You can't argue with the results, however.

After jumping out to a 14–0 lead, the Redskins gave up a touchdown and a field goal. Momentum seemed to be swinging in the Cowboys' favor. "Seemed to be" is the operative phrase here. From that point forward, the Cowboys were inept and seemed to lose their cool. White threw the third of his interceptions. The Redskins defense held Dorsett to 34 yards rushing. In the fourth quarter, Danny came to line on fourth down and called an audible. On the sidelines, Tom Landry shouted, "No! No! No!" The play failed and the ball went over on downs to Washington. Dorsett got so frustrated with being stymied and harassed that he threw the ball at the Redskins' Darryl Grant.

The Redskins' Fun Bunch, a package of five players who came in together in certain situations and had their own choreographed high-five end zone celebration, angered a couple of Cowboys who tried to stop their performance. Things got so bad that the Cowboys only had ten men on the field for an extra-point try.

We sat in the booth pondering what was going on, but in the end we had no answer. The Cowboys lost, 31–10. I didn't know it then, but that was the last time I would do a Cowboys game as their voice. If there was one consolation to the playoff loss it was that even though the Redskins made it to the Super Bowl, they ended up losing to Al Davis's Raiders.

As fierce as that rivalry was, I admired Joe Theisman. He later became a very good broadcaster himself. As a player, he had the knack of getting under the opposition's skin. Still, he was a gunslinger of the old-school variety, the kind of guy you wanted on your team but hated to play against. The image of him having his leg snap two years later when they squared off against the New York Giants on another Monday night is indelibly seared into many minds. Football can be a brutal game.

The Cowboys' season ended on a brutal note. Following that loss to the Redskins, they took it on the chin in another *Monday Night Football* telecast. That 42–17 loss to San Francisco had no real impact on the playoff picture. The Cowboys would host the Los Angeles Rams in the wild card round. Dallas turned the ball over four straight times, and the Rams capitalized on three of them in a 24–17 win. Tom Landry later said that he knew that his football team was not in the right place mentally entering the playoffs. He felt they had lost their mental edge.

White's three interceptions offset the 330 passing yards he amassed. Perhaps more significant, Dorsett was held to 59 yards rushing, his third sub-100-yard game in a row. This was his sixth year in the league. He enjoyed another Pro Bowl season, rushed for 1,300-plus yards, and scored 8 touchdowns. His 4.6 yards-per-carry average was second in his career to his rookie season, when he averaged 4.8. His 289 carries that year seems like an enormous tally today, but in the next two seasons, he'd carry the ball more than 300 times and finish both those seasons with more than 1,000 yards gained. Tony was as durable as they come.

Lots of questions faced the Cowboys. A season filled with so much promise had ended on a sour note. That was a familiar song to Cowboys fans, a country and western tune about someone or something having done them wrong. As the golf season got into high gear that summer, I was already thinking about the Cowboys and their chances for taking that next step and getting back into the Super Bowl. The team had no glaring weakness, save its propensity to turn the ball over, and that could be remedied.

As it turned out, though, I wouldn't be in the broadcast booth to witness those remedies firsthand.

IN JULY 1984, I WAS in Oak Brook, Illinois, for the Western Open when I got a phone call from Jim McKenna at CBS. He was one of CBS's vice presidents and he wanted to inform me that at a staff meeting earlier in the week, the team had made a decision: I was being taken off college football and put on NFL games. My initial reaction was to be greatly pleased. The NFL was the jewel in the crown of the sports department. The NFL was still in ascendance in those days and was on its way to supplanting baseball as America's most popular sport. That initial pleasure took a hit a moment later. I would have to end my professional association with the Cowboys. That was the price I was going to have to pay.

Further, Jim told me that I was going to be paired with Terry Bradshaw. To that point, Bradshaw had not announced his retirement. It was widely speculated that he would hang them up, but nothing had been formalized. In this pre-Internet, pre–social media era, rumors would circulate but there wasn't the constant attention on everything. I knew Terry, superficially, having interviewed him briefly when he was the quarterback opposing the Cowboys in Super Bowl X and XIII. My brief conversations were both conducted on media day, when the players were subjected to hours of answering either the same questions or the most inane ones that a journalist could come up with. I had no way of knowing if he'd even remember me. I did appreciate the irony of the Steelers' former quarterback and the Cowboys' radio guy being joined together in network matrimony. Based on past experience and promises made and broken regarding who I would be working with, I was skeptical about how long this thing could last.

After the Western Open ended, I went back to Steamboat to share the news with Nancy. On the three-hour drive from Denver's Stapleton Airport to our small vacation home I had a lot to think about. With no more professional obligations keeping us in Dallas, we could move anywhere we wanted to. As much as I enjoyed the convenience of living in the Dallas–Fort Worth area, cruising along Interstate 70 through the mountains, enjoying the vistas from atop Rabbit Ears Pass and all along the route, an idea began to form. I'd first gone to Steamboat Springs in 1971. Steamboat was a skiers' paradise even then. While it lacked some of the high-end amenities and luxury accommodations as Vail and Aspen, the skiing was world-class, the people friendly, and the home prices manageable. I had returned to Steamboat a couple more times over the years. In 1975 I got a chance to play a round of golf on a newly constructed Robert Trent Jones course, and the experience was mesmerizing. The beauty of the surrounding area, the loveliness of the course, and the gorgeous weather had me hooked.

With my second wife, Kathy, I had bought a simple A-frame house there in 1978. Nothing extravagant by any means, more of a simple chalet, it offered us easy access to the slopes and to town. We'd purchased it with another couple, but when Kathy and I divorced, and the other couple expressed interest in divesting themselves of the investment, I bought them out.

By the time I reached Rabbit Ears Pass and began the descent into the Yampa River valley, I'd convinced myself that Nancy and I were going to become full-time Coloradans. Nancy was thrilled to learn about the change in my assignment and what that might mean for my prospects at CBS. She was less thrilled about the idea of moving to Steamboat. In my mind, it was a no-brainer. Who wouldn't want to trade suburbia and congested traffic, the threat of tornadoes and excessive heat for breezes whispering among the ponderosa pines and the yellow-gold aspens and bluebird days when the sky is a nearly indescribably beautiful shade of blue? It took me a week, but eventually Nancy saw the wisdom in the move. She was a lifelong Texan and her roots there ran deep. Transplanting her to another locale was going to take time, but fortunately for us, we were able to sell our house in Texas, purchase one in Steamboat, and be moved in by Labor Day of 1984.

If Nancy expressed trepidations, then Frank Chirkinian expressed outright hostility: "You'll live in Steamboat Springs only until you miss your first golf tournament because you can't get your ass out of that town." My commute was going to be more complicated, but the beauty of the place more than made up for inconvenience. Over the years, I had a couple of close calls in getting to my assignments on time. We live here part-time and I still have a deep and abiding affection for the place.

In the midst of all that house selling and moving, I had to go to New York in late July for a press conference. There, Terry announced his retirement, and CBS introduced the two of us as an announcing pair. The event was held at the '21' Club, one of the swankier New York City restaurants. A substantial group of journalists were present, and after Neal Pilson of CBS introduced Terry, he demonstrated the glib and downhome charming nature that would keep him in the business for the next thirty-plus years. For my part, I stuck to my usual script, spoke briefly, and understood full well that no one in attendance was there to hear from me.

Terry and I got a chance to speak to one another a few times before our first assignment. I related to him some of what I laid out earlier—my humble beginnings in radio, my time in Davenport, Iowa, subsisting on Ritz crackers and peanut butter. Terry smiled at those recollections and added that when he was thirteen, he and his family—his parents and his two brothers, Gary and Craig—had lived for a time about thirty miles north of Davenport. That little small-world-after-all connection helped our relationship. In early August, Terry and I received our first assignment. We were to work a preseason game in San Diego. The game was being televised by CBS, and John Madden and Pat Summerall were in the broadcast booth. Terry and I, Dick Vermeil and Frank Glieber, were all there as well. We were there to do a "rehearsal game." All three teams would cover the game live, but only John and Pat's version would go out over the air. For us "rehearsers," our call would go to the production truck, where it would be recorded. Later, CBS management types would listen to it, critique it, and deliver us notes we could use to help us in future broadcasts.

This was a routine procedure for new teams, and if you weren't able to do well, or you didn't get with the program and improve based on their feedback, most often you didn't get another chance. Terry was about to receive a real education. Dick Vermeil is one of the finest people I have known. He brought to the booth the kind of preparedness that made him a success in coaching the UCLA Bruins, the Philadelphia Eagles, and the Kansas City Chiefs. The man was meticulous. Almost an hour before game time, he came into the booth Terry and I were sharing. He asked if he could be of any help. He offered to show us his spotting board. This was an absolutely essential tool that broadcasters relied on. The board came in many forms but the information it contained was the same: one side of the depth chart lists the first, second, and third teams of, for example, the Chargers' offense. On the other side was the opposition's defense. There was enough space for the broadcasters to add personalized notes and whatever information they felt was germane.

Dick set his spotting board in front of Terry and the poor guy audibly gasped. There in front of him sat a masterpiece. Dick had color-coded his information. The roster information was fairly straightforward, but the "extras" were a marvel. Red indicated information about a player's NFL career; blue keynoted college history and statistics; green was for high school; magenta revealed something personal about a player's life—some tidbit about his wife, mother, father, children, hobbies, shoe size, or anything else that might bring that person to life. Terry sat there wide-eyed but silent, nodding like a man who had just been hauled into the police station and was having his rights read to him. He knew the information was important but it was all just too much to take in at that moment.

When Dick exited the booth, Terry stared at me, still not speaking. I watched as beads of perspiration formed on his brow and then all over his face. I believe the term "flop sweat" applied in that instance. Finally, he shook his head. "Gawd-aw-mighty," he stammered. "Am I supposed to do somethin' like *that* every week?"

Terry never approached that level of preparedness but then, few did. Dick's spotting boards so impressed me that I asked him to send me copies, which I shared with Terry. Terry would fill his out, in black ink only, with minimal information. He was more extemporaneous and that seemed to work well for him. I copied Dick's color coding. I never got the magenta level in full detail like he did, but his example served me well. In fact, from that point forward, mid-August 1984 to December 2016, when I called the Army–Navy clash, my last NCAA game, I used Vermeil's board. I never totaled all the games during that thirty-two-year span, but I suspect it's more than a dozen.

Terry and I were both new kids in the booth, and I like to think that played a part in our standing with the network. Making the transition from radio to television was fairly easy. The audience, obviously, had the visual component in front of them, so I just had to be less descriptive and keep things more fact based. Terry was rough around the edges, and rough in the middle, too, but that was to be expected. Today, new analysts are schooled, taped, analyzed, retrained,

A publicity photo of me for WOC Radio, my first radio job, in Davenport, Iowa. September 1962.

With the Milwaukee Braves manager Bobby Bragan, in Austin, Texas. 1964.

On active duty, the USAF Reserve, Kelly AFB, San Antonio, Texas. June 1966.

Frank Glieber and me on the rooftop of the Orange Bowl for KRLD radio broadcast of Superbowl V in Miami, Florida. January, 1971.

Interviewing Howard Cosell in Dallas, Texas, 1972.

Broadcasting my first national football game on Thanksgiving weekend with Frank Broyles in College Station, Texas, 1975.

Talking to Jack Nicklaus at the Byron Nelson Classic in 1976.

At a live telecast for WFAA-TV Dallas with Craig Mortin (Denver Broncos) and Roger Staubach (Dallas Cowboys), on the Friday night before Superbowl XII in New Orleans, Louisiana.

With soccer superstar Pelé and his interpreter Julio Mazzei. Dallas, 1976.

Laughing with Pelé in Dallas, Texas, 1976.

An offscreen chat with Craig Morton and Roger Staubach in New Orleans, Louisiana. January 1978.

With Ara Parseghian in the Superdome in 1979.

With Igor Rostov our interpreter in Moscow, Russia, for the ABC Sports USA-USSR boxing show. January 1980.

Halftime at Auburn—Alabama with Bear Bryant in Birmingham, Alabama. November 1981.

During a live shot for WFAA-TV in Texas Stadium, August 1982.

With Tom and Alicia Landry celebrating my last day at WFAA-TV in December 1983. Next up —CBS Sports!

Cruising around with Nancy at a charity golf tournament in Fort Worth, Texas. Summer 1983.

Me with Nancy in autumn of 1985.

Cozying up with
Nancy.

Hanging out at the Mile High Stadium in Denver, Colorado, with Terry Bradshaw during our first year together! September 1984.

During my first event with Scott Hamilton, the European Figure Skating Championships in Leningrad, Russia. 1990.

With legendary sportscaster— and my mentor — Ray Scott. Steamboat, Colorado. January 1999.

With Heisman Trophy winners from the military academies at the Doak Walker Awards in Dallas in 2002. From left to right: Joe Bellino (Navy), Roger Staubach (Navy), Pete Dawkins (Army), Glynn Davis (Army), and Doc Blanchard (Army).

Nancy and me with Lamar and Norma Huni at the Doak Walker Awards in 2002.

Celebrating the Sun Bowl in El Paso, Texas, with Todd Blackledge and Tracy Wolfson. December 2004.

At the first Walker-Lundquist golf tournament in Steamboat Springs, Colorado, with none other than Doak Walker (1947 Heisman winner). There were fifteen in all, the last held one year after Doak's death.

With college football analyst Gary Danielson in 2006. *Courtesy of CBS; Craig Blankenhorn /CBS*

At the 2014 NCAA Basketball Seminar with analysts Grant Hill, Steve Smith, and Bill Raftery. 2014. *Courtesy of CBS; John Paul Filo/CBS*

With Bill Raftery at the A-Ten Championships at the Barclay's Center in Brooklyn. 2014.
Courtesy of CBS; John Paul Filo/CBS

bottom left-hand page: With Billy Packer, CBS's lead college basketball analyst for thirty-four years, at the NCAA Men's Basketball Championship, at Louisville-Kentucky in 2008. *Courtesy of CBS; Jeffrey R. Staab/CBS*

At the 2014 NCAA Final Four in North Texas with Wisconsin coach Bo Ryan (left) and CBS Sports announcer Jim Nantz (right). *Courtesy of CBS; John Paul Filo/ CBS*

Practicing my commencement speech at Texas Lutheran University in Seguim. Texas. May, 2014. The mascot's name is Lucky.

and all the rest. Terry was thrown into the pool in the tried-and-true sink-or-swim method. He thrashed around a bit but never drowned.

In baseball terms, we were the seventh team in a six-team rotation. John and Pat were at the top of the heap—deservedly so—and got the games of greatest interest for the week. Terry and I toiled in relative obscurity. We were assigned what were called "point-to-point" games—those that were only being broadcast in the areas nearby the two teams playing. Our first assignment in 1984 was Detroit at New Orleans. That year, both teams' prospects for success were bleak. I can't remember if New Orleans fans had taken to wearing paper bags over their heads yet.

The game would be a kind of homecoming for the Louisiana-born Terry. Our first production meeting on the Saturday evening before the game was held in our hotel. Nearly everyone involved was new to working with the others. We made our introductions and moved through the agenda.

At one point, a propos of nothing, Terry spoke up. "Fellas, I've got an idea. Let's invent us a football player."

I took one for the team and asked, "What do you mean?"

"Well, here's my idea. You all know what happens. In every punting and kicking situation everybody gets told the name of the kicker or punter and the return men. But when those collisions take place in the middle of the field, nobody is really sure who is doing what to who."

He paused briefly. He was making some sense.

"Hell, we're only going to be seen by a few thousand people, several cowboys, some pigs and sheep. Let's have some fun!"

Fun meant creating a faux football player. He was the guy we'd credit with being involved in those special teams tackles. Regardless of who was playing, Willie Anderson, a free agent defensive back from Colby College in Maine, would be in on the tackle.

I would do the call straight up and then Terry would chime in, "I'll tell you what, Bubba, that was some lick that Willie Anderson of the Lions laid on the return man. That free agent out of Colby College sure can hit!"

We never mentioned Willie's number.

The next week we were in Tampa Bay for a game against the Falcons, another point-to-point telecast.

I decided to get in on the action, "It's fourth down and eight. The Buccaneers are in punt formation. Elmore Leonard is back to punt. He sends it high and deep and it's grabbed by Mickey Spillane for Atlanta at his own twenty. He's got some room! The forty; he gets a tremendous block at the forty-five, is across midfield, and is finally tackled as he reaches the Tampa forty-yard line."

"I'll tell you what, Bubba, that was a sensational block by Willie Anderson, the free agent defensive back from Colby College in Maine."

Willie Anderson played in all fourteen games that year, becoming the first player in NFL history to suit up for a different team each week.

We were never found out. I can't imagine what would happen in today's branded and packaged NFL.

Things got complicated only once. The last game of the year was the rematch between Atlanta and Tampa. I had to be sure that Willie showed up on my spotting board on the Buccaneers defense this time. Mike Burks, our terrific producer, wanted to present each of us with a memento to commemorate our first year together. We may have been the point-to-point leaders among CBS's NFL broadcast teams but we had a lot of fun. Mike called the sports information director at Colby College. He wanted to buy eight Colby T-shirts to give to members of the team and present them to us at the production meeting.

He reached the SID's office in Maine. He introduced himself and his affiliation with CBS.

"CBS Sports! Can you tell me what the hell is going on with you people! We get phone calls all the time from people wanting to know more about some guy named Willie Anderson!"

He went on yelling, insisting that he'd scoured the record books and couldn't find the guy. Mike felt bad for him, and he wanted the T-shirts, so he confessed to the deception. The SID was a smart man. He realized that the school was getting free publicity. He was also grateful that the mystery was solved. The T-shirts arrived at our hotel room in Tampa. We all wore them to the production meeting—held aboard a yacht owned by the founder of Krispy Kreme donuts—and had a photo taken. I don't know how Mike got us on that boat, but like any good producer, he was a master of resourcefulness.

I don't know if it is because we were both members of the Third Time's a Charm Club, but Terry and I got along very well. Our wives also became close friends. Charla even invited Nancy to be present in the delivery room when she gave birth to her youngest daughter, Erin. Nancy was touched by the kind gesture, and she cherishes the experience to this day. Charla always impressed me with her intelligence and her drive, things she put in practice on her way to a law degree and a career as a prominent attorney. Sadly, Terry and Charla's marriage ended in divorce in 1999. My professional relationship with Terry lasted only two years. At the end of the 1985 NFL season, I was informed that I would be returning to college football. Terry was paired with Tim Ryan for most of his assignments.

I did PAC 10 games with Pat Haden, a brilliant guy who'd quarterbacked the USC Trojans to three Rose Bowl appearances and two national championships. He went to play in the World Football League for a season before joining the NFL's Los Angeles Rams. Pat's decision to play in the WFL was motivated by a desire to take advantage of a rare opportunity: he was named a Rhodes Scholar while at USC and was able to study at Oxford University. Pat's NFL career wasn't stellar, but he seemed to have aspirations beyond the gridiron.

He earned a law degree, was partner in a firm, and chose broadcasting when CBS approached him at the end of his playing career.

To say that Terry and Pat were a study in contrasts would be an understatement. Pat has a great sense of humor, but I don't think he would have come up with the "invent a player" scheme as Terry did. Pat's later role as the athletic director at USC solidified his reputation as one of the real outstanding minds in collegiate sports.

Just as I was given no explanation as to why I was pulled from the NFL broadcasts to the PAC-10 games, in 1988 I was told that Terry and I would be reunited to do the NFL again. The previous year, I'd done a mixture of NFL and NCAA games, but this time would be different. Not only was I back to the NFL exclusively, but Terry and I weren't going to be seventh of six. We got bumped all the way to number two behind Pat and John. No more point-to-point games, no more Willie Anderson gags. I was thrilled when Ted Shaker at CBS informed me of the promotion.

Terry and I reunited in Gothenburg, Sweden. The NFL had decided that Nordic folks needed an introduction to the game, so they had the Bears and Vikings travel there for a preseason game. Gothenburg is a gorgeous city, situated on the country's West Coast. It sits on the Götta älv River, and you can ply it and a system of canals as you meander the city. The game was played in 19,000-seat Ullevi Stadium, built for soccer. The stands were not full that night, no matter the novelty on offer. Those in attendance cheered wildly anytime a foot came in contact with a ball. Oh, to be a place-kicker or punter at that latitude. They seemed to give the players extra points for extra-point conversions. Long passes, convoluted runs, and big hits were met with near silence.

The whole broadcast enterprise was a bit of a smorgasbord. Vic Frank, one of our associate producers, had spent a fortune on an opening tease to begin the broadcast. The video began with a map graphic that traced the route of the Vikings to Newfoundland in the eleventh century. We had purchased the rights to use a snippet from an old movie called *The Vikings*. It featured former Los Angeles Rams standout defensive lineman Deacon Jones. He sat in the prow of a Viking ship clad in furs and armor with a horned hat atop his massive head. I saw the tape prior to broadcast and it was, shall we say, memorable. I will protect the identity of the individual involved in this because this was a rare case of him not doing a wonderful job. Five minutes before kickoff, he stepped outside the trailer for a last-minute cigarette. When he came back in, he closed the door of the trailer not realizing that it had come in contact with one of the reels on the tape deck that held the tease. David Michaels, our producer and Al's brother, called out, "Roll tape."

Nothing.

Ten seconds went by.

Twenty seconds went by.

In living rooms across America folks wondered if their sets had gone on the fritz as they stared at the black hole in front of them.

"Say something!" Dave yelled at me through my headset.

"About what?" I asked, nonplussed.

"Just talk. It's what you're paid to do."

For the next what seemed forever but was likely only a minute or so, I entertained America with facts about Gothenburg, my family's coming to America, and a list of states I knew that one Lundquist or another had settled in. Gratefully, that bit of ad lib work done, I introduced Terry and we got to talking about football. The Vikings wound up winning, 28–21. To celebrate the discovery of a small but hardy band of Swedish fans of American football, the network had set up a celebratory postgame buffet at our Sheraton hotel digs. The Bradshaws and Lundquists found a corner table and began reminiscing and filling one another in on the events of our lives from the last two years.

The subject turned to Terry's thoughts about his possible induc-

tion into the Pro Football Hall of Fame. He was a four-time winner
of the Super Bowl and seemed a lock to enter. At least I thought so.
Terry thanked me for the vote of confidence. He then mused about
whom he might ask to present him on that future date. Art Rooney,
the beloved owner of the Steelers, was his first choice but was in poor
health. Terry crossed him off the list. Most everyone knew that Terry
and his head coach, Chuck Noll, did not see eye to eye. Terry ruled
him out.

What a lot of people didn't know was that with the exception of
Mike Webster, his center, Terry had not gotten close to many of his
teammates. Choosing any one of them wasn't feasible. He thought of
his father, but the man had never given a speech in front of a large
group. Terry wanted to save him the anxiety of doing so and allow
him to just enjoy the day.

"Bubba," Terry said, eyeing me, "you might be the one."

That "might" hung over us awhile longer. Nancy and I hadn't
given up on Dallas completely. We purchased a small apartment, a
winter escape when Steamboat's weather was proving to be too much.
The Bradshaws were living in a rental home in nearby Irving while
their permanent residence was being built. We gathered for Christ-
mas dinner. The Hall of Fame voting was coming up in a few weeks.
Terry did as he had in Sweden. He listed and crossed off candidates
one by one. Finally, turning very serious, he said to me, "Verne, you're
my guy."

The culmination of our reunion season was to be assigned to our
first playoff game together. The Philadelphia Eagles and the Chicago
Bears were squaring off in Soldier Field. The main story line that
everyone got their hooks into was Buddy Ryan returning to Chicago
to lead his Eagles against Mike Ditka and the Bears. Buddy had been
the defensive coordinator for the Bears and its record-breaking and
headline-grabbing defense that tore up the league in 1985. He inno-

vated the famed 4-6 defense that wreaked havoc on the New England Patriots in winning the Super Bowl title that season.

The scuttlebutt was that Ditka did not appreciate how much attention Ryan received. He didn't like how loyal those defensive players were to his subordinate. Ryan didn't have much good to say about his former boss. Things festered and by the time New Year's Eve in 1988 rolled around, those two old acquaintances would have loved to be able to forget each other. No one was going to let them do that.

The Bears came into the game tied with the Bengals and Bills for the best regular season mark at 12-4. The Eagles were only 10-6. They won the division in a tiebreaker over the Giants. The "Punky QB" Jim McMahon had been injured and split duties that year with Mike Tomczack and Jim Harbaugh. Walter Payton had retired, but Neal Anderson had a 1,000-yard season. The defense was still outstanding. Philadelphia's Randall Cunningham, a remarkable athlete and underrated quarterback, would face them. No one had any sense that another opponent would figure largely in the game's outcome.

New Year's Eve began in atypical fashion for Chicago in late December. Blue skies, temperatures hovering around the freezing mark, and the real rarity—no wind along the lakefront. That all changed with 2:21 remaining in the first half. Mike Tomczak had started for the Bears, and he led them to a touchdown on their first possession, throwing a long touchdown pass. The teams traded turnovers and field goals, with the Bears taking a 17–9 lead. Just before the two-minute warning the fog rolled in. We'd had our eye on some weather phenomenon, or perhaps we speculated that it was smoke from a fire. The dense fog rolled in and enshrouded Soldier Field.

The rest is a mystery.

Terry and I could see no more than six feet in front of us. We had no idea how the game could continue, but it did. The NFL was monitoring events, of course, but never postponed or delayed the game.

I didn't know how the players were dealing with the fog, and many voiced their displeasure later, but somehow Cunningham managed to throw for more than 400 yards that day. The Bears' defense managed to keep the Eagles' offense out of the end zone.

Terry and I saw none of that, really.

David Michaels made the call to put our two minicam operators on the field in between plays. They could show the huddle and the spot of the ball but little else. They had to leave the field when a play was run. For much of the second half, I removed the left side of my headset. I could hear a voice giving the down, distance, and time on the clock. I presumed it was the public address announcer, who had moved to the sidelines to make those calls. I later learned that it was the referee, Jim Tunney, who was keeping those in attendance up to date. Viewers at home, much like they had when tuning in to our Swedish black screen, were treated to gray and little else. Our *NFL Today* hosts, Brent Musburger and Irv Cross, were on hand, standing fifty feet from the end zone in one of the tunnels. NFL rules at the time prohibited sideline reporters, so they were helpless.

Terry later told me that he was more frustrated by this situation than any he'd faced as a player. He wished that he had gone down to field level with a microphone, taken a position on the sideline, and reported what he could see from there. He'd deal with the rule and Mr. Rozelle later.

We learned the oddest thing. We assumed that the entire Chicago area had been socked in by fog. As we drove along Lake Shore Drive, we had no reason to think otherwise. Once we headed away from the lake and west toward the airport, the skies cleared and it was back to that lovely day. It was as if we'd been in a tiny snow globe. The fog only covered a tiny portion of the city. We got to the airport and back home in time to celebrate the new year.

Several months later, in August 1989, I stood up in front of a packed house in Canton, Ohio, to introduce my friend Terry Bradshaw as an inductee into the Pro Football Hall of Fame. An estimated twelve thousand fans were gathered in front of the hall, most in black and gold. In addition to Terry, his teammate Mel Blount was also being honored. Joining the two Steelers were Green Bay's Willie Wood and Oakland's Art Shell. I'd labored over my remarks, wrote and rewrote, rehearsed and memorized. I spent five minutes extolling the personal and professional virtues of Terry.

When Terry stood and approached the microphone, the crowd erupted. I could see that he was deeply touched but that big grin of his didn't waver. Terry launched into his speech with no note cards, paper, teleprompter, just his natural gift for speaking. I thought I was in the presence of a Baptist minister of the fiery type. Terry plucked at each emotional string, weaving those notes into a joyful, funny, and tender song. The place went up for grabs when he said, almost shouting, "Do I miss it? Of course I do. What I wouldn't give to have my hands under Mike Webster's butt just one more time."

Better his than mine, I thought at the time—words that would come back to haunt me later.

Terry was a hit and I can see why he's much in demand as a motivational speaker to this day. Heck, he almost had me wanting to put on a set of pads and go out there to capture some gridiron glory for myself. As many people have pointed out, Terry's good-old-boy persona was mostly an act. He did have southern roots, of course, but the not being able to spell *cat* if he was spotted the *c* and the *t* was not Terry at all. He was an intelligent man, had a keen understanding of football, and was very competitive. All of those contributed to some of his frustrations with his role on CBS. Pat and John were number one in the network's mind and there wasn't much that could be done to dissuade them. That didn't stop Terry from trying. If John had his telestrator, a high-tech gizmo at the time but a ubiquitous part of broadcasts now, Terry went old school, and we carted around a blackboard—a real blackboard, the kind found in schools and in locker rooms. Terry would pick up his chalk and his eraser and diagram plays. His X-and-O show was the antitelestrator.

One Sunday in Minnesota, Terry decided to put to use the actual football that he always insisted should be in our booth. The Vikings offensive center was Kirk Lowdermilk. Tall and high-waisted with the length of an NBA center, Kirk presented problems for a quarterback. Terry related that he had a hard time with tall centers. He also had a problem with more diminutive centers—like his pal Mike Webster. We went to break and I had in mind a kind of Goldilocks scenario of discovering someone who was just right. When we came back after the 2:40, we were in the on camera position. Terry had that huge grin splitting his face. I stood there with the ball in my hand looking serious.

"Okay," Terry said. "Now you're going to be Mike Webster. Squat like a frog and snap the ball to me on two."

I did as instructed, my forty-something-year-old butt as close to the ground as I could manage. Terry had to practically get down on his knees in order to receive the snap. Next, he asked me to Lowdermilk. I kept my legs as straight as possible while bending at the waist. Show-and-tell was over. The lesson delivered. I'm still hoping that at some point on Fox's *NFL Sunday,* Terry will erupt and say, "What I wouldn't give to put my hands under Verne Lundquist's butt just one more time."

As a colleague and friend, I had only one gripe about him. He lacked "courage." That failing came into sharp focus during the famous Bounty Game of 1989 in Philadelphia, when we came under fire and Bradshaw was nowhere to be seen.

The Bounty Game will stick in most people's memories because Buddy Ryan, while coaching the Eagles, put out a bounty on the Cowboys' kicker Luis Zendejas. Now, Zendejas was no bigger than I—a media-guide five feet, nine inches tall. Luis had made the mistake earlier in the season of going low on a block of an offensive line-man on a kick return. He took him down and injured him. Buddy offered five thousand dollars to any of his players who could teach Zendejas one of the unwritten rules of the game.

In my memory, the game is more famous for another incident. The game was played in Philadelphia's Veterans Stadium. It was one of the worst facilities in the league, one of those dual-sport monstros-ities favored in the 1970s. Philadelphia fans take great pride in having booed Santa Claus. In this last game of the season, there wasn't much on the line for either team—except for the health and well-being of Luis Zendejas. A foot of snow had fallen overnight. Crews got the field ready, but there wasn't enough time left to clear all the snow from the stands. As sometimes happens, fans began lobbing snow-balls on the field, targeting players and officials.

Terry and I were in the broadcast booth for most of the game. However, because of how long and narrow the booth was, anytime we did something on-air, we had to turn our sides to the field. Any military strategist will tell you to avoid being pinned down with-out escape routes. It's also not a good idea to turn your side on said enemy. Terry and I were forced to do both. Snowballs whizzed past us, hitting the wall and revealing rocks at their center.

To their discredit, the snowball throwers weren't very smart. They stood and laughed and pointed at us, making it very easy for anyone to point them out as the offenders. Police came and hauled them away. With about four minutes left in the game, however, the barrage resumed. I don't know if it was the same four, but Philadelphia at one point had a jail and judge located inside the stadium to speed process-ing offenders, but the effects were the same.

One of my lasting memories of my time with Terry is of him crouching below the low ledge that ran along the front of the broad-cast booth. An assistant had placed his monitor down there so that he could view the action. He did those last four minutes on his hands and knees. Tough place, that City of Brotherly Love.

In the spring of 1990, Terry and I were asked to represent CBS Sports at the NFL Spring Meetings in Orlando. While we were there, we had a thoughtful discussion about his continued frustration at being second string behind Madden. He told me he was going to ask to be moved into the studio to join Greg Gumbel on the pregame, halftime, and postgame shows. I told him I thought he would have greater impact in that role than he would as an analyst. To truly appreciate all that Terry brought to commentating, he had to be seen. His nods, his winks, his laugh, his whole larger-than-life persona worked so much better when he was on camera. Clearly I wasn't alone in that assessment. He left the booth for the studio and he and Greg enjoyed a terrific four-year run.

After that stint, he headed for the different pastures of Fox, and truthfully, because Terry was at Fox and I remained at CBS, we traveled in somewhat different circles for a while. We reunited in 2003 when Terry was named the third recipient of the Davey O'Brien Legends Award. Roger Staubach and Bart Starr preceded him. I was asked to present the award to him at the annual dinner held in Fort Worth. I could hardly believe that fourteen years had passed since that afternoon in Canton. It was a great evening honoring a great man.

Fast-forward another thirteen years. In the midst of the 2016 college football season, my final year helping CBS cover the SEC, Nancy and I were enjoying what had become a ritual for us. We ate our lunch at a Cracker Barrel restaurant. Here's my unsolicited recommendation: great food, generous portions, but expect a bit of a wait on a Sunday. This particular visit was on a Thursday and we were somewhere between Atlanta, our SEC home base, and Birmingham. My cell phone rang.

"Hey, Bubba. How you doin'? This is Terry."

He was visiting the new Cowboys headquarters being constructed north of Dallas in the city of Frisco. His tour guide was Brad Sham, my dear friend and radio partner who had replaced me in 1983. They were chatting about the good old days and my name crept into the conversation. Terry wondered how to reach me, and Brad obliged. For the next five minutes, somewhere just off Interstate 20, Terry and I talked and laughed. He asked to speak to Nancy and she beamed and nearly blushed. It was almost as if Terry had made the intervening years collapse and we were back in Chicago simply trying to see our way through the fog.

CHAPTER 9

The Gang's All Here

As is true of any relationship, chemistry and communication are the keys to success. Communication without chemistry is like, well, a lecture on organic chemistry—a bit dry. Chemistry without communication can be fun but not very enlightening. As football broadcasters, our job was to entertain and inform. The pictures could tell only some of the story. With Terry, I knew my role and enjoyed it. He was great at being both entertaining and informative.

Sad thing is, over time I would rely more and more on the monitor to watch the action. My poor eyesight, even aided by corrective laser surgery and then cataract removal procedures, couldn't keep up. I began this book by talking about getting the names right, and one of the other lasting memories I have of my time in the NFL is of doing a Vikings game and misidentifying Jake Reed as the receiver who had gotten loose behind the secondary to haul in a long pass. To my chagrin, it was actually No. 88 and not No. 86 who made that reception. I tossed and turned all night over my failure to adhere to one of broadcasting's cardinal rules. I was the play-by-play guy, after all, and it was incumbent upon me to get the facts straight.

I don't know how Terry would have felt about my mistake, but he would have taken it somewhere fun. I can be pretty sure that Dan Fouts, my next partner, would have refrained from saying anything on-air about my eyesight. He would have waited until later to get his digs in. As much as I cherished my relationship with Terry, Dan ranks right up there as a broadcaster and a lifelong friend. One of the reasons why Dan would have given me a pass on that misidentification is that he came to broadcasting with a greater appreciation for the art and craft of it than most. Dan's father, Bob Fouts, worked in sports television and radio for more than fifty years. For many years he worked in the Bay Area doing 49ers games and local television. I met Bob years before I worked with Dan when I was still doing radio for the Cowboys.

John Madden was responsible in a way for arranging my first meeting with Dan. As the number one guy, John exerted considerable influence on CBS Sports management. In the off-season before the 1990 frame, John expressed his displeasure with some of CBS Sports activities. He believed that we weren't focusing enough of our collective resources on pro football. John only did football, of course, and the rest of us play-by-play guys spent the football off-season covering other events. John felt that we needed to have a kind of preseason ourselves. John brought a coach's mentality to broadcasting. We all needed to be prepared. We all needed to work together toward a specific set of aims and objectives. We needed to have a greater command of the fine points of the game so that we could better teach the American public its nuances. We all needed to attend a summer symposium on football.

The powers that be agreed and so they flew many of the broadcast teams out to Carmel, California, where all the broadcast teams would meet and share intel and insights about the game we loved. This symposium—and I'm repeating that word because management insisted that we were attending a *symposium* and not a *seminar*—would consist of morning presentations and sharing sessions.

It was really a boondoggle of the highest order. We'd sit around in the morning and try to bluff each other about how much homework we did and then play golf in the afternoon. We did that for five days. I can recall a few of the skulled chip shots I struck but very little of the football talk.

Dan and I spoke and hit it off. Of course, I had followed his career and done a few of his Chargers games. Famously, Dan was the key pilot in the Chargers offense that came to be known as "Air Corryel." Offensive coordinator Bill Walsh heavily influenced San Diego's deep passing attack. That kind of passing game required a quarterback who could stand tall in the pocket to wait for receivers to free themselves or for the tight end to get open. Dan took a pounding, but boy was he prolific. He was the first player to throw for more than 4,000 yards in a season. He did that in 1981 and then repeated that accomplishment the next two seasons as well.

Dan Fouts attained nearly everything you would want in an NFL career, but he never got to play in the Super Bowl. He came close in 1982. The Chargers squared off in a first-round game against the Dolphins in Miami, a game that entered NFL legends as the Epic in Miami. The Chargers outlasted the Dolphins, 41–38, with Dan throwing for 433 yards while completing 33 of 53 passes. It was one of those hot and humid days in Florida, despite the calendar reading "December." The following week, in the AFC title game, they lost to the Bengals in Cincinnati. The game-time temperature was 92 degrees lower (accounting for windchill) than it had been in Miami. Thus that game became known as the Freezer Bowl.

We had no such issues as we strolled the fairways—well, some of us were in them—on Spyglass and Pebble Beach.

I look back on those days at CBS, which some of you may remember being known as the Tiffany Network, with real fondness. I don't know if the purse had any strings, but if it did, they untied easily. The following year, John had another brilliant idea. We needed to focus on football. Because the previous year's intel gathering hadn't quite gone to plan, like any good coach John devised another scheme. Instead of a large group of forty or fifty going somewhere to "sympose," we could do small group sessions. Divide and conquer was the idea behind this, I believe.

After making a smooth transition to working with Dan, who was the consummate professional and a much more straightforward and traditional analyst than Terry, we were going to work together the following season. That meant that, according to Madden's plan, Dan and I and our producer and director, Mark Wolf and Larry Cavolina, would travel to three NFL training camps. While there, we would interview the head coaches and a few players, observe some practices, and drill down past the usual Xs and Os to what I thought of as the Zs—as in snoring. No matter; duty called. We were assigned to Seattle, Arizona, and Denver.

In Seattle we met briefly with Chuck Knox, interviewed a couple of players, and then took a boat to Fort Ludlow for a fine afternoon out on the links. We flew to Phoenix. Joe Bugle, the head coach, was quite busy but accommodating, so we didn't go to Flagstaff to the team's camp. We did a conference call with him and enjoyed a nice round of golf. The same was true of the last city. Denver's Dan Reeves couldn't meet with us in Greeley, Colorado, as scheduled, so we had a free day. We flew to Steamboat, got in a round of golf, and enjoyed a fine luncheon that Nancy prepared. We met with Reeves the next day.

In their wisdom, CBS decided that with all these teams of broadcasters scattered about, it made sense to have some kind of convocation or colloquium in New York City. We'd assemble there and do presentations sharing what we learned on our reconnaissance missions to each of the team's preseason camps. I don't know if the borough of Manhattan, in all its history from the time it was a small burg known as New Amsterdam to when Wall Street gained renown as one of the world's great financial capitals, has ever been inundated by so much bullshit. Everyone, with the exception of John Madden, pulled information from orifices that weren't normally data generators. Hank Stram, the Hall of Fame coach turned broadcaster, brought a steam shovel while the rest of us used spades. Even members of the production staff joined, concocting elaborate presentations where they demonstrated their mastery of rosters, among other things. I should add Pat Summerall to the list of exceptions. He didn't prepare at all for his time to talk. He was so naturally gifted and knowledgeable that his off the cuff remarks should have been preserved for posterity.

If nothing else, those two research projects illustrated a couple of things that I already knew. John Madden had considerable pull with the network executives. John took his job seriously and demanded excellence of himself, the crew he worked with, and of everyone associated with all NFL telecasts at CBS and not just the ones he worked on.

I worked with John on-air a few dozen times in my career. For later summer and early fall Pat was still doing golf and then the U.S. Open tennis tournament. I filled in for him. John loved his work, loved the game, and loved the NFL. His passion for all three came through in every broadcast. John would have loved if everyone around him felt as deeply as he did. I can still picture his look of dismay when, following a game, everyone went about their business of wrapping things up to get out of the stadium to get to the airport to get home. John didn't fly, of course, and he hoped that we could all get together after the conclusion of the broadcast to revel in the game play or talk about the finer points of the production that we might tweak to get it better next time.

He had the unique ability to find some minuscule bit that most of us wouldn't have noticed and bring it to viewers' attention and riff on it. That was his genius. Pat's was that he could call the game straight up and also somehow manage to wrangle John back to the main focus of the game. They were extraordinary together, the best I've seen, and surely deserved to be the number one broadcast team that CBS has ever had. Like Howard Cosell, John had the ability to not just keep an audience, but to *bring* an audience to the game. Even if you had no rooting interest in a particular contest, John and Pat were, as the expression goes, appointment television.

One thing I found interesting about John is that he came to broadcasting after a playing and coaching career. John was a lineman, and so many of the analysts I worked with were quarterbacks—Terry and Dan, of course—but also Todd Blackledge, Pat Haden, Gary Danielson. Maybe I was predisposed to working with former signal callers or maybe it was just coincidence. In reflecting on this, three things come to mind. First, quarterbacks have to have vision. Their ability to scan the field is essential on the field and in the broadcast booth. (Clearly John Madden's ability to do this means this trait isn't the exclusive domain of quarterbacks.) Second, as far as networks are concerned, recruiting quarterbacks makes sense. They are names, known quantities among fans, and therefore may bring more eyeballs. Lastly, the quarterbacks I worked with were used to thinking on their feet, communicating succinctly, and had a better understanding of the big picture and little pictures in the game. I don't want to paint with too broad a brush here because I worked with Matt Millen and Dan Dierdorf, two outstanding nonquarterbacks who had the skills, if not the name recognition factor, that I listed above. Maybe this is somewhat like the belief that catchers in baseball, because they are the only players looking out on the whole field, make better managers and even broadcasters—think Tim McCarver, for example.

Along with being the best analyst in the game, John is the most idiosyncratic person I've ever met. Some of his quirks are the stuff of legend, but once you're involved personally in them, they take on a new light. I was fortunate that Nancy frequently traveled with me to games. During one of those preseason/early season substitution scenarios, Nancy flew with me to New York for a game I did with John. Our next assignment was in Pittsburgh.

John graciously offered to let us join him on his famous tour bus that Greyhound provided. A lot of people assume wrongly that John was afraid of flying. That's not strictly true. What John didn't like was giving up control. That might have been part of his coaching mentality bleeding over into another area of life. Come to think of it, him leaving coaching might have had something to do with those control issues. John likely would have been fine flying if he could have been his own pilot. John likely would have been fine with traveling by train if he could have pulled the cord so that the train could stop whenever he wanted it to so that he could grab a cup of coffee, at a convenience store, have a meal, or whatever suited his fancy at that moment.

Traveling by bus provided him with that level of control. Nancy and I found out the hard way that if you traveled by bus with John, you should know John's Rules of the Road. On that trip we discovered that John, a large man, needed the bus to be chilled to an unpleasant for most 55 to 60 degrees. When we entered the bus and took our seats in the first section of it—behind the driver's compartment and where a café table and chairs, a sofa, and an easy chair were positioned—we didn't feel the chill at first. By the time we crossed the George Washington Bridge our gooseflesh let us know that something was afoot. We'd dressed and packed for August heat and humidity, not the tundra. We looked around and saw that John's regular traveling companions, CBS broadcast associates—young men low on the corporate totem pole—must have been Boy Scouts. They came prepared. John had three full-size monitors suspended from the ceiling and a satellite dish on the roof. He watched tape, other broadcasts of games, and whatever else he wanted for entertainment.

John's entourage included the two bus drivers. One drove while the other rested so that the bus could be in motion continuously except for fuel stops and at John's request. Sandy Montag of IMG accompanied John as well. Sandy is the most powerful agent for sports broadcasters today, but back then he was an assistant. I was glad that Sandy was along. He did what a good agent does—he negotiates. He knew that Nancy and I were on the verge of becoming frozen fish sticks. He mentioned this to John, and, knowing that turning the temperature up was not an option, suggested John allow Nancy to go to the back of the bus. There she could settle under the sheets and blankets of his queen-size bed. John agreed to that accommodation. Dave Anderson, a Pulitzer Prize–winning journalist, was also along. He was working on a book with John but was also still writing a column. He reported that Nancy was the first woman to sleep in John's bed while he was on the road.

A small claim to fame, I suppose, but still noteworthy.

Once we arrived in Pittsburgh and were properly thawed out, I went with John to Three Rivers Stadium. It was another of those horrible circular stadiums with sight lines from the booth that could disorient anyone. John was dressed in usual track suit type leisurewear, and we ambled across the field toward one of the baseball dugouts. John suddenly stopped. He turned to the Pittsburgh equipment manager, "Dirt" DiNardo, who had been talking with John. (John was a very friendly guy.) He pointed into the dugout and asked, "Is that the one?"

I had an inkling of what "the one" referred to.

In 1972, his Oakland Raiders had come into Pittsburgh for a playoff game that became known for the Immaculate Reception. That disputed play cost the Raiders the game, and has been enshrined in NFL history as one of the greatest plays and one of the most controversial calls ever. Volumes have been written about it, generations have feuded over whether or not Franco Harris's catch of a deflected pass should have been ruled a touchdown, and sixteen years after the fact, John was still steamed about the call that went against him. What particularly irked him, and accounts vary about just what exactly referee Fred Swearingen said or asked chief of officiating Art McNally, was that the officials on the field seemed not to agree on the ruling. Swearingen used a telephone in that dugout to call up to the press box to speak to McNally. He learned that it was a legal catch.

Once John got confirmation that the offending phone was still extant, he stomped over and tugged and pulled and dislodged it. I worried that he might try to kick it, given John's habit of always wearing tennis shoes. He tucked it under his arm and continued along his way, saying something about how he was finally going to get something from this damned stadium. The phone eventually took up a prominent place of (dis)honor on the bus.

John and I got along well, but it was clear that he was most comfortable working with Pat. The two of them were a great team, but I can't say that they were buddies. Pat suffered from alcohol addiction, and John didn't seek out the nightlife. He had a routine in place wherever we stayed. He did not want to be on a high floor, generally asking for no higher than the third. He and the broadcast associates, one of whom was Richie Zyonts, who went to Fox with John and rose through the ranks there to be a lead producer, would order takeout dinners. They had their cuisine on rotation and enjoyed hanging out in a meeting room playing poker. I wasn't a gambler, so I never joined them. John said that he didn't go out to dinner because fans would inundate him and he wanted to be left alone. Yet he frequently sat in public places in the hotel and was warm and receptive to the people who would recognize him and chat him up. We're all complicated individuals and have our contradictory ways, but I always noted that particular trait in John—he didn't like to be alone. Some of that was likely his predilection for bus travel. The rest of us got to go home to loved ones between games. John was on the road, and his wife, Virginia, seldom joined him. His two sons, both Ivy League–educated young men, also were seldom on scene.

John was diligent and well prepared. I only really saw him sweat once, and that had nothing to do with preparation. John didn't like tight spaces, and one preseason game in Wisconsin put him to the test. Instead of the Packers facing off against the Giants in Green Bay, the Packers scheduled it in Madison. I've already said how much I liked Camp Randall Stadium and how big a role that Illinois–Wisconsin game played in advancing my career. In the intervening years, Camp Randall had undergone a renovation. A second deck was added and a short roof was constructed that jutted out over the broadcast positions. I walked into that small space with the canted roof and had the feeling that I was looking out on the field through the opening of a football helmet. John showed up after me, and I could immediately sense he was uncomfortable. After a minute or so, à la Terry Bradshaw, John broke into a flop sweat.

He got in touch with the production staff and they put in a few calls to the Packers. They contacted the university's facilities management folks and a few minutes later, workmen showed up. They knocked out an adjoining wall, extending our broadcast spot into the one beside it. John breathed easier, and I marveled at how quickly a solution was found. I'll admit that I was a bit envious. John meant a lot to the company and the financial benefits of having him on our team are immeasurable but substantial. I should have been, I can see now, a bit more grateful and a little less dismayed.

I have similar feelings about the position I was often placed in when taking over for Pat when it wasn't another sporting event that prevented him from partnering with John. Pat was remarkable at what he did, especially considering that he was given a pass on attending our production meetings. He'd been at it so long, I suppose, that he didn't feel the need to go and CBS wasn't going to force him to do anything he didn't want to do. I could understand and accept that. I struggled with other of Pat's absences.

Pat's battles with the bottle have been well documented, and I won't dwell on them too much here. I tell this only to illustrate the

.effects that his drinking had on me directly. I was frequently called in to replace Pat when he "went down." I'd get a call from one CBS executive or another letting me know in that coded language (as we would say of a player who was injured) that Pat was in a bad way and couldn't do a broadcast. I understood the disease nature of alcoholism, and I had worked with and otherwise seen a lot of individuals who were afflicted with it. I was no teetotaler, but I was always able to do my job. This may sound harsh, but it sometimes rankled me that Pat's struggles necessitated him receiving treatment I doubted I would have been given.

His problems once offered me an opportunity that I might not have ever received. At the end of the 1990 season, just before the playoffs, Pat went down again. Midweek before the second to last weekend of the regular season, I got word from Neal Pilson that Pat had checked into the Betty Ford Clinic. That alcohol rehabilitation center was renowned for its effective treatment. I was sorry to hear that Pat was in tough shape again but glad that he was getting the best of care. I was also glad to hear that I was going to be moved from working with Dan Fouts to do play-by-play alongside John Madden. We'd be paired for the last two games of the regular season plus the playoffs. I'd done playoff games before, but only one round of them. Neal assured me that the switch was going to be in effect throughout the playoffs. I'd be doing the most high-profile games and that was a thrill. Jack Buck was going to be shuffled over to work with Dan.

I was pleased to have the opportunity but it didn't sit well with two other members of my team. Wolf and Cavolina were understandably upset. Breaking up an announcing pair that late in the season would upset the rhythm of the entire broadcast team. Heated exchanges ensued. Regardless of how upset they were, the final decision had been rendered. I reported to Chicago for a January 6, 1991, playoff game between the Bears and the Saints. Minutes before kickoff, the phone rang in our booth. John answered it. He let out a big "Hey!

How are you! Glad to hear from you." Then he hunched over and turned his back to me and continued the conversation. I figured it was Pat and that he was likely just calling to wish John well. We did the game. The Bears won, 16–6. We had a nice, tight broadcast, and I was looking forward to going on to New York the following week to cover the Bears versus the Giants. Two storied franchises. Two huge markets. Another opportunity to be on the first team.

Before the game, I was down on the field. Neal Pilson walked up to me and put his arm around me. He said that he had some good news. Pat had been released from Betty Ford. He was doing well. His doctors okayed him leaving. He was going to New York and would do the game with John. I was not happy. I said so. I probably used far stronger language than that. I regret how I acted. I should have been happy for Pat and for the network. Pat was beloved among most of the folks at CBS Sports. I liked and respected him. I should have been more concerned about his welfare and less about my career prospects.

That said, eventually my feelings about the Pat situation played a large role in another career decision I faced.

Toward the end of the 1993 season, I was working with Dan Fouts again. We were doing a Cowboys–Jets Saturday afternoon football game at Giants Stadium. We stayed at the Hilton in adjacent Secaucus, New Jersey. Dan and I, along with our producer Mike Burkes, were having our production meeting. At one point we were waiting around for Jimmy Johnson, the Cowboys' head coach, to join us. While we were waiting, Mike took a call. He excused himself for a moment and when he came back into the room, he delivered the news. CBS, after thirty-eight years of televising NFL football, had lost the broadcast rights. Fox, the upstart network, had outbid us. We barely had time to let those words register when Jimmy came into the room. We all recovered enough to greet him. He looked at us one by one and said, "What's with you guys? You look like you've seen a dead man."

"Kind of," Dan said, "but we're the dead guys. We just lost the rights to the NFL."

Jimmy, glib as ever said, "Goes to show you, boys, it's a tough fucking business on both sides of the ball."

Amen to that.

We finished out the season. Speculation about who would make the move to Fox ran rampant. Pat was the first to sign and despite what many believe, he wasn't a part of a package deal. John was nearly signed, sealed, and delivered with NBC. At the eleventh hour, Rupert Murdoch, the chairman and CEO of parent News Corporation, called John. He asked John if his decision was about the money. John reportedly said, "Isn't it always?"

For me, it wasn't about the money. I was contacted about going to Fox and assuming my role as the number two guy there. I thanked the folks at Fox and said that I needed some time to think about it. That's as far as it got. They inquired. I thought about it briefly and declined before any negotiations began.

Why did I reject the idea?

This may sound bitter, but it also has the ring of truth to it. Very high on my list of reasons was my desire to get out from under being number two to John and Pat. I didn't like the idea of going to a new network and assuming the same responsibilities. I was okay with being number two, but I had enough of being called on to clean up other people's messes. I understand how that sounds, but that was how I felt then. That said, that doesn't diminish my feelings, more so now than then, that I should have been more concerned about Pat and what he was facing. Not for the first time in my career or in my life, I had to come face-to-face with my selfishness and my ambition.

The good news is that I don't regret turning down Fox's overtures. I took a substantial pay cut as a result of my diminished role at CBS. I was working more but being paid less since those NFL advertising revenues weren't rolling in. I think that had I gone to Fox, I would have had at least one regret.

One of my earliest assignments with CBS following the announcement that we would no longer cover the NFL was to do the narration and on-camera work for a nonsports project. To commemorate the fiftieth anniversary of D-Day CBS did a piece on Lynn "Buck" Compton. There was a sports connection because Buck played baseball at UCLA and was a teammate of Jackie Robinson. He left school to join the U.S. Army and was a member of the 101st Airborne Division. He parachuted in during Operation Overlord—the code name for the Normandy invasion. He performed heroically and was later a member of the unit depicted in *Band of Brothers.* He later became an attorney and prosecuted Robert Kennedy's killer Sirhan Sirhan. I got to travel to France and in addition to doing the voice-over work, I did on camera segments at various places where he'd acted heroically.

I rank that special as number two on my list of all-time favorite productions I've been involved in. As I said, striking that balance between entertainment and information is crucial in becoming an effective communicator. I'm pleased that I was able to be a part of that examination of history. That memory takes the sting out of another from that period. I did a tennis tournament at Stratton Mountain in Vermont. My partner was Mary Carillo. The only trouble was, in doing the taped opening, I called her Mary Catillo. Twice. Mary has one of the great minds in all of sports broadcasting, and I've always greatly admired her work. I think she finally forgave me for violating that cardinal rule of broadcasting. She joked that if she was an NFL football player I would have gotten it right the first time.

With no more NFL games on the horizon for me, my brain space was going to be occupied with other sports and other names. As it turned out, I wound up enjoying greatly my time in NFL exile.

CHAPTER 10

Live from Lillehammer It's Verne and Scott Meet Tonya and Nancy

I'm grateful that Mary Carillo was able to forgive me for not getting her name right. She understood that we all make mistakes, and as egregious as mine was, she still found a way to let me know that we could move on and have a good working relationship. And we did, though we didn't do many events together. Holding a grudge would have been unproductive and unhealthy. How do I know that? Because for a long time after I was let go by Chuck Howard and ABC in 1982, I often fantasized about what I would say if I ever saw that man again. I'm not a violent person by nature; when I considered all the perceived injustices I suffered at the hands of ABC and Chuck, I could work myself into a real lather. I may not have wanted to literally cut him off at the knees, but to do so verbally would have given me great satisfaction.

Shortly after learning that we'd lost the NFL, I was in Los Angeles International Airport. I was on one of the long escalators heading to baggage claim. Something caught my eye. A man on the floor below was wearing lime green slacks. I also caught a flash of white and tan—a bit of ankle and white Gucci loafers. I thought, Only one man in America dresses like that. Sure enough, my nemesis Chuck Howard was waiting to claim his bags. He was with another man I recognized. Chet Forte, the great director of *Monday Night Football*, was with him. Our paths had crossed but I didn't know him well.

My mind reeled. Here was my chance. I could really give Chuck a piece of my mind. I'd had great success with CBS. Enough time had passed that my revenge dish was quite cold despite my hot emotions. Plus, I'd be able to lay into him in front of one of his peers.

Delicious.

I walked up to Chuck, juggling malicious metaphors as I did. Which weapon would I play first?

"Hi, Chuck." I nodded like a gunslinger. "Hi, Chet."

Chuck greeted me. Before I could draw my weapon, he said, "You know, Verne, this is a business where you have to make judgment calls. Sometimes we make mistakes. I made a huge mistake with you. I want to apologize for not keeping you on the staff."

All my anger and resentment washed out of me. I dropped my weapons. I thanked him for his apology. I left my entire "why me" whining baggage there unclaimed. I didn't spend any time ruing what might have been or chastising myself for a waste of time and energy. That would have defeated the purpose of the chance encounter. I fairly skipped through the airport to a waiting vehicle that took me to my hotel. Life was good.

I felt the same about my career prospects. Sure, I had to take a substantial pay cut, but Nancy and I would be more than fine. We tried to spend as much time together as possible, even when I was on the road working, and with my Sundays likely open, we'd be able to spend even more time together. As it turned out, that wasn't quite the case. CBS had a Sunday afternoon time slot to fill and they engaged in a counterprogramming effort that proved to be successful: figure skating.

As it so happened, my unlikely love affair with figure skating had begun even before we lost NFL football, but it deepened into something greater as a result. It also gave me an opportunity to work on a regular basis with Scott Hamilton, a man I still respect, admire, and love. Since I've stepped away from the regular broadcasting duties in the last year and half, I've been asked many times, "If you had one chance to do one event before you die, what would it be?" People expect that I'd want to call the Super Bowl or I'd want to call the college football championship or I'd want to be at the tower at 18 at Augusta. And none of those things is true. I mean, I've had a very, very, very full career and very rewarding, but if somebody pinned me down and said, "One more event," I would say I'd like to do another Winter Olympics. And I would like to do it with Scott Hamilton.

I didn't always love figure skating, but I did always aspire to cover the Olympics. In the summer of 1989, when I was first given my Olympic assignment for the 1992 Olympic games, I worried I wasn't being utilized in the way I thought made the most sense. Given that I lived in Steamboat Springs and had become good friends with the resort's director of skiing, Billy Kidd—the first American ever to medal in an Olympic alpine skiing event—it made sense to me that I'd be covering the downhill, the giant slalom, and the slalom. I had the interest and the aptitude and that should have been enough.

It wasn't. When I got the call and learned that I was to cover figure skating, I could barely keep the disdain out of my voice. Tim Ryan, who had done skiing before and with Billy Kidd, got the assignment I wanted. That didn't take the sting out of their decision. Nancy spoke up as the voice of reason: "You know what? Calm down. You're going to love it because of your equal respect for athleticism and music and your involvement in both, and this combines the best of both, because the music is so important and the athleticism should never, ever be understated. These young people do amazing things, and they do it all by themselves on a sheet of ice that's very long, and they're on a four-inch blade."

So I calmed down. I got Scott's number and talked to him. He was quite pleasant and enthusiastic. We were going to meet in Colorado Springs at the 1989 Junior World Championships. With the exception of going to a skating rink once as a kid, I'd never seen a competition. All I remembered was people going around in slow circles while calliope music played. I got to Colorado Springs and went to the old World Arena, at the Broadmoor Hotel. The arena has been razed but reminded me of a large warehouse. I walked into its dim interior and there was a rectangle of light ahead of me. I got to the edge of the rink and it was crowded with young skaters practicing. What I can't ever forget was a young guy skating backward toward where I was standing. He was moving at a high rate of speed and I had visions of him crashing into the boards. Instead, four feet from the edge of the ice, he extended one leg behind him and then stabbed the tip of his boot into the ice. The next thing I knew he was rising off the surface, spinning three times in the air, and landing what seemed to me yards away from where he took off.

The young man, it turns out, was Elvis Stojko of Canada. He went on to become a three-time world champion, two-time Olympic silver medalist, and seven-time Canadian champion. He was renowned for his athleticism and still is. He introduced me to the sport up close and personal and I was mesmerized.

Scott joined me and began my skating education. I pointed out before that Frank Glieber gave me great advice about studying film and learning the rules. That all worked for me, but having an understanding and knowledgeable partner can make up for any deficiencies you might still have. I was used to working with highly accomplished athletes, and Scott was certainly that, but he was also an impassioned advocate for his sport. He was a great believer that the theatrical elements of the sport—costumes and music primarily—shouldn't ever overshadow the grace and athleticism on display. Scott won four straight U.S. and world championships from 1981 to 1984. He also won the Olympic gold medal in 1984, capping off a remarkable run.

One reason I admired Scott was his perseverance. At the age of two he displayed mysterious symptoms of a condition that took a long time to be adequately diagnosed. The most obvious symptom was that he stopped growing. When he was winning all those championships, he was only five feet two and weighed just over 100 pounds. By the time we worked together, he added another two inches in height and a few more pounds. Scott didn't have the most telegenic voice—his condition and size affected his vocal cords—but he more than made up for that with his enthusiasm and expertise. He first really made a name for himself in 1980 when he finished third at the U.S. Figure Skating Championships. He made the Olympic team and in recognition of his accomplishment his fellow Olympians selected him to carry the U.S. flag in the opening ceremonies.

Scott not only had to overcome that rough start due to health concerns, but he almost had to give up the sport because his parents couldn't afford the high cost of training. Scott was adopted by two professors, Dorothy and Ernest Hamilton, who taught at Bowling Green State University in Ohio. Frank and Helen Lorraine helped out financially and Scott would later work with them to find funding for other skaters and the sport itself. Not long after Scott and I first worked together, he was inducted into the United States Olympic Hall of Fame.

Despite Scott's tutelage I made a hash of that first broadcast. Scott explained to me that there were only six jumps in the sport. Only one of them had a forward takeoff—the axel. For the rest the skater turned around and faced backward before launching. I got that straight, but I had a hard time recognizing a triple from a double jump. That became apparent when I conducted a postcompetition interview with a young American named Jessica Mills. I asked her the most basic questions, and erred in stating that she had completed all her triples when she hadn't. That interview never made it on air.

It was a good thing that we still had two years until the Olympics in Albertville, France. To familiarize us with some of the competitors from the rest of the world, CBS sent us to the European Championships, being held in Leningrad. I was sad that Nancy couldn't join us. We'd spent our honeymoon cruising through Eastern Europe and Russia. That was in 1982 when hotels in the Soviet Union weren't really up to tourist standards. By the time Scott and I got there in 1990, the hotel where Nancy and I had briefly dropped in had been upgraded but was still little better than an economy motel in the States.

What the Soviet Union lacked in pleasant accommodations it more than made up for by their excellence in figure skating. The connection between ice skating and dance, particularly the ballet, and the Soviet Union has been well documented. Soviet skaters dominated the podium in all the events. Names that would become familiar to viewers in the United States—Viktor Petrenko won the men's competition and Ekaterina Gordeeva and Sergei Grinkov the pairs'— rolled off Scott's tongue.

The event was held at Yubileyny Arena, site of the volleyball match I'd covered years earlier. The atmosphere wasn't as raucous, but, boy, those Russian fans crowded in there and responded with great gusto to the performances. I was amazed by how highly regarded Scott was. We arrived at the arena, got our credentials, and Scott then spent the next twenty-five minutes signing autographs as he made his way to our commentary location. Folks shouted his name and lined up for autographs. He refused no one. He stopped for photographs and was as gracious as could be. Keep in mind that I'd just spent four years working with Terry Bradshaw and Dan Fouts—Hall of Famers both—and the reception that Scott received from non-American skating fans was greater than what those two received in stadiums throughout the NFL.

It was there that Scott and I developed our rapport both on and off the air. More important, Scott devised a system that enabled us to function very well as a broadcast team. He watched all the practices and memorized the competitors' routines. Once the music began and the familiar slashing sound of skates on ice started, I knew I was in good hands. I would do my spare bit and when an important element was coming up, Scott would place his hand on my forearm. That was my cue to be quiet and let him take over. I was happy to cede the stage to Scott and let him describe it. I would jump back in with some bit of storytelling: "So-and-so's mother drove her a hundred and forty miles round-trip to the rink for training each day." People still laugh about my inserts.

Scott and I spent ten days in Leningrad and I learned so much about the sport in that short span. Scott introduced me to a woman who proved to be an invaluable resource. Tamara Moskvina spoke seven languages, competed in both ladies' singles and pairs, made the Russian Olympic team, and was then a highly regarded coach. Among the things I learned was that the Yankees–Red Sox rivalry was nothing compared to the one between skaters and coaches from Leningrad and Moscow.

In March 1990, the stakes were higher when we traveled to Halifax, Nova Scotia, for the World Championships. We were joined by a third on-air commentator. Sandra Bezic was the ice-dancing aficionado who worked with us. Scott confessed to me that he had little interest in the ice-dancing competition. The Canadian Broadcasting Corporation was also televising the event. Scott pointed across the ice to their broadcast post and pointed out a young woman by the name of Tracy Wilson. Like Sandra, Tracy was a former skater and we'd eventually work together at CBS. She won a bronze in ice-dancing at the '88 games in Calgary.

Scott and I did a few more events before we finally went to France for the Games. I was like a seven-year-old kid who'd just gotten a puppy. Nancy was with me and we sat in the third row for the opening ceremonies. I didn't know whether to gawk at Prince Albert of Monaco, who sat a few seats in front of us, or the brilliant presentation that one of the founders of Cirque du Soleil had created. You just about needed to be a circus performer to fit into the tiny hotel rooms we were booked into. Albertville was a small host city, and the only two suites in the place were reserved for Scott and CBS News' Charles Kuralt. Katarina Witt, the West German skater who was in some people's minds the last of the elegant ladies of figure skating, had been hired to provide commentary, but with her limited English, she was there more for name recognition and to add some glamour to the booth.

Besides all of us hanging out at a lovely hotel bar each night after the skating concluded, I remember feeling out of my depth. I think that most of us on the production side did as well. Scott, Tracy, and Katarina weren't really aware of this, but CBS struggled to get a fix on how to present skating to the American public. We hadn't covered the Olympics since 1960 when Tex Shramm was the executive producer. We had a bit of new-kids-on-the-block anxiety. As I've said, I see myself as a storyteller, and the success of a multisport, multivenue, multimillion-dollar venture like covering the Olympics comes down to creating some cohesive narrative to tie together all the different elements of the Games. This was the Olympics during which I first met Nancy Kerrigan and Tonya Harding, but of course the real drama with them was still a couple of years down the road. I do recall, with some slight embarrassment, and a sense of someone being prescient, that CBS promoted one of the U.S. pairs figure skating teams as the "waitress and the truck driver."

In truth, Rocky Marval did drive a truck—he owned a trucking firm with his brother—and Calla Urbanski did work as a waitress and a barmaid to support herself while skating. Still, the idea that we were hoping to lure people to the event by featuring skaters who had little chance to medal strikes a wrong note with me more so now than it did at the time. We were a business operation, to be sure, and earning ratings was the way to get the advertising dollars. But those promotions of Rocky and Calla, the attempt to make them into household names and stars in some way, was a part of the business that made me uncomfortable.

What I remember most wasn't the action on the ice. We had a wonderful time hanging out at the hotel bar afterward. We all needed a few drinks. Katarina's spotty English proved to be a real liability. At first she was reduced to taping a one-minute introduction to each of the events. It became clear that those bits were beyond the scope of her language skills. Management decided to put her in the studio with Tim McCarver and Paula Zahn. I love Katarina, and it pains me to say this, but she really was little more than set decoration. She was put in an impossible situation but soldiered on and was delightful company, especially when one night she resisted the charms of Jim Lampley.

For our part, Scott and I muddled through. Even before the first event, Scott said to me, "You do realize that I'm the first guy to analyze Olympic figure skating besides Dick Button?" Dick Button was a fixture on American television as the Voice of Figure Skating. He was much beloved. I told Scott that I knew that was true, and I also understood that I was taking over the role of the much-beloved Jim McKay.

That's no excuse.

The critics initially panned us. I'm okay with that especially because of what happened on the second Saturday night of the Games. My father called me in Albertville the following day to mention that I'd been on *Saturday Night Live*. I wasn't, of course, but I was in a way. You know you're a pretty big deal when you are featured in the cold open of *SNL*. That introduction of five or so minutes is often water-cooler talk on Monday mornings. Apparently Scott and I were so memorable that the Not Ready for Prime Time Players, as the cast was once known, decided to spoof us to nail home the point that we weren't ready for prime time, either. Dana Carvey played Scott and the late Phil Hartman played me. When I later saw it, I was thrilled. Both comics nailed the performance. My inserting personal stories to give viewers someone to root for came under fire hilariously.

Jason Priestly played an inept skater who wound up flopping all over the ice. Julia Sweeney was amazing as Tracy Wilson. I laughed until my eyes teared up. I still have a video of that piece and frequently use it to close speeches I give.

Scott loved it, too. Somehow the folks at NBC were in touch with our people at CBS. They sent us a copy of it. Pat O'Brien, who was just starting to earn the notoriety that would make him a household name, was hosting the late-night recap show in Albertville. Scott was his guest on the Sunday following *SNL*. He showed it with Scott sitting right there. Scott was roaring with laughter and Pat commented that my partner seemed more excited about being sent up that way than he had been when he won gold in Sarajevo. Scott agreed. That is the power of television, I guess.

That power is not to be taken lightly, though it too often is. I'm told that the *SNL* cast reprised the bit with different players for each of the next Olympics Scott and I covered. There was something about the freshness of the first one that couldn't be recaptured in subsequent versions. See? Everyone's a critic.

What no one could criticize, along with Paul Wylie's stellar performance, was Kristi Yamaguchi's gold-winning efforts. Even though she didn't skate a clean program—she lost points for touching down on a shaky triple toe loop—she had a comfortable enough lead after the short program to hang on for the win. At four eleven, Kristi presented a small figure out on the ice, but she had a huge heart. Born to a mother who was put in a World War II internment camp for

Japanese Americans and to a lieutenant in the U.S. Army, she was the first American woman of Asian descent to medal at the games. Kristi dreamed of being a figure skater from a very young age.

Like many little girls at the time, she was inspired by seeing Dorothy Hamill win gold in the 1976 Olympics. One of the oft-told stories had her carrying around a Dorothy Hamill doll incessantly when she was a child. Dorothy was in Albertville and met briefly with Kristi before her winning performance, urging her to go out and have fun. Winning is certainly one way to do that. I don't mean to diminish her accomplishment in any way, but I don't think that anyone in the skating world considers that Olympic Ladies final to be a classic. It seemed as if one by one each of the medal contenders fell, ruining their chances for the top spot. As Scott pointed out, Kristi skated a conservative program that night in France, but it proved enough. What the final may have lacked in outstanding performances, it didn't lack for drama. I can still hear the crowd voicing its empathetic disappointment as clean programs fell by the wayside. Idori Ito of Japan finished second and Nancy Kerrigan won the bronze, slipping one spot from her position going into the final. Tonya Harding finished just off the medal podium in fourth.

SEEING THOSE THIRD- AND FOURTH-PLACE finishes by Nancy and Tonya, I don't believe that any of us who sat in the bleachers at Le Halle Glace Olympique could have guessed how things would play out in two short years. The International Olympic Committee decided that rather than have the winter and summer games held in the same year, they would be held separately every two years. The good news for 1992 Winter Olympians was that they would only have to wait until 1994 in Lillehammer, Norway, to bring their dreams to life.

In the run-up to the Olympics, Tracy Wilson and I were present at the World Championships in Lausanne, Switzerland. Scott hadn't been feeling well, so he didn't make the trip. Shortly after we arrived, we received a phone call. Scott had been diagnosed with testicular cancer. I felt a sickening drop in my stomach. Tracy and I went about business, but we were both in a daze. Our partner was hurting and many miles away physically, but very much on our minds and in our hearts.

Of course, I knew logically that life isn't fair and that cancer, as awful as it is, neither plays favorites nor targets anyone. Still, Scott had dealt with a lot as a kid and now here he was, still a young man, dealing with another tough situation. I knew that if anyone had the spirit and will to battle back, it was Scott. He would work with Tracy and me again in 1994, and I find it interesting and instructive to note the contrast between his personal struggle and what transpired on and off the ice before and during the Olympic skating.

I know that I've said that one of my goals as a broadcaster was to give viewers a reason to root for someone. The Kerrigan-Harding debacle suffered then and continues to now from too much oversimplification. I hope Scott will forgive me this costume-themed metaphor, but too many people were too easily placing white hats and black hats on the heads of the main participants and assorted others.

On January 6, 1994, shortly after finishing a practice at Cobo Arena in Detroit, the site of the U.S. Figure Skating Championships, Kerrigan was assaulted on the leg with a police baton. Her unknown assailant escaped. Very quickly, suspicion fell on Tonya Harding, her ex-husband, Jeff Gillooly, and Shawn Eckhardt and Shane Stant. Eckhardt acted unofficially as Harding's bodyguard. On February 1, 1994, accepting a plea deal, Gillooly acknowledged that he conspired with Eckhardt and others to have Kerrigan injured. As a part of his plea, he agreed to testify against Harding, implicating her in the planning.

Kerrigan couldn't compete in the U.S. championships that determined who would make the Olympic team. Harding won the event, but Kerrigan was voted onto the squad in recognition of the unusual circumstances that resulted in her inability to perform. The two would travel to Lillehammer. At home and around the world, a media frenzy began the moment the public learned of the attack. A video of the aftermath of the attack fired our collective imagination. This was a train wreck of Olympic proportions and rubbernecking became a national pastime here and elsewhere. From the onset the two women were hounded by fans and the media and that would continue until the Olympics and beyond. The good-versus-evil element was too juicy and too clear to be spun off the news cycle and replaced by anything else. Thuggery and figure skating? What an odd pair.

I will say this, however: As much as the sound bite of Nancy Kerrigan postattack crying out and saying, "Why? Why? Why? Why me?" is indelibly imprinted in the minds of so many Americans, a short time later she was better able to put things in perspective for all of us.

"That's not the most important thing, skating. If I can't [skate], I'll deal with it. I'm okay. It could have been a lot worse," Kerrigan said.

Even later she was quoted as saying, "The most important thing is to be happy and healthy."

Amen to that.

In the media blitz that followed Kerrigan being attacked inside Cobo Hall in Detroit, Nancy became even more of a media and fan darling than she had been before. What I find interesting is that if the lunacy hadn't taken place, I would have chosen Tonya Harding as the one whose cause I would have championed. America loves an underdog. We root for those who overcome tough circumstances with grit and determination. Nancy Kerrigan was fortunate to be raised in a somewhat stable household. Long-limbed, graceful, and attractive enough to have once been named among *People*'s 50 Most Beautiful

People in the World, she seemed to lead a charmed life. That wasn't entirely the case, and her mother's vision issues and other troubles weren't part of the usual fairy-tale plot line. The fact that her father, Daniel, would eventually be killed by Nancy's brother Mark in 2010 suggests that there were more dark things afoot in Nancy's home life.

That's not to say she didn't have to work hard to be among skating's elite.

It was more obvious that Harding's family life was anything but stable, including frequent moves, a product of a broken home, a mother who remarried for the sixth time shortly after she split with Tonya's father. Tonya was short and squat, a fireplug powerhouse who never seemed to be able to find favor with skating judges who acknowledged her prowess as a jumper but dinged her on presentation scores. On and off the ice, she seemed rougher around the edges, less polished and poised. She wound up in a disaster of a marriage, had to petition for protective orders against her husband Gillooly, and the on-again-off-again nature of the relationship and eventual marriage had to be as much a puzzle to the two of them as it was to outsiders.

The blunt and inaccurate assessment that many in the media made was that this was a case of blue blood versus white trash. Distilling their histories to fit into those neat but mean-spirited categories may have made for good TV drama, but it hardly captures any of the nuances of American society or the sport of figure skating.

I also can't easily place a white or a black hat on any of the media outlets that covered the story. Playing up the differences between the two women, pitting them against one another, playing up the whodunit elements of the scandal, all made for great television. And it wasn't just American media. When Scott and I showed up in Lillehammer to view a practice session, we were two of four hundred media members there. Scott summed things up neatly and angrily in stating that the worldwide media attention was turning the skating into just another tabloid event. CBS wasn't immune to the fevered fascination. The network assigned its lead anchor, Connie Chung, to come to Lillehammer and shadow Harding.

As Scott said to me at that practice in defense of all the other competitors, "Someone has lost sight of the fact these young men and women have worked their whole lives for this. We shouldn't focus on this cartoon."

We did our best in the face of competing interests. To ignore that "cartoon" wouldn't work at all. Acknowledging its existence and moving on was going to be a fine line to walk. I believe that's what we managed to do. All we could control was the minutes when we were broadcasting the skating. What the network chose to do outside of that was out of our hands—as was frequently the case even when there were no real controversial circumstances to deal with. We also felt an obligation to the other athletes and their compelling stories. They didn't deserve to be shunted aside; that would have been nearly the equivalent of taking a club to their chances to shine in the biggest competition in their careers. In our minds, Tonya and Nancy were *a* story. They weren't *the* story.

The medal winners would be determined by combining judges' scores from the shorter technical program and the longer free skate. In the first of the events, the skaters were all required to complete three required elements: a triple Lutz/double toe loop combination as well as a double flip and a double axel. In between those they also did spins and spirals and other maneuvers. As Nancy warmed up before her short program, the atmosphere inside the Hamar Olympic Amphitheatre, also known as the Northern Lights Hall, turned electric. A large contingent of Americans waved flags and the loud and sustained applause Nancy received upon being introduced contributed to my opening remark. Just before the first strains of "Desperate Love" began, I said, "It's been a long wait." I was, of course, also referring to the time between her attack on January 4 and February

23. Oksana Baiul and Surya Bonaly, her two main competitors, had already skated and were first and second. Nancy stood at center ice frozen in time in a black and white dress, breathing deeply before she began. Scott waited some fifteen seconds or so before he first spoke, saying that, "This program is everything it needs to be. Artistic. Speed skating, but she has to get past this combination." His comments previewed the first major element that Nancy would do, the triple Lutz into a double toe loop. When she completed it, Scott's voice rose in excitement: "Beautifully done."

We let the cameras do the talking for nearly a minute until Nancy approached the double axel, which Scott succinctly described as the most difficult. Nancy landed it perfectly and went on to complete the routine with a beautiful spiral. Nancy was clearly pleased, beaming and smiling and waving to the appreciative audience as she made her way to the so-called kiss-and-cry area just off the ice. There her coach, Evy Scotvold, and his wife and choreographer Mary Scotvold, wrapped her in an embrace. Nancy's high-wattage smile was still on full display.

Scott and I opted to continue to let the images carry the day, with me merely making the identification of those on-screen. We then went to a brief replay of the tougher elements of the routine, which Scott called a "beautifully delivered technical program." The director cut briefly to a shot of Tonya Harding sitting and watching the action and applauding Nancy's efforts. With just a brief ID of her, we moved on. When we cut to Nancy's parents, I had to do more than merely introduce them. Nancy's mother, Brenda, was shown standing in front of a large monitor on which she viewed the proceedings. I said, "Her mother is, as I think most of you know, legally blind," and then added, "she can sense beauty."

We remained silent while Nancy took a seat, chatted with her team, and awaited her scores. When they came up, Scott said with hardly a second elapsing, "I don't know what Great Britain and the

Czech Republic were looking at. There were no deductions in that program." Those first set of scores were for technical merit, how the athlete executed all of the elements. I had to agree with Scott and trust his judgment. Nancy's first set of marks looked like this:

5.6	5.9	5.6	5.7	5.9	5.9	5.9	5.8	5.8
GB	POL	CZE	UKR	CHN	USA	JPN	CAN	GER

With the graphic showing, we offered no further comment and continued to show and listen in on Nancy and her team. The boom mic wasn't able to pick up much of what they were saying given the crowd noise, but no one looked demonstrably upset. Her marks were strong. A few seconds later, her presentation scores came up. As before, the British and Czech judges awarded her the lowest scores among the nine of them.

5.6	5.9	5.7	5.7	5.9	5.9	5.9	5.8	5.8
GB	POL	CZE	UKR	CHN	USA	JPN	CAN	GER

The judges also listed their ordinal scores. With the obvious two exceptions each of the judges had rated her first. Nancy's marks were good enough to put her in first place. I slipped into a bit of golf lingo stating that she was "atop the leaderboard." Nancy stayed there, and went into the long program, which would commence two days later on the twenty-fifth in first place. In the time that followed, we got caught up a bit on Oksana Baiul. We'd seen her at various competitions and she had a compelling story of her own. Her parents divorced when she was only two years old. Her father left their home in Ukraine and wasn't a presence in her life. Her mother, Maria, raised Oksana until she died in 1991, when the young skater was only thirteen. At sixteen, Oksana was among the younger women in the competition. I always chafed at the description of various young gymnasts as "pixieish," and will say that Oksana looked very much like what she was—a young teenager. In comparison, Nancy looked like what she was—a young woman of twenty-four.

Just about everything you need to know about the contrast in the two can be summed up in the marks they each received in the short program.

Required Elements or Technical Merit	5.7	5.8	5.4	5.7	5.7	5.6	5.7	5.6	5.5
Presentation	5.9	5.8	5.7	5.9	5.9	5.8	5.9	5.9	5.9
	GB	POL	CZE	UKR	CHN	USA	JPN	CAN	GER

Oksana's presentation marks, sometimes referred to as artistic impression, were clearly higher than Nancy's. That said, Nancy was rated first on seven of the nine judges' cards. What these scores also show is the aspect of figure skating that can either fascinate and enthrall or frustrate and disillusion skaters and fans alike—the great artistry versus technical mastery divide. *Divide* is too strong a word. Everyone agrees that skaters need to have both of those characteristics in their routines or programs. Which matters most to you, and to the judges, will nearly always be variable. On Pat O'Brien's late-night recap after the long program was concluded, Scott summed up this enigmatic aspect of the sport, "On a night when a decision had to be made it came down to two skaters and they both skated their hearts out. How do you compare? It just depends on how you feel at the time."

I want to be clear here: I'm not putting words in Scott's mouth; this is my take on what he said. Please also keep in mind how much I loved working on these events. A competition whose results depend on how a group of nine judges is feeling at the time is always going to be fraught with controversy. Maybe that's the appeal of it for some. It isn't as cut and dried, you scored more points, more runs; you ran/

swam/biked/skated/skied/drove or whatever faster than everyone else. Some people are sports fans because they love the black-and-white nature of the results. In the rest of their lives, the reasons behind wins and losses are often murky and complicated.

As murky and complicated as the Kerrigan–Harding drama was, so was the result of the Baiul–Kerrigan battle. It saddens me that too often the topic is the attack and not the competition. In recent years, and particularly lately with a new film out about those events, I've read timelines and other forms of coverage of the attack and the Lille-hammer competition. Very often the skating is reduced to a single line: "Nancy Kerrigan won a silver medal." Now, for fans of the sport, that simple summary falls short of what they recall of the night of the twenty-fifth when the two young women took to the ice.

CBS's ratings for the short program and the long program remain among the top fifty or so for any broadcast in American television history. An appetite existed and CBS was there to whet it and feed it. For our part, Scott and I had to deal with the on-ice drama far more than we did the rest. That was how we both wanted it. In our introduction, we showed Oksana Baiul entering the rink. She was the world champion. We showed Nancy Kerrigan, the leader going into the long program, and we highlighted Katarina Witt, a longtime star and sentimental favorite who was likely making her last Olympic appearance on ice.

Harding wasn't really in medal contention after the short pro-gram, finishing tenth. Still, she was going to be a part of our broad-cast, as were other skaters down the ranks. That was always a part of the plan. What none of us could have anticipated was how much drama would surround her effort. Tonya came out on the ice for her warm-up and seemed to have trouble with her laces. When it was her turn to compete, I made a brief mention of the tortured path that she had taken to get to the Olympics. We showed her off the ice furiously working on her skate, and I mentioned other times when costume difficulties and other distractions had figured in her competition. Scott added that Tonya was experiencing every skater's nightmare—to have an equipment or costume issue just before going out onto the ice.

The public address announcer introduced Tonya but she didn't step out. The crowd grew restless but the rules stated that Tonya had two minutes to take her position following her introduction. As the countdown went on, Scott said that he'd never seen anything like this before at any competition. The bizarre nature of the Harding saga could potentially lead to her being disqualified. Things got even stranger.

Tonya got out on the ice in time, started her program, and then stopped. She skated over to the judges and showed them her broken skate lace. Per the rules of the competition, she was allowed to make the repair and come out later to skate again. When Tonya's skate lace broke, we had to be the ones to deliver the rules and policies to an audience that was composed of far fewer knowledgeable viewers than ever before. That kind of audience is typical for an Olympic broadcast, which draws in casual sports fans. Because of the suspicions that fell on Tonya and her group, a far greater number of viewers was drawn in. That increased the pressure on us to make them feel comfortable.

I have a great deal of sympathy for the Canadian skater Josée Chouinard, who was forced out of her routine and rushed onto the ice after Tonya Harding cut short her program to ask for, and receive, a "do-over" that was within the rules. In many battles there is always collateral damage, and Josée was, in Scott's and my estimation, treated unfairly. As for Tonya, despite all the anxiety the equipment failure produced, she skated decently, ranking seventh in the long program, good enough to place her eighth overall.

As for the performances of Oksana and Nancy that night, words wouldn't do them justice. As Scott said, both women skated their hearts out and skated beautifully and demonstrated great mastery.

The atmosphere was electrifying and each set out to do what they had planned to do and trained to do for years. I wrote earlier that for a competition to truly become a classic, a lot has to be at stake. Seeing these two athletes rise to the occasion still causes the hairs on my arm to rise in appreciation and wonder at their abilities. With so much on the line, with no one else out there but themselves, they each blocked out all the distractions and immense pressure to perform as well as they possibly could.

I have no real understanding of the physics involved in burying a metal pick attached to a blade, attached to a boot, attached to a foot, that's attached to the rest of a human body that can propel it several feet into the air. Never mind how that human body can also spin and land. Never mind how it can rotate at such a rate of speed without disorienting the brain that controls that body. In terms of the mastery and manipulation of physics, we might as well be talking about a particle accelerator and how it operates. Both have some element of danger involved as well. To be honest, I don't really want to fully understand at a granular level *how* these marvelous athletes do what they do. I want to, and do, *appreciate* what they do. I have a fairly firm grasp of what's involved in making a tackle, rising up to fire a jump shot, rolling a putt, but how you do a quadruple toe loop is beyond me. I like that about the sport. I like the speed, the precision, and the grace and the violence that precedes the grace. I would much rather marvel at how these athletes perform a death spiral than marvel at what must have gone on in someone's life that they would even contemplate the assault of another competitor.

What took place on the ice that night embodies what I love about sports. Both Oksana and Nancy had to overcome adversity. Nancy's was well documented, while I'm not certain many remember that on the day before the final, Baiul suffered a cut in a collision with another skater during practice. There was no Curt Schilling bloody sock on display, but her grit can't be questioned. Worse than the cut, she wrenched her back so severely that she needed two legal painkilling injections in order to compete the next night. Had I slept funny and woken with a stiff back, I would have likely needed similar treatment just to go to breakfast, never mind propel myself around the ice.

All of the women in that final, including Tonya Harding, transcended the sometimes mean-spirited, misguided, and, frankly, malignant fascination that had become *l'affaire Harding-Kerrigan*. I'd rather talk about the controversy over the final determination of the victor than what led up to it.

In the end, attempting to quantify the decision that saw Oksana Baiul crowned Olympic champion is difficult. It would be nice if there were some unanimity in the appraisal of that result. I know that both of them rightly believed that they had done enough to win. The judges declared for Oksana versus Nancy. I suppose that growing up in the sport and getting to the level of achievement each had, they had a better understanding of the nearly nebulous differentiations that separate gold from silver. It's not like you can, as in chemistry, assay the difference between the two metals.

Just so you can understand how close it all was, here are those quantitative results based on qualitative evaluations of their performances:

Oksana Baiul

Jumps	Triple Lutz, Triple Flip, Triple Loop, Triple Salchow, Double Axel, Double Toeloop, Triple Toeloop, Double Axel + Double Toeloop								
Judges	UK	POL	CZE	UKR	CHN	USA	JPN	CAN	GER
Required Elements or Technical Merit	5.6	5.8	5.9	5.8	5.8	5.8	5.8	5.5	5.7
Presentation	5.8	5.9	5.9	5.9	5.9	5.8	5.8	5.9	5.9
Ordinal	3	1	1	1	1	2	2	3	1
Rank	1st								

Nancy Kerrigan

Jumps	Double Flip, Triple Toeloop + Triple Toeloop, Triple Loop, Triple Salchow + Double Toeloop, Triple Lutz, Double Axel								
Judges	UK	POL	CZE	UKR	CHN	USA	JPN	CAN	GER
Required Elements or Technical Merit	5.8	5.8	5.8	5.7	5.7	5.8	5.8	5.7	5.8
Presentation	5.9	5.8	5.9	5.9	5.9	5.9	5.9	5.8	5.8
Ordinal	1	2	2	2	2	1	1	1	2
Rank	2nd								

In the end, that all came out to a 5–4 decision in favor of the young Ukrainian. After the competition was over, Scott and I went to do post-production work in the truck. Our live to tape efforts were done, but we needed to do voice-overs to augment the graphics and scores and replays that would be added to the telecast. By four A.M. we were nearly done. In the last segment, Scott was going to explain that the difference between gold and silver came down, arbitrarily, to what the German judge had decided. He was judge number nine and had gotten that number nine by the luck of a draw—a number pulled out of a hat that put him in the ninth chair. His name was Jan Hoffman, a former skater who had competed against Scott. He'd given Baiul a 5.9 for presentation and Kerrigan a 5.8. That was the margin of victory. Of course, he did his scoring simultaneously with the other judges and didn't know that his was the "deciding" score.

Just as we finished up that final segment, we got a call from a production executive in Lillehammer. He told Scott that he should identify whether the German judge was from the East or the West. The implication was clear. Baiul was from the Ukraine. An East German judge might be biased toward her because of the communist connection. Scott tried to refuse, but in the end Scott had no choice, and he reluctantly and subtly referenced Hoffman's ties to East Germany. On the drive back to our hotel, he was still upset, thinking that he'd done Hoffman an injustice. What difference should it have made which Germany the man was from? Scott believed that the judges had gotten the decision right. Why did politics have to enter into it?

As it turned out, the East vs. West question was the first one I encountered when I returned to the U.S. No one wanted to seem to talk about the fact that the judges, in Scott's mind and in the minds of many other experts, had made the right call.

Later, the Swedish referee spoke with Jeré Longman of the *New York Times* and other journalists to shed some light on the final, controversial result. She didn't vote, but she was the one who supervised those who did. She stated that in performing her role as a judge for thirty years, she'd never faced such a difficult decision. When pressed for specifics, she cited Nancy's decision to reduce a planned triple flip to a double near the beginning of her program. Nancy's speed was somewhat slower than her fellow competitor's as well. Both those actions left the judges with the impression that she was being cautious. That presumption influenced their marks.

What I found interesting was a few of her other statements. She believed that Oksana was "an artist on the ice," Nancy was a "little more cold," Oksana's presentation comes "from the heart, the inside," Nancy's was "nice." Others, including those in Nancy's camp, were stunned that Baiul received some of the marks for technical merit that she did. Nancy's program was more difficult; despite that early doubling of a triple flip, she did two triple jumps in combination—no step in between. Oksana did no combination triples. Nancy skated clean while Oksana had two slight bobbles that resulted (or should have) in a deduction of points. Ms. Lindgren, the Swedish referee, made an important distinction between clean and good. She stated that in the judge's minds, the other elements of the program besides jumps—spins, spirals (a move in which the skater's body is 90 degrees to the ice and a leg lifted overhead), and footwork—all needed to be considered. In her estimation, that was where Oksana edged Nancy: quality, not quantity, separated them. Lindgren equivocated on that as well. She said that either of them could win but in the twenty seconds allotted for the judges to produce their scores, a choice had to be made.

Those assessments are arguable, but in the end no one needed to shed any tears for Nancy. A couple of days after the competition ended, her agent announced some of the endorsement deals she had signed. She was also set to host *SNL*.

I don't recall how well received her performance was. To be honest, I don't have the heart to judge her. The same is true for how she and Tonya conducted themselves on and off the ice: it is not for me to criticize or praise. Being forced to do so would be a real nightmare. I prefer to just remember living out my dream.

CHAPTER 11

Conference Lines and Passions

As much as I enjoyed covering figure skating and other events for CBS, along with the network I felt the absence of NFL football in my life. So, when CBS began covering the NFL again in 1998, I was very happy. I got to work with Dan Dierdorf, the former St. Louis Cardinals lineman, as the number two team. Dan broke my streak of primarily working with former quarterbacks, including Pat Haden. Though we were no longer working together, Pat and I remained good friends. Pat phoned me in the spring of 1999. At the time he was under contract at NBC. He and Dick Enberg were doing Notre Dame football. Pat and I exchanged pleasantries and then he got to the point of his call. He had it on good authority, his own, that Dick Enberg wasn't completely happy at NBC.

Dick was enjoying an amazing career, but I could understand his feelings. He and Bob Costas had equal stature at NBC. Having two big dogs living in the same house can cause problems if both of them want to be the dominant one. I could see Dick's point. He'd been brought on to be the number one guy and now he had to share some of that spotlight with Bob. I could see NBC's point, too: Bob is one of the best broadcasters the industry has ever seen. Something had to give, and Pat wanted me to be aware of the situation. He urged me to keep my eyes open for any signs that Dick Enberg was making himself available to CBS. The repercussions of that might be me losing my number two standing in the ranks of our NFL broadcasters.

Ultimately, though, I dismissed either scenario as highly unlikely. Dick had been with NBC for years. He was a valuable asset. Why would they let him go? With John and Pat entrenched at Fox, CBS had Greg Gumbel and Phil Simms at number one. They worked well together and seemed poised to become a fixture in the booth for years to come. Would CBS upset that?

I didn't think so, but ours is a complicated business.

In late October 1999, Dan Dierdorf and I were in Foxborough, Massachusetts, for a game between the Patriots and the Broncos. Lance Barrow, my producer at the time, wasn't with us when we arrived on-site. He was down in Augusta, Georgia, meeting with CBS executives. They did this frequently so no alarm bells went off. When he arrived, he took me aside and said, "I just want to give you a heads-up. I think they're seriously talking to Dick Enberg, and it may affect you. So just be aware that that is going around." I thanked him but didn't lose any sleep over it. It was inconceivable to me that Dick would leave NBC. Even when Rudy Martzke, the sports media reporter for *USA Today,* also ran a few lines in his column echoing what Lance had just told me, I was still nonplussed. His version was slightly different. Dick was making himself available to CBS. Either way, I saw Dick's move as a 100-to-1 longshot. We had a new favorite in the starting gate anyway. Jim Nantz had taken over as the number one guy for all of CBS sports coverage. Why would Dick Enberg want to come here and end up in the same position he had with NBC?

By the time the NFL season was entering its stretch run, the answer to that had drilled its way through my thick skull. As John Madden had said to Rupert Murdoch, it's always about the money. That's when I really started to worry. I put in a call to Sean McManus, the

President of CBS Sports. I told him, "I just want to talk to you about these rumors that I keep hearing about Dick coming over to CBS. I certainly can't imagine that that would affect me."

He said, "Well, let me explain. We are talking to Dick, and he has made it known that he would be available to come with us. But I don't really see it happening, because he's so established at NBC. He's a big-ticket item."

I wanted to put in my two cents: "But, you know, I'm the number two guy, and I can't see him as number two."

Sean said, "Well, I don't think it's going to happen."

The line went quiet. Something told me there was a "but" about to make its presence known. "But, in the unlikely event that he did come over, how would you feel about switching back to college football and becoming the lead voice on the SEC?"

Being the team player that I am, I said all the right things. However, in the back of my mind, I saw this as a demotion. The SEC was a great NCAA conference. CBS and Sean McDonough had been covering the league since 1996. Still, if you were going to fly that pennant on the CBS flagpole, it would have been hanging well below the NFL.

Sean said, "Well, good. I'm glad you called. I'm glad we talked about it. I'll keep you informed."

I hung up the phone, turned to Nancy, and said, "Honey, pack your bags for Tuscaloosa," because from the tone of Sean's voice it was obvious that something was happening.

And it did.

Sean McDonough left CBS. I took over his slot as the voice of the SEC, and Dick Enberg came over and worked with Dan Dierdorf in the number two slot.

I was not thrilled but what choice did I have?

From 1995 to 1998, I'd actually made a change myself, leaving CBS to work at TNT doing NBA games, the NFL, and whatever other assignments they had for me, often track and field. My time there was okay, with the exception of working on the NBA telecasts with Doc Rivers, Chuck Daly, and Danny Ainge, which was absolutely wonderful. Coming back to CBS after that brief hiatus didn't give me much leverage with the network. I'd just have to see how things played out.

My broadcast partner was going to be Todd Blackledge, another in my succession of quarterback analysts. Todd had worked with McDonough so he was familiar with the SEC and that made me feel comfortable working with him. Todd had been an outstanding college quarterback at Penn State. He helped the Nittany Lions win the national championship in 1982, the same year he won the Davey O'Brien Award as the nation's best quarterback. Todd was the seventh pick of the first round of the 1983 draft, going to the Kansas City Chiefs. You may have heard a thing or two about that year's NFL draft. Todd was part of a class that had six quarterbacks drafted in the first round. John Elway, Jim Kelly, and Dan Marino were among them. I used to kid Todd that he'd not kept up with those guys given their many Super Bowl appearances and later induction into the Pro Football Hall of Fame. Todd took the ribbing well and we remain good friends today, long after our six-year partnership ended when he moved on to work at ESPN.

We started the 2000 campaign in Knoxville, Tennessee. I'd been around the country a lot but had never been to Neyland Stadium before. I'd seen it on television a bunch of times, but you can't appreciate what a bowl full to its 105,000-seat capacity looks and sounds like until you're there in person, perched among that full-throated throng. The Volunteers were taking on the Florida Gators.

Steve Spurrier brought his sixth-ranked Gators into Nyland with a 2-0 record. Phil Fulmer's squad had won its only game and was ranked No. 11 in the country. The two teams were in the Eastern Division and one or the other was regularly in the SEC Championship Game. The first half ended with the Volunteers leading, 12–7.

They had rolled up nearly 200 yards of offense on their four field goal drives. Their failures to convert in the red zone would haunt them.

Florida took the lead near the midpoint of the third quarter. Lito Sheppard of Florida intercepted an A. J. Suggs pass and returned it 19 yards for a touchdown. Neyland went quiet, but not for long. Travis Henry, who still holds the record for most yards rushing, attempts, and 100-yard-plus games, scored from the one and a field goal put them up 23–17 early in the fourth. I felt like the sound of the fight song "Rocky Top" could cause an avalanche. The Gators got a field goal to bring them within three points. A fine punt pinned the Gators back on their own nine-yard line with 2:14 to go in the game.

Jesse Palmer, who later went on to fame as television's Bachelor and now works for ESPN, was the Florida quarterback. He quickly got them to fine scoring position inside a minute to play. He hit Reche Caldwell on a touchdown pass, but a flag was thrown. Florida was penalized for an illegal man downfield. On second and goal with only 14 ticks left, Palmer dropped back and threw to a well-covered Jabar Gaffney. The ball and Tennessee's Willie Miles arrived simultaneously. The defensive back slapped the ball away. After a brief conference, the officials ruled that Gaffney had held on to the ball long enough for it to be ruled a completion. The Gators won, 27–23, and that game has gone down in history with its own version of "the Catch."

Tennessee fans, and rightly so, were incensed by the call. They'd dodged one touchdown bullet as a result of the Florida penalty, but they believed that they'd just been robbed by the same officials. It was a thrilling and controversial finish to my first game as the voice of the SEC.

When we got off the air, I looked at Todd and asked, "Are they all like this?"

Grinning, he said, "Well, enough of them are."

I had no way of knowing this then, but making the move to the

SEC was the most significant assignment in my career. More than anything else I've done, I believe folks will remember me for having covered the SEC. Some of that has to do with the fact that I went on to enjoy seventeen years of life in the Southeast. The football was always competitive in the SEC but I think the regular national exposure that CBS gave it enhanced its reputation, made recruiting outside the region easier—though most rosters are dominated by players from within the Southeast—and exposed the rest of the country to what had been going on below the Mason-Dixon Line for all those years. Some have pointed out the National Hockey League has been influenced by the SEC's success and traditions—chant-cheers in Nashville and Vegas in the '18 Stanley Cup finals were a new twist for an old league.

While I've lived in Texas most of my life, I've been all around the country, and the passion for college football in the Southeast is unequaled by any other passion for the sport in any part of the country. That includes in the Big 10, the Big 12, and every other major conference or independent. Allegiance runs deep. When I meet people, no matter the circumstance, the first thing after the introduction is made—if they're from the Southeast—is their loyalty to whichever program. I don't hear that from people from other parts of the country who may identify themselves as Patriot loyalists, Bear fans, or adherents to some other professional sports team. You have to have strong ties if you're going to be in Neyland and hear "Rocky Top" thirty-eight times a game. My dear friend and statistician Chuck Gardner made a study of the song's frequency for three years and he arrived at that figure as an average. Similarly, I can't go anywhere in my travels and not hear someone say to me, "Roll Tide," or "War Eagle," or "How 'Bout Them Dawgs."

I've been lucky. I've done the Texas–Oklahoma game probably eight times. I thought that was the greatest rivalry in college football I'd ever seen. But, in my view now, as a guy who is still loyal to the state of Texas, it doesn't compare with Alabama–Auburn. It just doesn't. The passion in that state for that game is unequaled in the country. Georgia–Florida is something else, too. The rivalries are just amazing.

That said, I really don't pull for a single team. I never have. My wish is always that good people win, and so I'm loyal to men and women I've met in sports whom I consider to be loyal, honest, and who play within the rules. The last of those can get me in trouble and greater minds than mine will have to figure out a way in all of college sports to sort through its many challenges.

One of the challenges I faced in my first ten years of doing SEC games was commuting from Steamboat to Atlanta and then on to wherever the game I was assigned was being held. I kept thinking of Frank Chirkinian chastising and threatening me for the move and issuing a dire warning about what would happen to me if I missed or arrived late for an event. In 2009, while at Augusta, Sean McManus, who was the chairman of the Sports Division by then, asked me to join him for a ride in his golf cart. He told me that he could see that travel was taking a bit of a toll on Nancy and me during the SEC season. I was told to find a place in Atlanta to rent, as well as a car, and CBS would pick up the tab for both. Spending that much time in Atlanta gave me a real appreciation for life in the South. For one thing, reading the Sunday college football section in the *Atlanta Journal-Constitution* was a real treat. I can now say that it is unrivaled in my estimation, even better than the one in the *Dallas Morning News*. How's that for a switch of allegiance?

Living in Atlanta and being immersed in the culture of college football in the South gave me a greater appreciation of how important it was to so many people. I didn't know this before we moved down to Atlanta. Georgia–Georgia Tech is a really big deal. And it never had been to me. But in Atlanta, the Georgia Tech people are as fervent about their team and as anti-Georgia as can be. In Baton Rouge, the Saints have a very fervent fan base. But I don't think it equates at all with how people feel about LSU football. That's the loudest stadium I've ever heard anywhere, when they've got 93,000 in there and they've been drinking all day. And they especially hate us if we do an afternoon game in there because it cuts into their enjoyment of adult beverages. But when we do a night game, it's some kind of experience.

One of my top five favorite SEC contests ever was the 2007 Florida–LSU game. That first Saturday in October, Les Miles had the number one team in the country, sitting atop the polls with a 6-0 record. They were the preseason number two and had traded places with the preseason favorite, the University of Southern California, despite the Trojans also being undefeated at that point. The 2007 season would go down in many people's minds as the Year of the Upset—a moniker that could be applied to nearly every Division I season in my memory. But that year it was particularly apt. Fifty-nine times it would see an unranked or lower-ranked team knock off a favorite. More significant, 13 of those upsets occurred to teams in the top five.

Florida was among those thirteen victims. The week before taking on LSU, they lost, 20–17, to unranked Auburn in Gainesville. Urban Meyer was in his third year at Florida and had named Tim Tebow his starting quarterback when the latter was a sophomore. To that point in the season, it looked like a very wise decision: Tebow came in with 1,300 yards passing, 11 passing touchdowns, 2 interceptions, 433 yards rushing, 8 rushing touchdowns. Talk of him winning the Heisman Trophy had already begun. Despite Tebow's gaudy numbers, Florida's offense couldn't generate much against Auburn.

In my time covering SEC games and college football generally, I was the play-by-play man for twenty-three of Tebow's games. I first heard about him when he was an eighth grader. Gary Danielson saw tape of him as a youth league player and noticed how the lefthander dipped his elbow when he threw. That flaw in his delivery, as well as some footwork issues when throwing, would plague him throughout his career. Later, Gary said that we shouldn't dwell on that fact. The kid was as competitive as anyone I'd ever seen, and he overcame those technical flaws.

As a person, Tim was hard to find fault with. I first met him when he was a high school senior on an official recruiting visit to the Alabama campus. Mike Shula was the head coach back then and was hoping to bring Tebow there. He was a very gracious, very assured young man even then. His faith in God plays an enormous role in his life, and at one point when we were speaking with him on campus before one SEC contest or another, Gary asked if his stated favorite thing to do, going to prison to preach to convicts, had produced any results.

Tebow looked very thoughtful and then said it hadn't. He added, "But I'm going to keep on trying."

The previous year, when Florida won the national championship and Tebow was the quarterback, he impressed the heck out of me in the Tennessee game. On fourth and two with two to go in the fourth quarter, out of shotgun formation, he ran the ball and I swear he moved the entire pile backward to get the first down in a demonstration of brute strength. I also recalled him throwing a few old school jump passes that brought me back to my days as a kid watching the University of Washington's Don Heinreich doing the same thing.

I also loved his attitude when LSU fans somehow got ahold of his cell phone number, had it published in the school newspaper, and inundated him with calls. Tim was not pleased. He scored the game's first touchdown, set the ball down, and then pretended to punch in the numbers on an imaginary cell phone and hold it up to his helmet's earhole. He got a big laugh from the LSU crowd for that one, deservedly so.

Entering that 2007 game, Florida was the defending national champion. They were riding an 11-game winning streak before a last-second Wes Byrum field goal as time expired split the uprights for the 20–17 victory. Auburn had been an 18-point underdog and the loss reverberated throughout the league and the country. Auburn didn't have much success against the Gators in Florida at that time, but they had knocked them off the number one spot in 1994. We would have loved to have featured two undefeated teams going at one another, but Florida's loss didn't take much of the shine off what we expected to be a terrific competition.

The game didn't disappoint. LSU hadn't been the top team in the Associated Press poll since 1959, and it seemed for much of the game that they weren't going to stay there much longer. With runs of his own and passes, Tebow led the Gators to a field goal on their first possession. LSU's tough defense prevented Florida from capitalizing on a Matt Flynn interception, but on their third possession, covering 77 yards in 12 plays, Tebow threw a two-yard touchdown pass. The play before, he'd been stuffed on a run, and the short pass caught LSU's defense by surprise.

Five different LSU runners gained 49 yards on their touchdown drive that pulled them within seven. Setting the tone for the rest of the game, Les Miles rolled the dice on fourth down and goal to go from the one with backup quarterback Ryan Perilloux sneaking into the end zone with 6:08 left in the half. Florida scored again before the intermission to lead, 17–7. Colt David missed a 43-yard field goal inside a minute to go that could have brought the Tigers closer. If LSU was going to maintain their footing then they were going to have "geaux" all out in the second half.

Just as the LSU fight song takes a while to build in tempo, so did its football team. The Tigers scored on a long drive to open the second half chewing up more than seven minutes. On fourth-and-5 from the Florida 25, Matt Flynn managed to gain 8 yards on a run to keep the drive alive and the fans in a delirium.

The Gators came back in just 2:33 with Tim Tebow hitting Cornelius Ingram for a 33-yard touchdown pass to go up 24–14. Those were the last points they would score. Two turnovers in the third quarter, a Kestahn Moore fumble that LSU failed to convert on a second missed field goal, and a Tebow interception that they did capitalize on for a touchdown saw the game enter the fourth quarter with the score 24–21. During that postinterception scoring drive, Les Miles went for it again on fourth down to score. This time it was a four-yard Matt Flynn throw that brought the crowd noise to a crescendo.

Todd and I both questioned the wisdom of those fourth-down calls, but in a postgame interview, Miles indicated that he'd gone into the game thinking that he'd have his Tigers going for it on fourth down. He believed that the Gators' offense was a ball-possession offense, thus limiting the amount of time that his offense would have. His players certainly appreciated the trust he placed in them and the fans loved the gambles—especially since they paid off. This fourth-down trend continued when the Tigers took over on their own 40 with 9:10 to go in the game.

On second down with three yards to go for the first down, Matt Flynn dropped back to pass. The play resulted in a fifteen-yard penalty against the Tigers' Jared Mitchell for offensive pass interference. What could have been a backbreaker of a penalty instead was forgotten in what followed. Following a two-yard run, a hobbled Flynn managed to gain 15 crucial yards on a third-down run. Facing fourth-and-1 from their own 49-yard line, Miles kept his offense on the field. Jacob Hester moved the chains with a two-yard gain. A few plays later, Hester blasted his way from the Florida 35 to the 16. That 19-yard rush was a thing of, if not beauty, then certainly brutality as he broke through the line and took on much smaller defensive backs. Unfortunately for him, he was stopped on third down and one.

Again, Miles faced a tough decision, with 2:10 left on the clock. Kick a chip-shot field goal to tie the game or go for it? He went for it and Hester again came through, gaining two tough yards. Following a first-down incompletion, it took Hester two more carries to get into the end zone. Florida's last-gasp drive ended with an incompletion and the fourth-down fortunes of LSU had produced a classic game, 28–24. Five for five on fourth-down plays is pretty special, especially in a game against a top rival, and especially in a season that sees your team go on to win the national championship.

LSU's victory over Florida was just one small part of the story. The following week, the Tigers traveled to Lexington, Kentucky. Gary Danielson and I, along with sideline reporter Tracy Wolfson, were there. Demonstrating the strength of the SEC, the Wildcats were ranked No. 17 and they pulled off one of those many 2007 upsets. It took them three overtimes, overcoming a 13-point deficit, and some poor execution on LSU's part, but they won, 43–37, stopping LSU without a first down on their last possession of the third overtime. LSU suffered a second triple-overtime loss, this time against Arkansas after the Tigers had regained the top spot in the polls in this season filled with so many upsets.

Despite their two losses, LSU advanced to the SEC Championship Game, beat Tennessee, and then was named to the BCS Championship Game. There they beat top-ranked Ohio State, 38–24, to win the national championship. Seemed appropriate in a season that began with tiny Appalachian State knocking off the behemoth Michigan Wolverines, that the twice-defeated No. 2 team in the country should be crowned the national champion. Les Miles and his bunch were deserving champions and their season of close victories and losses provided the nation with a lot of thrills.

I was excited that season to continue my working relationship with Gary Danielson in our second year together covering the SEC. Like Todd, Gary was a former NFL quarterback for the Lions and the Browns. He showed an early interest in broadcasting. While still actively playing in the NFL, he worked on television in both Detroit and Cleveland. He came to us after a relatively brief stint at ESPN as a college football analyst. A former Purdue Boilermaker, Gary has a deep love and understanding of NCAA football.

It always takes a bit of time to develop a rhythm and a rapport with an analyst. Trust is a major component in any relationship and it's no different with an on-air partner. I've been privileged to work with some great analysts, and with their backgrounds trust has not been an issue. As I've said before, I'm there to tell you the story, give you the facts you need to know where we are in the game, and I leave the analysis entirely to my partner. Gary played thirteen years in the NFL and he knows the game inside and out. Todd had that same level of knowledge and expertise, and this is no knock on him, but Gary brought a slightly different perspective. From working with him, I have a better understanding of how an NFL player goes about his business of being a professional athlete. Much of that has to do with establishing and following a routine.

For the SEC games, we all arrive on Thursday. Gary will get in before noon so that he can attend a practice session. I don't have the same eye for the game as he does, so for me watching a practice won't tell me much. I check in to the hotel and review my notes and my boards. All of my memorization of depth charts and board preparation has been done earlier in the week. Prior to the economic downturn in 2008, we used to all gather on Thursday night for a dinner with the entire production staff getting together. After the recession hit, we were given a per diem rather than the blank check our producer Craig Silver used to cover that team dinner. I loved and looked forward to those meals together. I believed they helped establish camaraderie, an essential component of a great production. Building relationships is key. CBS understood that to a great degree. Having the same broadcast team covering the SEC made a lot of sense. We got to know the coaches, athletic directors, sports information directors, and players better from being around them more often. The better we built those relationships, the more information and insights they were willing to share.

Gary understood that and being a presence at the practices was one part. Gary was also all about being as productive as possible. On Fridays we met with staff and players at both schools. Coaches could feel like those meetings either were an obligation or an opportunity. Prior to Gary's arrival at CBS we'd been doing conference calls on Tuesday instead of those in-person meetings. Anyone who's sat in on a conference call versus a face-to-face meeting will tell you that the level of involvement is incrementally greater in the latter.

Gary gently insisted that we end the conference calls and only conduct the meetings. He saw the calls as time wasters. He'd learn far more from watching film, and I benefited from having more study time. Being in a room fully engaging with coaches proved to be very fruitful, particularly with the player interviews. These are young men and they had a lot of other things on their mind. For a long time, many of them seemed uncertain, or indifferent, to who Gary and I were. We weren't big names that they recognized. We were just a couple of guys in pants and collared shirts asking them questions, to which they frequently gave monosyllabic responses.

Gary was good at establishing his authority with them—not in the sense of being in control of them, but letting them know that he knew his stuff and that he understood some of what it was like to be a student-athlete. The same was true with coaches. The great thing was that he never resorted to referring to himself or his career or his past accomplishments in order to build that rapport. It's a delicate art that is part of the craft of being a good reporter and Gary possesses that ability. He comes into the games as prepared as anyone I've worked with. He is the driving force behind how we televise the games and is always coming up with ideas to enhance the viewers' experience. It sounds somewhat contradictory to say this, but keeping to the same routine as much as possible is a part of that—that holds true for the rest of the staff and technicians. Once you've got most things nailed in place, that allows you the mental space to consider other options. I know that Gary and our producer Craig Silver talked every day, starting on Monday, until we went on-air, and were always looking for ways to improve the telecast.

Like me, Gary is supported in the booth by someone you at home never see but who plays an invaluable role in making us look good. I have Chuck Gardner, my statistician and my spotter Butch Baird without whom I would be lost. Gary has an assistant, David Moulton, in the booth with him for every game. David is a radio talk show host and columnist in Fort Myers, Florida. Gary wouldn't be able to do what he does without David's capable assistance. While we're doing our thing, David sits behind us. Depending on what goes on down on the field, David will pull out one of the blue index cards he's prepared and hand it to Gary. On it could be a pertinent statistic, an anecdote, anything that will help Gary deliver the message in the most interesting way. Obviously I didn't cover the SEC during the 2017 season, but I watched the games at home and I could visualize David leaning forward and handing Gary one of those cards as he relayed some additional information. It sounded seamless on air, but having been in the booth with him for as long as I had, I could detect David's welcome presence and input.

As much as we prepared each week and as much as I maintained my stance as a neutral observer with no rooting interest other than that we have a compelling game, there were those who believed I was biased toward one program or another. Gary does a weekly guest spot on Paul Finebaum's radio show which was then out of Birmingham. Paul is enormously popular and after being on the show, Gary would come back with his scouting report on what people felt I'd miscalled.

"Verne, you really pissed them off in Tuscaloosa when you said X," or "The Dawgs are really barking at you in Athens after you said Y."

I appreciated the heads-up, but nothing anyone might say or do diminished the thrill from my feet to my head during our drives to and from the games. The atmosphere was electric.

The football being played in the SEC was the best I've seen in the college ranks. Oh my Lord, the speed at which these players move! That is particularly true on the defensive side of the line. And it's also true as you move down the depth chart. One amazing athlete after another.

At the risk of inciting the ire of fans of other programs, I will make note of what Nick Saban has produced at Alabama. I met Nick when he was the defensive coordinator for Bill Belichick in Cleveland. I'd also covered him when I did my first NCAA football game for ABC, Ohio University at Kent State, where he was a graduate assistant at his alma mater. I was there for some of his games as LSU's head coach, and I had to shake my head over the story of how Alabama athletic director Mal Moore got him and his lovely wife, Terry, or "Miss Terry," as Nick calls her, out of Miami, covering them with hooded jackets to attend secret negotiations and all the rest of the deception and fake hiring committee and the rest of the nonsense that went on in getting him to Tuscaloosa.

People forget that Nick Saban lost to Louisiana–Monroe at home in his first year in Tuscaloosa. But from that point on, what he has accomplished makes him arguably the greatest college football coach ever.

What's most impressive is Alabama's consistency at such a high level. Saban may lose four or five defensive players to the NFL, but because of what he calls "the Process" he just plugs another guy in the next year who was on the third team the year before.

When I first spoke with Nick back in 1991 when he was with the Browns, I didn't recall that he'd served under Don James as a graduate assistant at Kent State back in 1974. Eventually we figured out the connection. In a way, I'm surprised he didn't remember because he is the master of minutiae. He learned that from Bill Belichick during that four-season stint in the NFL. He has described those years as the "worst of his life," but that is both a tribute to the affection the two men have for one another and their mutual desire to tease the media—particularly local media.

I know that Nick can seem cantankerous. I've seen him come close to blowing a gasket on the sidelines. He can be tough on himself, his assistant coaches, and his players. But I also know this Nick Saban. When we are in Tuscaloosa and have our meeting with him, he's always in a sport coat and tie. That's a sign of respect. Not that he hasn't always been respectful of my partners—in fact, I'd say it is because of Todd and Gary that I'm a beneficiary of the doubt— Nick's clothing choices have to do with his respect for the Roll Tide fans. No matter where we are in our conversation, at 11:30 sharp, his personal assistant will interrupt us, politely, and Nick will end things right there. Has to get off campus and over to his long-standing engagement—a Nick at Noon luncheon. There, he regales the all-female audience assembled and engages in a candid question and answer session. I've also witnessed him do the same thing on his local Thursday night radio show. During the commercials he will mingle with the live audience, then get back on stage just in the nick of time to be back on air. Attention to detail. Meticulous preparation.

Nick isn't the only good coach in the SEC. Les Miles was sometimes a bit difficult to get a handle on because of his personality quirks, but he accomplished great things at LSU. I remain a big fan of Mark Richt and what he achieved at Georgia. I was very sad to see how things ended for him in Athens when he was let go. It is a tough business but because of its prominence, the moth-to-flame phenomenon applies. Gus Malzahn at Auburn and Will Muschamp at South Carolina are also high-quality coaches with high-quality programs. The question is if they can sustain the level of excellence that Saban and Alabama have. That guys like Les and Mark had to move on makes Nick's accomplishments shine a little brighter.

One of my other all-time favorite SEC games became so because of the circumstances surrounding it as well as what happened during it. My second year covering the SEC was 2001. We all know what terrible tragedy befell this country that September. Wisely, commissioners of various leagues in various sports postponed games. We were supposed to open with Tennessee and Florida, but after the tragedy, it was moved to the first week in December in Gainesville.

The 2001 SEC season opened with high hopes for the conference. In the preseason polls Florida was ranked No. 1 in the country and four other teams—Tennessee, LSU, South Carolina, and Alabama—were all in the top twenty-five. Steve Spurrier was in his last season at Florida and many believed that this was the finest team. They easily won their first three games against two nonconference opponents and Kentucky. Their first challenge came against the 21st-ranked Mississippi State Bulldogs at Ben Hill Griffin Stadium in Gainesville. We covered that game, and my word, 52–0 only begins to give you an idea of how dominant that squad was. They had lost to the Bulldogs the previous year and if this wasn't a case of payback, then I don't know what would be. They rolled up 640 total yards of offense. Rex Grossman, who would go on to throw for more than 4,000 yards that season, threw for 393 yards and 5 touchdowns. Rex was on a hot streak and he'd wind up throwing for 300-plus yards in four straight games.

Florida didn't let up the following week when they overpowered the 18th-ranked Tigers 44–15 in Baton Rouge. Grossman threw for a school record 464 yards in that one. Unfortunately for the Gators, they stumbled against the unranked Auburn Tigers, 23–20. They won their next four in a row, putting them at 9-1 and No. 2 in the country heading into their December showdown with the Volunteers. For its part, Tennessee started out the season ranked sixth in the nation. Their early season SEC schedule looked tough and it was. They were to face No. 14 LSU and No. 12 South Carolina. They won both of those but a tough, unranked Georgia bunch beat them, 26–24, in Neyland on a six-yard touchdown pass with ten seconds left in the game. That stunner dropped them in the rankings briefly, but winning their next six, they came into the Florida game at No. 4, also with a 9-1 record.

The Tennessee offense was led by quarterback Casey Clausen, and three other players—defensive tackle John Henderson, wide receiver Donté Stallworth, and defensive tackle Albert Haynsworth—would all be first round picks in the NFL. Seven other Volunteers would be drafted that season. (They also had on their roster a tight end by the name of Jason Whitten, who'd get some attention later on.) Despite their talent and their record, not many gave them a chance against the Gators in Gainesville. Experts believed that if given time, Rex Grossman and his talented pair of receivers, Jabar Gaffney and Reche Caldwell, would find openings. As Lee Corso of ESPN said before the game, "Forget about it. There ain't no way they're going to stop Florida's receivers." Yes, our competitors were there in Gainesville and anytime ESPN's *College Game* was on the grounds, the circus atmosphere got hyped up even higher.

Whether or not the Volunteers could contain Alex Brown, who would end up with an astounding 33 sacks on the season, was another key point. Casey Clausen was only a sophomore and this was to be his first visit to the infamous "Swamp." How he would handle the pressure, the crowd noise, and all that went with a game of this importance was subject to a lot of speculation coming into the week.

After the Friday afternoon walk-through, we were down at the Tennessee team buses. Todd and I were with Phil Fulmer and his wife Vicky. Phil said, "I know not many people like our chances here, but I like—I think we'll win this." Many head coaches publicly express thoughts like that. Somehow, something in Phil's voice made me believe that he believed. I tried to never make any kind of judgment. I was just going to call it as I saw it. I did suspect this: the winner of the game had a great shot at advancing to the Rose Bowl to play in the BCS championship game. Florida had beaten its SEC opponents by an average margin of 37 points a game. Tennessee had survived many more close contests, managing only a 12.8 margin of victory. It was easy to see why Florida, which many considered the only team capable of beating the top-ranked Miami Hurricanes, came into the game as a clear favorite. Obviously a lot was at stake.

Because the game had been moved to the end of the season, rather than its customary place in early September, it took on an even greater magnitude. It nearly always had huge implications for the SEC race. Since the league split into two divisions in 1992, either Tennessee or Florida had won the Eastern portion and advanced to the SEC championship game. In seven of those nine years, if you won this game, you went on to win the championship. Most often, it was merely a footnote worth mentioning during other late season contests. With the consequences being so immediately apparent, the tensions and the fun factor that came with a high-stakes game were even greater.

By the opening kickoff, the Swamp was as frenzied as I could ever remember it being. Tennessee's players, urged on by Phil Fulmer's pregame speech reminding them of how many had counted them out, came out of the locker room fired up and ready. The fans were in full throat, and so were the Tennessee Volunteers. They were doing their version of our broadcasting open. They recited General Robert Nylan's Seven Maxims:

1. The team that makes the fewest mistakes will win.
2. Play for and make the breaks and when one comes your way—SCORE.
3. If at first the game—or the breaks—go against you, don't let up . . . put on more steam.
4. Protect our kickers, our QB, our lead, and our ball game.
5. Ball, oskie, cover, block, cut and slice, pursue, and gang tackle . . . for this is the WINNING EDGE.

6. Press the kicking game. Here is where the breaks are made.
7. Carry the fight to our opponent and keep it there for
   60 minutes.

I love when all those prognostications and keys to the game are in our rearview mirror and the game reveals itself play by play like a taut thriller. The Gators went on offense first and a great stop for a one-yard loss on a third-and-one forced them to punt. Three and out. We wouldn't use that expression much in the roughly two hours that remained.

By the end of the first quarter the Vols were up 14–0. I don't know what Steve Spurrier said to his men, but the next quarter was all Florida. They ripped off twenty straight points to go into the locker room leading 20–14. The Gators held the ball for more than 13 minutes of that quarter, capitalizing on a Clausen interception. After the interception we showed Phil Fulmer embracing his quarterback and Todd suspected that he was telling his quarterback to hang in there. He'd had a good start to the game and they would need him later on.

At the half it was Florida up by 6. The Swamp was awash with jumping Gators on the field and off. I've seen so many games turn quickly. Usually it's mistakes and poor execution that lead to those kinds of turnabouts. That was certainly true then.

Tennessee came up firing, scoring a touchdown and keeping the Gators to only three points. During our half-time assessment, Todd had mentioned on air that the Vols' two big wide outs, Stallworth and Washington, had been fairly quiet. They needed to contribute more. Todd wasn't in the booth with Tennessee's offensive coordinator, but on the very first play of the second half, Clausen targeted Kelly Washington. He threw behind him, but later in the drive Stallworth and Washington each caught a pass. However, it was Travis Stephens who really delivered. His 35-yard touchdown run thwarted a Florida safety blitz. He evaded the blitzer and outran what remained of the

Florida secondary. The Gators would add a field goal in the third quarter for the only other scoring play. One of the most significant plays of the quarter was Spurrier deciding to go for it on fourth down from the Tennessee 36 with a little more than a minute to go in the period. Unfortunately for him, a false start on an interior lineman turned a fourth-and-one into a fourth-and-six. Todd astutely noted that Rex Grossman's hard count, trying to draw the defense offside and get the one yard needed the easy way, had backfired.

Florida went for it anyway.

Grossman dropped back to pass. The Tennessee secondary blanketed all the receivers, He moved around in the pocket before he was finally brought down for a sack by Will Overstreet. I pointed out that he'd suffered a severe ankle sprain four weeks earlier against LSU. I didn't say anything about how so many people had said that Tennessee's secondary was no match for the speedy Gators.

That's why they play the games.

On the next drive, Travis Stephens gashed the Gators for a 36-yard run, bouncing outside on a terrific cut before getting knocked out of bounds at the two. That set them up for the eventual score. During the drive, the Vols had gone for it on fourth-and-one from the Florida 46. Clausen's bootleg, a gutsy call, kept the drive alive. Stephens's contributions were a revelation—I always love it when a player who doesn't figure much in the pregame dialogue emerges and has a big day. At five nine and 190 pounds, he was quite the specimen. He was a senior running back who lived the dream of anyone who has stuck around a program for four years. He played sparingly for his first three seasons, mostly due to Travis Henry and Jamal Lewis also being in the backfield. Given a chance to start and to be used extensively, he ran for more than 1,400 yards his senior season, setting the school record. Someone to root for, don't you think?

After another Vols touchdown, they were up 34–26, and with exactly five minutes left the Gators took over on the change of possession from their own 33-yard line. We cut to shots of the Tennessee band and threw up a graphic identifying Todd and me as the commentators, then I noticed some activity down on the field. The officials were marching off fifteen yards against the Volunteers. At first I hadn't seen a flag, and my spotter hadn't, either. Fulmer wanted an explanation, and so did we. All we knew was that it was for a personal foul.

Before we could get that explanation, Florida snapped the ball and ran a trick play. A streaking wide receiver took a direct snap while in motion to the left side; he handed off the ball to a wide receiver on the right side, then threw a pass back across the field to another wide receiver. They picked up only nine yards on the risky call, and it's that factor again that came into play—speed. The Tennessee defense swarmed all over and kept that play relatively in check.

From that point on, what we had all said might happen did. Grossman led the Gators down the field, completing 5 of 6 for 54 yards and a touchdown to bring the Gators within two at 34–32. Eighty-six ticks remained on the clock. Spurrier didn't hesitate. We'd been saying throughout the drive that he had to go for the tie by attempting the two-point conversion. They needed two yards. Spurrier's offense came out in a four-wideout formation. Jabar Gaffney, an All-American, was lined up against Buck Fitzgerald. Fitzgerald had never started a game. He had only 26 tackles in his entire career. Those are the kind of match-ups you want. Grossman had thrown for 362 yards to that point. We didn't have time to set up all of that, and Todd and I just let the play unfold.

Grossman took the snap and Tennessee's cover guys were all over their men. He danced around a bit before firing wide of his target, Gaffney. The ball wasn't close. Gaffney signaled that he was held, but the play stood.

We broke away for commercial and did our usual game-scoring recap when we returned. A minute and ten seconds remained. Florida lined up for an onside kick. The ball bounced high in the air and

Tennessee's mountain of a block tight end, John Findlayson, leaped as high as Rocky Top and brought the ball down. Tennessee ran out the clock and won in the Swamp for the first time since 1971. Albert Haynesworth of the Volunteers later delivered a memorable line stating that the Vols had made it into "a little old pond."

The lasting image I have is of Casey Clausen climbing the bandleader's ladder and waving the baton to conduct the Pride of the Southland Band in "Rocky Top." I didn't mind that he'd exceeded the average number of times the tune was played. What a stirring ball game that was.

Only later did we learn that the two-point incompletion was more controversial than we thought. At least that was true in the mind of Spurrier and many Florida fans. Some went so far as to say that the no-call on pass interference was a makeup for what happened the previous year when Gaffney scored the winning touchdown on a ball that many believed he didn't catch. More than a decade later, in 2013, Jeremy Fowler wrote a piece that appeared on CBSSports.com about the no-call. He got in touch with the two coaches and their versions of that last-gasp effort are enlightening.

"Guy was hanging all over him, but no interference," Spurrier said. I believe that what he meant was that no interference penalty was *called*.

Fulmer said that it was great defensive play and added, "It kind of makes up for one in Knoxville where Gaffney dropped the ball and official called it a touchdown."

Nice to see that fans and coaches alike can stoke the fires of what might have been/what should have been. I'm glad that we didn't get into any of that. There were plenty of near misses—balls that could have/should have been intercepted, a penalty call or two that might have been on the edge. Instead, I prefer to think of what had happened and the excitement those plays generated in the moment.

As the saying goes, upon further review, they still thrill.

CHAPTER 12

The Tournament and the Shot(s)

I'd been calling NCAA tournament games for CBS since I started with the network, but it was a special thrill to partner with the legendary Al McGuire in 1999 for the opening weekend. During that 1998–1999 season, Bill Clinton was in the White House. Monica Lewinsky was in the headlines. The Broncos beat the Packers in Super Bowl XXII. The movie *Titanic* had all kinds of Oscar buzz. I wasn't on top of the world; I was in Charlotte, North Carolina. Still I was pretty thrilled to be doing my first tournament games with Al McGuire. Al had coached the Marquette Warriors for a number of years. He led them to the NCAA title in 1977 in his final year as head coach. He went into broadcasting with NBC and was courtside in 1997 for the famous Indiana State/Larry Bird versus Michigan State/Magic Johnson title game, which many say launched the NCAA tournament into the stratosphere.

Al's exuberant style stood in contrast to Billy Packer's closer-to-the-vest, analytical style. Dick Enberg kept the high-wire act from falling to the net. By the time I worked with Al for that 1999 tournament, he'd been doing games for so long that he believed he really didn't need to prepare much. He was a basketball lifer and he'd let the game come to him. That also included letting the names and numbers come to him—he didn't bother with memorization. I can kind of understand why. I've always said that the first two days of the tournament, with four games to do, are the longest day in sports broadcasting. They can take a toll on you. Even when you are at your best and most prepared, mental fatigue can set in and you can make mistakes.

We got through the first game, Delaware versus Tennessee, in decent shape. Following that, we had to endure what I still say is one of the worst college basketball games ever. Southwest Missouri State took on Wisconsin. It was almost surreal. The Badgers fell, 43–32, and during the intermission between games I felt like I'd been badgered into submission. At least the giant stack of papers that I had prepared with notes was then halved. Duke, the top seed in the regional, destroyed Florida A&M. That left us with College of Charleston against Tulsa. Bill Self was at the helm of a very good Tulsa team.

During the break, I approached Al and asked him, "Coach? Anything I can do for you in this last game?"

He shook his head.

I went about my business reviewing my now very thinned pile of papers. I looked over at Al and he was sitting and staring ahead, lost in thought. We made our way back to the broadcasting position. I noticed that Al had nothing in front of him. Not a roster. No notes. Nothing.

I thought maybe he had an eidetic memory or was somehow otherwise very familiar with the two clubs. Still, I wanted our coverage to be good, so I asked him again if I could do anything to help him out.

"No. They'll take their warm-ups off, and I'll get the names and numbers. You'll do the bulk of it for the first few minutes. I'll pick things up. I'll be okay."

Who was I to argue with a legend?

Just before tip-off, the Charleston players came off the court and stood near their bench. The starters slipped off their long-sleeved tops. I saw numbers. I saw no names.

I looked down the line at the Tulsa bench. Same thing. Numbers. No names.

Al leaned over to me and said, "Son, you might have to help me out. I think I'm screwed."

We made it through the game and on to the next weekend. Unfortunately, that was the last time Al would do an NCAA tournament game. We all knew he was ill, but as far as I know, no one knew how virulent the leukemia was that he was battling. That was his last broadcast, and, sadly, he died in 2001. I was grateful that I got to do those games with him, and have fond memories of him. He was one of the great characters in the game. So much so that the headline of his *New York Times* obituary was "Al McGuire, 72, Coach, TV Analyst and Character Dies." I don't know about you, but going down in history as a "character" sounds like a pretty good indicator of a life well lived.

Al was idiosyncratic, to be sure. That year we were working together we were in Chicago. I sat solo at a table for four. The rest of the space was nearly empty. Al strolled in, spotted me, and took a seat at an adjacent table. We exchanged greetings. I had to ask him: Why did you choose to seat yourself near me but not with me? "This way I can see the whole room." I raised an eyebrow. The "whole room" consisted of empty tables and chairs and a lone waitress who soon figured in our little drama.

Before she did, Al sat craning his neck and rolling his head from side to side. "I know you think I'm a bit unusual," Al said, "but I'll tell you this. I've made millions being this way."

I couldn't disagree with that.

Nor could I not take his side when he engaged in a debate with a waitress that reminded me of the famous diner scene in the Jack

Nicholson film *Five Easy Pieces*. Al's battle wasn't over a chicken salad sandwich but in his case a poached egg. It was lunchtime, the place was empty, but given the irrefutable logic of meal service, he couldn't get the waitress to meet his simple request for two poached eggs. Doggedly, Al labored on: "I'm a betting man, you see. I'm willing to wager that somewhere back there in that kitchen are some eggs. Dozens of them." He paused for dramatic effect. "You do have eggs back there."

The waitress blanched. "We do. But we don't serve them after eleven."

"I'm not asking you to serve the eggs. I'm asking you to serve me. Two eggs poached. I bet if you ask the chef, he'd be able to do that."

He was. Al never raised his voice or condescended. He just had to figure out the right approach.

It was a small victory in comparison to him walking away from his coaching job at Marquette after winning the national title. I admired him for making that move. As I've said, so few of us go out on top.

I was also privileged to work with Tommy Heinsohn, doing NBA and NCAA games. What a contrast to Al. If Al was a Tesla automobile—sleek, silent, and swift—Tommy was a muscle car—just as fast but louder and more what you see is what you get direct. Back in the 1980s, CBS used to do a late Thursday and Friday night NCAA basketball telecast. It started at 11:30 on the East Coast, so, by necessity, it generally featured teams from out west. We were sent to broadcast the game between Texas Western and LSU. That game was preceded by Bob Knight's Hoosiers taking on George Washington University.

Contractually, the winning coach in each of the games is required to come over and spend five minutes with the host television broadcast network. After the Indiana win, their PR guy stood with Coach Knight and pointed towards us. Tommy and I were standing on the court near the mid-court line. We watched as Knight shook his head emphatically.

I said to Ed Goren, our producer in the truck, that he's not going to come over; he's shaking his head. Ed replied that in New York they were demanding the interview. Knight has to come over. We had a deal. I suggested to Ed that he'd better send somebody from his staff into the locker room to explain this to Coach Knight. We had thirty minutes between games so we were out on the court and doing our rehearsal and our warm-up for LSU and Texas Western. The camera guys had to get it right because I'm five feet nine and a half, and Tommy is easily a full foot taller. All of a sudden, I said to the guys in the truck, "Roll the tape. Here comes Knight and he doesn't look like he's in a happy mood."

The cameras were rolling. Bob came up to the two of us and he looked at me; he didn't look at Tommy at all.

He said, "They tell me I've got to talk to you guys. Okay. Here's the deal. Verne, I will talk to you, but"—he touched Tom with his finger in his chest—"him I'm not speaking to."

Tommy was incredulous and said, "Do we have some kind of an issue that I'm not aware of?" Knight looked at him and got right in his face. "Yeah. I've got a beef with you. Did you just write a book?"

Tom said, "Yeah, it was just published about two months ago."

Knight shook his head. "Well, on page two hundred forty-nine of your book you said your son was a football player and not a basketball player but were he a basketball player you would never have allowed him to play for Bob Knight at Indiana."

By the time Knight got all that out, his face was crimson.

Tom said, "That's how I feel. I don't think you treat your players right. I think you abuse them."

That set Bob off and for the next two minutes they went at it, verbally, chest to chest like a baseball umpire and a pissed-off manager.

We chewed up a chunk of time and we had to get the interview done. I said as much to Bob. In a split second, Bob turned around to me with this big smile on his face. He put his arm around my back and said, "Now, Verne, what was it you wanted to ask me about the game we just played?"

That all happened that fast, and he just flipped the switch. As far as I know, he and Tommy never spoke again. Coach Knight and I always had a cordial relationship, but seeing how quickly he could turn on someone was a valuable lesson for me. For my part, Coach Knight and I always got along well. I kept my judgments about him to myself. He was a great basketball coach, but his temper did get the best of him at times.

In 2000, I was paired with Bill Raftery as my analyst. Talk about another character. Until I stopped covering the tournament in 2018, we worked together for 15 years. Ironically, Al McGuire's brother Frank, then the head coach at South Carolina, played a role in my first meeting with the Big Irishman. In 1983, I'd just started working for CBS and got a call from New York telling me to pack my bags and get to Columbia, South Carolina. A fascinating regional rivalry game between the University of Idaho and the Gamecocks. I'm sure that the East Coast was riveted to their tens of millions of seats. In any case, I was further informed that my partner would be a man named Bill Raftery. He was my age. He had once been the head coach at Seton Hall and before that, Fairleigh Dickinson.

If this sounds like the beginning of a story about a blind date, in a way it is. Bill and I met for the first time, he clarified for me that his name wasn't Rafferty, and the two of us became instant friends. I can't remember a thing about the Idaho–South Carolina game, but Billy and I were paired again in Columbia the following week as they took on Marquette. Doc Rivers was their point guard and the two of us would eventually be paired as broadcast partners years later during my TNT days.

Bill had said to me the previous week, "Listen, this is so much fun, I want you to meet Joanie, and I'm going to bring Joanie and I want you to bring Nancy, and the four of us will have dinner and the ladies will go to the game." So the two women came to Columbia, and Bill and his wife, Joanie, and Nancy and I hit it off right away. And one of the reasons for that is that Bill knows and knew everybody of any consequence in the sport. And among those who were living in Columbia was Frank McGuire.

Bill said, "I've arranged for the four of us to be hosted by Frank and his wife at their dinner club in downtown Columbia." So this was Saturday night, and the game was Sunday. First we met at Frank's house for drinks. Then we had dinner and cocktails. Then we went back to Frank's house for a nightcap. We stayed up and watched a late-night basketball game on something called ESPN. And I swear that was one of the first dozen times I had ever seen the network on the air.

Finally, we stumbled back to our hotel, and I learned then about Raftery's resilience. The next morning, I got up at seven thirty or eight o'clock with not much sleep, and I went down the elevator, and I looked like hell and felt like it. Still, I was determined to get the Sunday *New York Times* and the local paper and go up and shower and shave and do my notes and get ready. As the elevator got to the lobby floor, the doors opened and there was Raftery in his coat and tie. He held a cup of coffee, and he was whistling.

I said, "Where in the heavens have you been?"

He said, "I went to Mass at seven o'clock."

That was my baptism by firewater with Bill.

And we did the second game and we got a call from New York, one of the things that you always hope for. One of the executives said, "Boy, you guys sounded great together. We can't wait to hear you together again." That was in 1983. The next time we were assigned as partners—now, there was probably a game or two in the next seventeen years—but we did not become full partners until 2000. Maybe CBS was thinking of the health of our livers.

Even though we didn't become full partners until then, we kept in touch and whenever possible got together. A particularly memorable New York trip when Billy was working a game at Madison Square Garden and proved that he had the kind of staying power that he was so well known for. Dinner at eleven thirty. Drinks following. Sometime in the wee hours of the morning, I vaguely recall him calling Joanie from a phone at the bar and telling her, "I'm going to be a little late tonight."

Bill was, and is, a great storyteller and hugely fun to be around. In some ways, he carefully cultivates that barfly image. While he enjoys the nightlife, I can say this for him: not only does he outlast the rest of us, he always comes to the games prepared. Al Maguire was quite the character and could spin a yarn with the best of them, but Bill would never let himself get caught off guard the way Al did that memorable day in Charlotte.

Bill is a real student of the game, and he brought a coach's sense of preparation to the broadcast. In the midst of all the bubbling personality and the warmth and the Irish wit and the shtick, Bill Raftery is as prepared as any man I've ever worked with in any sport. And so I've often told people, "Don't let that Irish humor and that casualness deceive you. This guy is meticulously prepared." And in part, that has to do with his interaction with coaches and their willingness to share things with him. He doesn't rely on his memory or his partner. Like a baseball pitcher who keeps a book on all the opposing hitters, every year Bill gets a basketball scorebook and starts taking notes. It's got a basketball court diagram at the top of the page so he can illustrate to himself particular plays and defensive schemes. And then below that are small, tiny handwritten notes that only he can read. It's Raftery's way of using hieroglyphics to prepare for a broadcast. But he gets it all in. I mean, sometimes he just rushes to get it all in. He used to do the Maui tournament to kick off the season in November and he keeps that note-taking going through March. Keep in mind that he's a guy who will work every weekend throughout the season, sometimes doing more than one game. As you can imagine, that book is thick with insights, but I don't think anyone would ever be able to decipher any of it.

Bill carried it with him in his briefcase, and at one early season game we were at a practice, Bill was making his hieroglyphics. I was observing, looking for any physical characteristics of the players that would help me identify them quickly and aid my memorization. Famously, I was grateful one year that a St. Louis University player had dyed his hair blue—that helped him stand out and made it easier for us announcers to identify him. You're not always that fortunate. After practice was over, Bill and I returned to our hotel. I called him an hour or so after we got back. He was in a panic. He didn't know where his briefcase was. I told him not to worry. Someone would find it. Either we would be able to get it the next day or it could be sent to us.

Bill wasn't mollified. He did, however, agree to go to dinner. Throughout the meal, he kept talking about the darn notebook. I asked him if it had the country's nuclear codes written down in it. A map to the location of the Holy Grail? Had someone passed along the secret to transform lead into gold? A smile flickered across his face for a second before he got agitated again. I couldn't blame him, but still it was great fun to see him sweat like that.

I wish I could say that I had his briefcase and was holding it hostage. That would have been a great prank, but the story is more mundane than that. Some staffer at the arena discovered it and got it back to Bill in time for the game. I suggested that Bill invest in handcuffs so that he would always have his Bible and his Bible holder with him. He said that he didn't want to do anything that might inhibit him raising a glass.

At one point in our history, we had to worry about Mother Nature raising the roof on us. We were in Atlanta on March 14, 2008, for the SEC basketball tournament. The site was the Georgia Dome, and since it was primarily a football facility, temporary bleachers had been installed to bring fans closer to courtside. That night we were doing the Alabama–Mississippi State quarterfinal game. It was a tense affair and had gone into overtime. At about nine thirty or so, I heard something above the crowd noise and the action. I'd always heard that an approaching tornado sounded like a freight train. I can confirm now that it really does. I looked up and the scoreboard suspended from the dome began to sway like a pendulum. At that point I glanced to one side and Rick Stansbury, Mississippi State's head coach, had turned around and was gesturing to his family—his son and his wife. He led them off the court and I heard him say, "I'm going to find safety."

Just beyond him a temporary scoreboard had been set up for the tournament. It was swaying. The tornado hit the dome with a glancing blow, shearing off one of the panels in the roof. The public address announcer told us all to remain in our seats. We were told that it was safer to be inside than out in the storm. The tornado had passed but dangerous conditions still existed. The police department had instructed security personnel to keep us all in the building.

Bill and I did as instructed but our producer and director, Mark Wolf and Suzanne Smith, were worried about the status of our production staff and the truck. They came up to Bill and me to tell us that they were going outside to check on things. They later reported to us that the truck was fine. Debris had demolished Suzanne's rental car. Unfortunately, a few people who were outside the building when the tornado hit the facility were injured—none seriously.

Bill and I sat inside for twenty minutes or so. We weren't getting any more information, and we speculated on what all this meant for the game, the tournament, and, more critically, for Atlanta and its residents. Just how bad was this thing? It was clear that whatever had come through had gone, so we decided to join our colleagues outside. We went to the truck and saw Suzanne's car. At that point Bill realized that he didn't have his briefcase or his Bible. He went to the press entrance. There he was told he couldn't go back in. It was too dangerous inside the building. Well, not only did that contradict what we'd been told previously, but that was the first time anyone had said that. What about the others still inside? Were the coaches and players in their locker rooms? What kind of danger were they facing?

Apparently, the security person had bad intel. After an hour's delay the game resumed and we were there to broadcast it. Mississippi State edged Alabama 69–67. Afterward, Bill and I were driven by golf cart back to our hotel. The rest of the staff stuck around to make sure that everything was broadcast ready for the next day. That was one of the stranger moments in my broadcasting life. Our cart driver took us through Olympic Park. Light poles, power lines, and other debris littered the ground. It was only then that we had a sense of what had just happened, how potentially dangerous the situation was. When we got back to the hotel that was made even more apparent. We weren't allowed up to our rooms. Another tornado might develop.

Ever the Pied Piper, Bill suggested we go back out to get a bite to eat. The power outages were intermittent and we wound up at a Hooters eating burgers. Things were so surreal that that location seemed somehow appropriate for the evening. By the time we got back to the hotel, we were allowed to return to our rooms. The next morning we learned that the damage to the Georgia Dome was severe enough that the SEC had no choice but to change venues. The rest of the tournament would be held at Georgia Tech—an Atlantic Coast Conference school. For a variety of reasons, only the teams, family members of the players and university staff, the cheerleaders, accredited officials, and four hundred fans from each of the schools and the school's bands would be allowed to view the game live. Alexander Memorial Coliseum seated roughly 12,000 but I would say that

10,000 of those seats were vacant when play resumed that Sunday. That was a strange experience, playing to a mostly empty house. The ringing of the dribbled ball was audible even through our headsets.

The great part of the story was that the University of Georgia, which came into the SEC tournament with a sub-.500 record, won the whole thing. They advanced to the tournament as a result. Cinderella's slippers were duck boots, but still they got her to the dance. She didn't stay long. Georgia bowed out in the first round. There were no true Cinderella stories that year—as far as advancing to the Final Four. All four top seeds made it to the Alamo Dome, where Kansas took the title over Memphis. They won it in overtime thanks to what Kansas fan's now speak of as Mario's Miracle. Mario Chalmers hit a three-pointer with 2.1 seconds left to get the game to overtime. In retrospect, it was more of a miracle that no one was severely injured or killed at the Georgia Dome a few weeks earlier.

In the category of what-ifs, I had time to reflect on the events of March 14. We even taped an insert in which Bill and I talked about our experiences. It got plugged into CBS's coverage of other tournaments that weekend. Two people had been killed in Atlanta and that was a sobering reminder of everything that had taken place and how truly fortunate we were. Later, it hit me that if our game hadn't gone into overtime, a whole lot of people would have been outside or on the streets following the game. Alabama's Mykal Riley hit a clutch three-pointer with two seconds to go in the game to tie it. As Bill often said, "Onions!"

Just to lighten things up a bit, here's one of my favorite Raftery and NCAA tournament moments. I frequently give after-dinner talks, and of course I have to talk about my good buddy Billy. I also use video from the games I've covered to add flavor to the presentation. In 2009, we had Siena–Ohio State in an eight (Ohio State) versus a nine (Siena) in Dayton. Regulation came down to the wire. Sienna tied it on a made free throw, had a chance to go into the lead on a second free throw, but missed. Ohio State's Evan Turner missed a layup. Overtime.

In the first overtime, Ronald Moore of Siena bailed out the Saints with a three-pointer with three seconds left to again tie the game.

"Onions!" my partner said.

In the second overtime, the Saints were down by two with twelve seconds left. From the same spot on the court, Moore rose up again and hit the shot to win it.

"Onions! A double order!"

A great game, a great call.

I use that game in many of my speaking engagements. I love seeing the confused expression on the faces of some folks when Bill lets loose with his signature expressions. I'm tempted to say that it has something to do with Georgia and the sweet variety of that vegetable produced in my part-time home state.

It is safe to say that everyone loves an upset in the NCAA tournament. That is, with the exception of the team that was victimized. It's also true only to an extent at the network which hopes that the big-market or big-name teams make it through the early draw and deeper into the tournament. Billy and I were a part of a couple of thrilling upsets in our day.

In 2006, Steve Alford and his Iowa Hawkeyes were a third seed, and they took on the Northwestern State Demons out of Natchitoches, Louisiana, a 14 seed. We were in Auburn Hills, Michigan. In our pregame preparation, we got to meet the players and staff from the Southland Conference champions and they charmed us. This was only their second tournament appearance in the school's history. From head coach Mike McConathy to their sports information director, Patrick Netherton, I'd seldom come across a more accommodating group. With about seven minutes to go before the game, the two teams came off the court. The Demons went to their locker room but their coach went over to the broadcast table and sat down. He did an interview with their radio guy. Billy and I noticed that. Most coaches were too caught up in the moment to do that kind of thing. After the game, we asked Mike about that and he told us, "Well, I've coached them all I can. They're not going to listen to anything I've got to say right now, so they might as well go back to the locker room and concentrate on what the task is. I'm going to come over here and do the radio show, and it's my way of relaxing." That was enough to make a broadcaster tear up.

I think Mike wanted to tear up when his team was down by 18–4 early on and then by 54–37 later on. Still, they didn't give up. Thanks to better shooting and a frenetic defense that saw them force 19 turnovers, with just 14 seconds left, following an Iowa missed free throw, they were down 63–61. Jermaine Wallace got an offensive board off a missed three. He dribbled near the corner and with three seconds left put up an off-balance fadeaway jumper. He hit it. Iowa's desperation heave missed and one of the bigger upsets in tournament history was in the books.

What I remember most was the unabashed pleasure the Demon players took in their win. It was reminiscent of Jim Valvano's North Carolina State squad celebrating their national championship. That Northwestern State victory over Steve Alford's squad was one of the most thrilling things I've ever been a part of in the NCAA tournament. That's saying something.

Another one that Bill and I were very much a part of was George Mason over the University of Connecticut in 2006 in the Washington, D.C., regional final. George Mason wasn't very highly regarded and UConn was the No. 1 seed. In fact, Billy Packer had given George Mason very little chance of advancing. Jim Calhoun's squad had an air of imperiousness about them. George Mason stuck around, and the longer they did the angrier Calhoun got. He was a fiery competitor and was known to explode on his team and could be cranky with the media. I was the beneficiary of Jim respecting Bill because he was a former coach. It was because Bill was a coach that I think he became critical on-air of Calhoun's behavior. At one point he shouted, "Where are the assistants?" He felt they should have been better able to handle their boss. Later, he made some pointed remarks about Calhoun's behavior as well.

As the game unfolded in the final minutes, it was clear that George Mason's advancing as far as they had to that point was no fluke. Being from the D.C. area certainly helped have the crowd on their side. They didn't have UConn's size. They didn't have UConn's athleticism. They didn't have UConn's tradition. But they did have a lot of heart, and they fed off the energy of that crowd. I have to give UConn credit. They were down by four at 74–70 with twenty-three seconds left but managed to tie it. The game went into overtime and everyone expected that with momentum on their side, the Huskies would pull it out of the bag. They didn't. Never trailing in the overtime, George Mason won it, 86–84. After the final buzzer, two of George Mason's players came over to the scorer's table, jumped on it, and led the crowd in a well-deserved celebration. They had made it to the final four as a No. 13 seed. I don't know where to rank my statement, "By George, the dream is still alive." It was a bit hokey but it worked.

As CBS shuffled its broadcasting lineup and Billy Packer fell out of favor, Bill Raftery eventually got promoted. I was happy for him. That's an understatement. I thought that Billy often went underappreciated by his peers. In May 2017 I was honored with the Lifetime Achievement Award for Sports at the thirty-seventh annual Sports Emmy Awards ceremony at Lincoln Center. That was an unexpected and incredible honor. I was even more pleased that my good friend Bill Raftery was up for an Emmy Award as well. This was his first nomination, and I believed he should have been honored with one for years. When his name was announced as the winner, I jumped out of my seat and shouted, "Yes!" Cris Collinsworth, one of the best there's ever been as an analyst and who'd won the award multiple times, was seated a few rows in front of me. He turned to look at me. I may have violated the rules of decorum but Cris didn't seem to mind. He mouthed the words "I understand" and continued applauding. A great moment and two wonderful men who are a credit to the industry I called home for more than fifty years.

Though we don't work together anymore, our friendship has endured. Bill and I are in touch once a month, and he is among my dearest friends. Some of that has to do with our closeness in age. We spent fifteen wonderful seasons together, and you get to know a guy a bit when you spend that much time with someone. Bill tried to keep his age under wraps. I don't think it was out of vanity but necessity. This isn't necessarily a young man's game, but when you've been around a long time, it's pretty easy to hear the footsteps coming up from behind you.

CBS didn't seem to mind us two older guys working together. For most of the time Billy and I were together Mark Wolf, now the lead producer for college basketball, was our producer. Suzanne Smith made us look good as our director. Maybe four or five years into our tenure together, someone from the NCAA tournament organizing committee asked about the regional assignments. I don't know if it was completely off the cuff, but it came as a surprise to me when I later learned that Mark had dubbed Billy and me "the Sunshine Boys." CBS picked up on that and used it in some promotions.

I believe that it had its origins in two things—our generally upbeat disposition and a Neil Simon Broadway comedy turned feature film called *The Sunshine Boys*. It starred Walter Matthau and George Burns as a couple of vaudevillians of a certain age. I believe it has stood the test of time and is worth watching. I'd like to think the same can be said for Billy and me and the many years we spent together.

At CBS, one of my partners was Len Elmore. I had never seen

Len play in person when he was a standout at the University of Maryland or with one of five NBA teams. I knew he was a New York City guy and that he'd gone to Power Memorial High School, the same place Lew Alcindor, later Kareem Abdul-Jabbar, had attended. Like Kareem, Len is possessed of an amazing intellect. In addition to his exploits on the basketball court, he graduated from Harvard Law School, served as district attorney in Brooklyn, worked at a major New York law firm, is president of the Retired NBA Players' Association, and serves on the Knight Commission on Intercollegiate Athletics. Len is obviously an astute guy and his commitment to preserving the integrity of college sports in the face of so many challenges speaks volumes about him.

In 1990, Len and I were paired for another major upset. We were at Cole Field House on the campus of Len's alma mater. Syracuse was playing Richmond. For the first time in tournament history a No. 15 team, Richmond, knocked off a No. 2, Syracuse, in a first-round match-up. Following the game Len and I got one of "those" phone calls. Ted Shaker, the executive producer in charge of our NCAA basketball operations, let us know that we'd done a great job on the game and throughout the weekend. For a lot of us doing the first round, the goal was to get to the second week of the tournament. We knew that the Final Four were not in the picture. Despite what Ted had to say, we weren't advancing. Len and I were surprised, stunned, really, but Len took it well. I suppose it helped that he had all those other irons in the fire, but he had as much pride in doing the job as anyone.

After I covered Jack Nicklaus's remarkable win in the 1986 Masters, the great golfer told me that he and I were joined at the hip. He made the putt; I made the call. I feel the same about Len and me. I would feel that way because he is such a caring individual, but even more so because he and I shared one of the most amazing experiences of my life. We were privileged to call what many consider, as I do, the greatest college basketball game in history—Duke versus Kentucky in the regional semifinal in 1992.

Len and I got assigned to Philadelphia. Jim Nantz and Billy Packer requested Lexington. I'm not sure what influenced their decision. Ohio State, Oklahoma State, Arizona, and North Carolina were the 1–4 teams in the Southeast. Michigan, which would go on to face Duke in the final and had their amazing collection of freshmen, the Fab Four, was only a No. 6. Maybe it's true that the longer you stick around the better your chances are of having something great happen for you. Our top line was Duke, Kentucky, the University of Massachusetts, and Seton Hall. Talk about a Murderer's Row of programs and a hall of fame of coaching—Mike Krzyzewski, Rick Pitino, John Calipari, and P. J. Carlesimo, respectively.

Love them or hate them, the Kentucky Wildcats were a welcome addition to the tournament after a two-year absence following NCAA sanctions resulting from improprieties involving Eddie Sutton's previous coaching regime. To the Kentucky faithful, the team's four seniors—Richie Farmer, Deron Feldhaus, John Pelphrey, and Sean Woods—were victims of circumstance. They were also extremely loyal. Each of them opted to remain at Kentucky despite the postseason ban. You went to Kentucky to have a shot at a national championship, and the four of them, all but Sean Woods, a native of Kentucky, were denied that opportunity for two of their four years. As much as those seniors contributed, Jamal Mashburn was in his sophomore season, shooting .567 from the field and .439 from beyond the three-point arc.

Duke had won the title the previous season and came back with a talented and deep roster. All-Americans Christian Laettner and Grant Hill led the team. The gritty Bobby Hurley, a coach's kid, was their point guard. Grant's father, Calvin, played for the Cowboys back when I was their radio guy. Calvin and I were good friends, and when his wife Janice was pregnant, I asked Calvin to let me know as soon as possible when their child was born. I actually announced Grant's birth on October 5, 1972, to an audience in Dallas–Fort Worth on my telecast on that Friday night. At the conclusion of the Duke-Kentucky game, I shared that story and a bit more. Calvin wanted to name their son after his father, Henry. Janice couldn't see that. I do know that Roger Staubach visited the Hills in the hospital. He insists that it was he who suggested that Calvin and Janice name their only child Grant.

Regardless of his name, Grant Hill was a very, very talented player. He and his Blue Devil teammates ran off 17 straight, lost a close one to North Carolina, and then suffered only one other defeat, to Wake Forest, to cap a remarkable regular season. They earned a top seed in the East and were set to face Kentucky, with a record of 31-2. Comparatively speaking, Kentucky struggled a bit. They stumbled out of the gate, losing two games before SEC play began, but they handily won the SEC regular season title with four conference losses. They also won the SEC tournament. They were the No. 2 seed in the region and came into the regional final with a record of 29-6.

For so many, March 28, 1992, and the events at the Philadelphia Spectrum have similar staying power. That a regional final could eclipse in people's memory the championship game says a lot about what took place on the court during that 104–103 overtime win. I can, *almost*, say the same thing about one play that took up 2.1 seconds in that game and its power to overshadow the preceding 44 minutes and 57.9 seconds. That says something about the nature of certain moments, extraordinary efforts in athletic competition. I suppose that is why we say they transcend the game.

Down by one with just over two seconds left, Grant Hill was to inbound the ball for Duke at his own end line. Len Elmore pointed out that he suspected that Duke might opt to advance the ball past midcourt and then take a quick time-out. Going the full length of the court and getting a good shot seemed unlikely. Kentucky opted not to put a defender on Hill and he had a clear view down court. He threw the ball baseball style to Laettner, who caught it near the free throw line with his back to the basket. He turned and hit the jumper. The game was over.

As much as I remember what took place on the court, I also recall what many of you at home watching then or during one of the countless times it's been replayed may not have been aware of. Lesley Visser was with us in Philadelphia, and she prepared a tribute to the University of Kentucky's longtime radio broadcaster, Cawood Ledford. He was in his final season after being the voice of the Wildcats for thirty-nine years. We wanted to salute him, but we never got Lesley on the air. Nearly every play in the game was so compelling that we didn't want to disrupt the continuity of the broadcast with that kind of an insert.

We weren't the only ones who were aware of the significance of that game for Ledford. In the bedlam after the Shot, Mike Krzyzewski managed to make his way over to Kentucky radio's position to congratulate him and to thank him for his contributions to the game of basketball. That was one of the classiest gestures I've ever witnessed. Like I said, some moments transcend a game, and for Coach K to have the presence of mind to do that is one reason he's so highly regarded by so many.

At the conclusion of the broadcast, Len and I took off our headsets. We didn't say a word. We both knew that we'd been a part of something monumental. How could we not have? Bob Ryan of the *Boston Globe*, an award-winning columnist and widely acknowledged basketball guru, walked to our broadcast position. He said to Lenny, "Listen, I was at the Maryland–North Carolina State game in 1974. I've always thought that was the greatest basketball game I ever saw. Until tonight. Can you give me some context? Which one had more significance?"

Len had played in that game. What was at stake was a berth in the NCAA tournament for the winner of the ACC. North Carolina State had David Thompson, a guy whose leaping ability defied physics and our ability to capture his talent in words. The Wolfpack edged the Terrapins, 103–100, in overtime. What's remarkable is that there was no thirty-five-second clock, no three-point field goals, and, if you believe Len Elmore, who was a fierce shot blocker, both teams displayed great defense in that forty-five-minute struggle. North Carolina State was the top-ranked and Maryland fourth-ranked team in the country. And can you imagine this: Fourteen players participated in that game—seven for each team. Eight of them went on to be NBA draft picks.

Len, always one to consider a question thoroughly, paused for a good ten seconds. Then he answered, "This one."

Now, keep in mind that Bob Ryan's question was about significance. He didn't say "best," and that's what Len responded to—the impact the game had on the championship picture.

All I can urge you to do is watch that NC State–Maryland game yourself and compare it to what Kentucky and Duke offered. We live in a great time when such things are easily possible and you won't be disappointed no matter which of those two classic games you deem best.

I was able to intercept Coach K after he spoke with Cawood Ledford. Mike was trying to make his way to speak with the Duke radio people. I caught him and said, "That's just the greatest game I think I've ever seen, and especially the finish."

Mike said to me with affection, "I just knew if we could get it in the son of a bitch's hands, he would make the shot."

Unfairly or not, Christian Laettner has not enjoyed the greatest reputation. He could be a bit standoffish with the media, and I don't fully understand why he got so much grief throughout his career at Duke and later. Years later, the writer Gene Wojiechowski approached me to talk about the game and I obliged. I told him the story above.

Later, when I got a chance to review, prepublication, what Gene had written, I was taken aback. Instead of Mike calling his center an SOB, clearly a term of endearment in my mind, Gene thought that I, and Coach K, had said, "a-hole." I immediately got on the phone and cleared the matter up with Gene. I was glad I did, as was Gene, but no one was happier about that correction that Laettner himself.

I didn't watch the telecast for eleven years. I thought at the time that our broadcast was very good. I didn't want to see anything that might change my perceptions. In 2003, Raftery and I were in Minneapolis to do the regional final there. I was in my hotel room preparing for the Marquette and Kentucky matchup that would feature Dwyane Wade. The phone rang and Raft wanted to give me a heads-up. ESPN Classic was showing the 1992 game. I was hesitant at first, but I did watch it. I know that reality can intrude on memories and sometimes elbow aside our cherished ones. The game was about six minutes old. I sat enthralled by what was taking place on the court. In a way, Len and I were just white noise. I didn't pay attention to our commentary with the kind of close scrutiny that I often did when I was younger and so eager to learn. I'm not beyond learning, but given the circumstances, this wasn't a full-on study session.

I had a few nits to pick, but the most egregious one was that I knew that Christian Laettner had been 10-for-10 from the free throw line. The Shot made him 10-for-10 from the field as well. I also recall that he had 7 rebounds. Missing out on the opportunity to point out that he'd been faultless from the field—even the sound of those words as I type them give me pleasure—upset me. I hold myself accountable for that mistake but know that I wasn't solely responsible for it.

On the twentieth anniversary of the game, CBS rented a suite in the Waldorf-Astoria hotel in Manhattan. I was in town for the National Football Foundation annual banquet, which was always held there. Len worked in the city. CBS flew Christian Laettner up from his home. Lenny and Christian and I were videotaped as we watched the telecast of Duke–Kentucky.

The one response from Christian that I most remember is when he felt like he had been roughhoused at the Kentucky end of the court, that someone had grabbed him around the neck and hauled him out of bounds. He believed that it was a Kentucky bench player by the name of Aminu Timberlake. On a later trip down the floor, Timberlake was sprawled on his back under the basket. Laettner put his size 14 rather abruptly down in Timberlake's midsection. Lenny said, "I'm not so sure he meant to do that," and I said, "Oh, yes, he did." And replays were pretty conclusive that he did.

So when we were watching the retelecast, we got to that moment in the game and Christian said—and they had him on camera for this—"I just knew you guys would feel compelled to show that." And I said, "Well, Christian, why would we not? It was one of the more memorable aspects of a game, and you probably should have been ejected." And then he explained his version of why he had done it, that he felt like he had been roughhoused and thrown to the floor on the defensive end, and that Timberlake was the guy who had done it. It turned out that was not true. Regardless, even if he had been the one who fouled Laettner, that didn't excuse what Laettner did in re-taliation. He was fortunate not to be ejected from the game. Another whole string of what-ifs could be spun into something very different from the eventual outcome.

I also was amazed by the shot that Sean Woods of Kentucky hit with 2.1 seconds left in overtime to tie the game at 100. If it weren't for what transpired in what little time remained maybe we'd all be praising him and saluting him for hitting the shot in the greatest college basketball game ever. Woods had a tremendous game, scoring 21, with 9 assists. On a pick-and-roll play they'd run many times, he released a hook shot that hit the backboard before going cleanly through the net. Maybe in a game of H-O-R-S-E the shot wouldn't have counted because he didn't call the bank shot. In Wojiechowski's book, a few of the Duke players made pointed reference to that bank shot, but in reality it was a more difficult "look" than Laettner's final shot that ended the game. Besides, it's not really how but how many that matter—except when you're talking about one of the greatest moments in all of sports.

The Shot was as much about strategy as it was execution. That doesn't diminish the skills of the players; it just supports the truism that it is a coach's job to put players in the right position to succeed. That meant Coach K deciding that rather than have his point guard, the NCAA's career assist leader, take the ball out from beneath their own basket, Grant Hill would be there. Surely, if Hurley were back there, Rick Pitino would have put one of his taller frontline players on the baseline to harass the Duke point guard. Instead, with Hill back there, he opted to put all of his men back in a basketball version of a prevent defense.

As so often happens when football defensive coordinators opt for that approach, a great pass and catch defeated that strategic decision. The ball was on the money, just beyond the outstretched hands of Feldhaus and Pelphrey, two of the been-done-wrong Kentucky seniors. Pitino's strategy was sound. Double-team the player who was perfect from the floor for the game. Double-team the guy who was an All-American. Double-team the Player of the Year. Don't foul him. If he makes the shot, he deserves all the accolades.

He did make the Shot and Duke went on to win back-to-back championships, the first team since John Wooden's legendary UCLA teams dominated the sport like no one before or since. Even if he hadn't, you might be able to make a case for this being the most compelling college basketball game ever. Combined, the two teams shot 61 percent from the field. Duke's Bobby Hurley played all 45 minutes of the contest, putting up 22 points while dishing out 10 assists. Jamal Mashburn played 43 minutes, made 11 of 16 field goals, hauled down

10 rebounds, and was 3 of 4 from three-point territory and was 3 for 3 from the line. John Pelphrey was 5 of 7 from the field, including 3 of 4 from beyond the arc. You could say that Duke's 19 turnovers kept Kentucky in the game, but in watching it again, and at the time, I was struck by the high level of the play. Time and time again, Len and I found our voices rising as we witnessed the call and response that makes basketball and its alternating possession of the ball so compelling. In what other sport can thirty-five seconds elapse, as it did at the conclusion of this one, with the ball changing hands five times, and each time it did so the team scored and the lead changed?

Strategy figured throughout. Coach Pitino felt that his Wildcats were more fit, had better stamina, and at the end of the game that would make a difference. Full-court man-to-man pressure proved to be the ticket when Kentucky found itself down by a dozen. When he switched to that attacking style, the game turned. Kentucky ran off eight straight points in the second half to pull within four at 67–63. We could feel a shift in the intensity of the game. That run came off a time-out and it seemed as if Duke lost its focus and Kentucky made them realize what a lapse like that could mean. Then came Laettner's poor judgment. Mike Krzyzewski yelled at his star, "That was unbelievably dumb." Yes, it was. Why risk fouling out or playing cautiously on the defensive end to avoid that fate by exacting revenge?

The game went on, relentlessly forward. Pelphrey, with four fouls, drew a charge on the exhausted but still driving Hurley. Thomas Hill contributed two big buckets. In overtime, Hurley missed a three and Grant Hill grabbed the backbreaking offensive rebound. He got the ball back to Hurley, who didn't miss the second chance. And before the Shot? Laettner hit two free throws to tie the game at 98. He was the only player to score for Duke from that point on. One of them was a bank shot off a partial block and reload, but style points don't really matter. That bit of good fortune was followed by those five possessions, the lead changes, and then the moment in time. Laettner dribbled once, faked right, and spun left and then rose up, falling away.

As much as the Shot itself, we all remember the Reaction. Kentucky players stunned, on the floor or with hands on heads as if to keep their skulls intact from the mind-blowing drama they'd just participated in. Len and I stayed quiet for more than a minute. What was there to say? Wasn't it obvious? A great game. A great team pushed to its absolute limit by another. One team overjoyed, the other disconsolate. Coach K would later say that he felt guilty that he and his team had caused the Kentucky side so much pain. Coach Pitino didn't want 2.1 seconds to dictate his kids' basketball life. Maybe it did. Maybe it didn't. But if your life is going to be dictated by any one small bit of time, isn't it better to be a fragment from a beautiful whole? If only you could see that small piece like a shard in a kaleidoscope, how by just turning that tube slightly, how it reflected or refracted would produce another thing of beauty.

CHAPTER 13

In Your Life:
Tiger and Other PGA Tales

I've collected a lot of memorabilia over the years. Opposite that signed Jack Nicklaus photo in my office, I've got another signed classic picture hanging on the wall. Tiger Woods holing out a chip shot on 16 in 2005 ranks right up there in a lot of people's minds as one of the greatest shots in Masters history.

The 2005 Masters was, for me, the tale of three "marks." A ball mark, spike marks, and Chris DiMarco. All figured in what was an amazing week of golf. It began as a variation on a horror story: It was a dark and stormy morning. Heavy rains delayed the start of the tournament by five hours, and 68 of the 93 players starting the tournament wound up having to complete their first round on the second day of the tournament. Chris DiMarco took advantage of the soft conditions and fired an opening-round 67 to lead after the first round. Tiger struggled out of the gate and shot a 74.

Stop me if you've heard this one before: Tiger was under the microscope. He'd gone ten straight major tournaments without a win. He'd gone thirty-four months without a victory in one of his sport's big four. He'd revamped his swing. He'd switched equipment. He'd gotten married and had maybe lost his edge, his competitive fire. He'd become distracted with the work of his foundation and other endeavors.

For those into the minutiae of the sport, Tiger took a big step toward accepting the reality of the game. Other players had already switched to drivers with longer shafts made of space-age composites and heads nearly the size of, well, human heads. Tiger was monstrously long, but others were catching up to him. In 2005 Tiger joined the ranks of the high-tech hitters. Rain softens greens but slows fairways. Tiger was back to bombing the ball beyond most of the competition. That increased distance paid off for him in round two when he fired a six-under 66. DiMarco, not known for his length, shot another 67 to be ten under going into the weekend.

During Tiger's so-called major drought, the pundits had decided that the gap between Tiger and the rest of the golfers on tour had closed. In fact, they then touted the Big Four—Woods, Phil Mickelson, Vijay Singh, and Ernie Els. The middle two of the four extended a figurative, and perhaps literal, middle finger at one another over marking up the greens with metal spikes in their shoes. The offender was Mickelson. He chose to wear old-school metal spikes to help his footing in the soggy conditions. Singh, playing in a group behind Phil all three days, didn't take kindly to Phil's perfectly legal footwear choice. He complained to tournament officials. Phil took exception to this. Why hadn't Singh spoken to him directly? Round three had a lengthy rain delay and rumors swirled about a clubhouse dustup between the two men that nearly had them come to blows. Perhaps it would best be settled with a duel at dawn with drivers fired at twenty paces?

Nothing could distract from the marvelous golf being played. Because round three got off to such a late start due to round two being completed in the morning, DiMarco only got to play nine holes. He carded a 33 on the front nine, putting him at minus 13 through 45 holes. Remarkable. Tiger, however, was even better. He was five shots under par through nine, bringing him to nine under par after that tough start. Tiger got on a roll in that round, and continued it on the back nine on Sunday morning. Seven birdies in a row put him on top of the leaderboard. DiMarco struggled coming in on Sunday morning. A double bogey on his first hole of the day (at 10) set the tone. What was remarkable was that the over-par score was his first in 44 holes. Tiger made up seven strokes on DiMarco. As the final round opened, Woods was at minus 11, three shots ahead of DiMarco, four shots ahead of Thomas Bjørn, and six shots ahead of Mickelson. Fittingly, Phil and Vijay were paired for the final round. Neither man, nor Els, would figure much in the final round. It became a two-man story with Woods and DiMarco now dueling for the championship.

They came to the 16th tee with Tiger up by one stroke. They'd each birdied the par-five 15th hole. How they each played that hole was a study in contrasts. Tiger hit a mammoth drive that left him with an eight-iron to the green. DiMarco laid up and pinpointed a wedge within a few feet for a short putt. He had the honors at 16 and hit a solid shot to the traditional Sunday back left location—21 feet from the bottom edge of the green, 4 feet from the left edge. He landed it in the center of the green and the ball took the slope and rolled down it to about 18 feet, leaving him a putt straight up the hill.

Tiger stood over the ball and tugged one left and long, off the green. It rolled downhill and came to rest on the fringe but nearly resting against the second cut of rough. That increased the degree of difficulty immensely. He was going to have to bring the club nearly straight down on top of the ball. The 16th slopes precipitously back to front toward the pond and from right to left as viewed from the tee. The following year, I walked to the approximate spot where Tiger's ball came to rest and paced it off. I had it at ninety feet away. Regardless of how imprecise my distance estimate may be, nearly everyone would agree that he had missed in the worst possible location. We showed the tee shots live, cut away, and then came back.

That year, former tour pro Lanny Wadkins had joined Jim Nantz in the booth at 18 as the analyst. He had succeeded Ken Venturi in that role. I asked him to assess Tiger's shot—that's his job. He said that it was probably the most difficult chip shot on the course. I mentioned that Davis Love III had chipped in from a somewhat similar position. After a bit more back-and-forth between us, Lanny stated that he doubted Tiger would be able to stop the ball from going down that slope and finishing inside DiMarco's mark. I waited for Tiger to get over to the ball and complete his practice swings before I said, "Well, here were go."

Tiger had to aim some twenty-five feet left of the hole. I didn't know this at the time, but later on, Steve Williams, Tiger's caddy, said in an interview that Tiger had picked out an indentation on the green, a ball mark, as his chosen landing spot. Well, as Tiger eyed that spot and then the pin, I went silent. For a good five to ten seconds, it was just the camera on Tiger, the late afternoon shadows, and the chirp of a bird. Once Tiger swung, the click of the ball and the murmur of the crowd chimed in. The ball landed far left of the hole. As it began its trip downhill and to the right, I said, "Well, here it comes." As it got nearer to the hole, I said, "Oh my goodness." By the time it got inches from the cup and then rested there on the lip, I let the patrons' oohs and aahs tell the story. For 1.8 seconds the ball rested there before dropping, and, as the crowd exploded, I added my "Oh wow!" to the chorus of cheers. Only when Tiger bent over to pull the ball from the hole did I say, "In your life have you ever seen anything like that?"

I knew that I hadn't, and I instantly knew that I'd been fortunate again to witness and give voice to a great moment in sports history. Tiger strode away, thrusting both arms skyward before high-fiving his caddie and letting out a roar of approval of his own.

As much as other people remember my call, I remember the great work that our team did in capturing those moments on-screen. Let me take you back to Wednesday of Masters week. Per usual, I climbed the tower behind the 16th tee and sat there with veteran camera operator Bob Wishnie. Bob had been at Augusta working that hole for longer than I had. That Wednesday he said to me, "I want to show you something." He showed me a camera. He told me that it had a 100×1 zoom and a horizontal stabilizer. He said that very often, holding the camera steady when something exciting happens is difficult. He hated getting yelled at for a shaky shot. He then pointed the camera toward the front of the green where one of the players had marked his ball with a nickel. He zoomed in and asked me, "What do you see?" On the coin, I could read, "In God We Trust, 2002."

The technology was clearly in place to capture that iconic moment when, in tight close-up, the Nike swoosh emblem on Tiger's golf ball as big as a boomerang on your TV set, it hung suspended for that moment. What was also in place was a human being's instincts. A whole team of people sit in the production trucks watching various monitors. Steve Milton was the director. He literally called the shots—the view from which at least five different cameras we had on that hole should go out on-air live. Norm Patterson, the technical director, who sadly is no longer with us, sat at the console to Steve's right and presses the button corresponding to the camera shot that Steve called out. In this case though, Steve called out, "Ready ten, take ten." Norm punched the button and Wishnie's 100×1 camera went from a long shot of Tiger's swing to a close-up of the ball rolling without losing focus. Try that sometime with your phone's camera. Steve then called out, "Ready six. Take six." That meant that he wanted to go to a flanker camera manned by Skip Shakleford to get a reaction shot of Tiger. Norm never punched that button. Something told him to stick with that close-up. Good thing he did. The ball wobbled nearly imperceptibly and then fell. We got that all live.

Truth is, Norm not doing what Steve had instructed could have gotten him fired. Instead he captured an iconic moment. The broadcast went on, of course, and none of you knew what was going on behind the scenes. I also don't think that many of you gave any thought to the fact that instead of immediately going to a replay of that great shot, Steve stuck with live shots of Chris DiMarco as he looked over his putt and then slipped it just past the hole. Seven minutes lapsed between Tiger's make and the replay. Steve's choice did two things. It showed a lot of respect for DiMarco, who was tenacious in battling Tiger. It also heightened expectations and kept the drama going. When can we see that again? That was all great visual storytelling and great teamwork.

I mean no disrespect to Steve in relating this behind-the-scenes action. I can't imagine doing the job Steve had to do that day. Sitting in front of a bank of monitors with more than fifty different views of the golf course and deciding which shot is *the* shot to go to would short-circuit my synapses. Covering one hole was enough for me, thank you very much. I always felt a mixture of relief and disappointment when the last group came through 16. Frequently the tournament was very much in play in those final two holes. That was the case in 2005.

Despite being behind by two with two to play, DiMarco didn't back down in the face of that miraculous shot. He tied Tiger with a birdie on 18, but eventually lost the playoff. Tiger recovered from his late-round struggles to birdie the first playoff hole—18—by draining a fifteen-footer. He earned his fourth green jacket and his ninth major title. Tiger was masterful in keeping to his habit of winning after leading after 54 holes but DiMarco showed a lot of courage in not backing down one bit. It's not as if his 2005 Masters performance was without precedent. He ranked in the top ten for quite a few weeks from 2002 to 2006. He took that punch from Tiger and battled back. He was great all week; Tiger was just a little bit better.

Tiger also proved to be a pretty good play-by-play man as well. In an interview his description of the chip on 16 bears repeating: "All of a sudden it looked pretty good. And all of a sudden it looked really good. And then it looked like how could it not go in, and how did it not go in, and all of a sudden it went in. So it was pretty sweet."

DiMarco's summation wasn't bad either: "You expect the unexpected, and unfortunately it's not unexpected when he's doing it."

How appropriate. Tiger's remarks were quite a bit longer, but DiMarco's were more precise.

The 2005 Masters also marked sixty-five-year-old Jack Nicklaus's final competitive round at Augusta National. He shot a 77-76 and missed the cut. On his final hole in his second round, he hit a six-iron to within a few feet but missed the birdie putt. Later that summer, he ended his run at the British Open with a birdie, demonstrating that sometimes you can really end on a high note.

Ultimately, these two moments at the Masters—Jack's 1986 shot and Tiger's 2005 one—stand at the forefront of my mind whenever I look back across the sweep of my career. I don't know if this is a valid indicator of the role that shot plays in the game's lore, but I'll share this story anyway. My brother Dan and his wife, Herbie Kay, have two sons who are avid golfers. Both played at my alma mater and earned small-school All American honors while at Texas Lutheran. Their aspirations of playing on the tour eventually didn't pan out, but not for lack of effort. The older of the two, Keith, says his major claim to fame is that in the medal (stroke play) rounds of a U.S. Amateur, he once finished four strokes ahead of Phil Mickelson. I learned to play the game later in life, and the lowest my handicap ever got was 14.

One day the two of them were at our home in Steamboat visiting along with their parents. I found them looking up at the two photos of Jack in '86 and of Tiger in 2005. I told Keith and his brother that when I'm gone the two of them can claim one or the other of the two large photos depicting those classic shots and two players who defined their respective eras. I told them they could flip a coin, arm-wrestle, or do whatever else it takes to decide who gets Jack and who gets Tiger. This was years before Tiger's fall from grace and his protracted slump. Shortly after the revelations of Tiger's infidelities, Dean called me and asked if his brother had been in touch about the two pictures. I told him that he hadn't. Good, he said, I want Jack.

No disrespect to Tiger, but I have to agree. Of the two players and the two shots, I'd have to say that Jack's putt and his overall career top my list of great golfing achievements. Don't get me wrong: Tiger's chip-in and his dominance and influence on the game are both unquestionably impressive. Jack's were just better. I enjoyed them both and they are both golfing geniuses, but just as I enjoy the music of Tchaikovsky over Stravinsky, Jack suits my sensibilities better than Tiger.

I also have to admit to a bit of an age bias. Jack and I are contemporaries. I first started following him when I was twenty-one. I was lucky enough to be in a position that he made the putt and took the lead and the abbreviated call of "Maybe," and "Yes, sir" seemed to find an audience. For all those reasons—drumroll, please—Jack's putt on 16 is my favorite moment in sports. Tiger's shot is tied for second. I'll leave it at that for the moment. You'll have to keep reading to learn what the others are. All I will say is that not all my favorite moments happened on the golf course.

That's what I'm hoping I can do by continuing to be a part of the Masters for the foreseeable future. I don't know how long I will continue at 16, but I know that every time I set foot on the grounds of Augusta National, I may not feel like a sixteen-year-old, but I definitely feel at least sixteen years younger.

I've loved covering golf for CBS, and I have so many fond memories of the events I've broadcast, the players I've come to know, and the people I've worked with and come in contact with at the various tournaments. I would have loved to report from the British Open, but that was not to be. I don't feel any kind of regret, but that omission in my résumé falls under the category of "It Would Have Been Nice, But . . ." I've got a few others in that column, but I prefer to focus on what I was fortunate enough to be able to do and not on what I wasn't able to do.

I saw firsthand how bitterness and regret could leave a mark on some people's lives. Ken Venturi was a wonderful broadcaster and an astute examiner of the game. That didn't bring him much pleasure. He was on the tour well before players began to earn huge incomes. I roomed with him for seven years while covering the Masters. He frequently reminded me that his career earnings totaled $238,000— roughly the amount that the eleventh-place finisher in the 2017 PGA Tournament earned. As prize money grew, Ken felt more and more like he had missed out.

At times I tried to give Ken a better sense of perspective. Yes, some of the top players earned millions and millions of dollars—as they should. They were at the pinnacle of their profession. There were a lot more other guys trying to hang on to their tour card, going down to the wire at the end of the season, staying at the Red Roof Inn, driving their own version of the beat-up Chevy I once had. That's how it is in any business. I could have spent my time lamenting the fact that I was born too soon to really enjoy the full benefits of the explosion of television outlets and the proliferation of opportunities afforded by cable, satellite, and streaming services. Ken really didn't want to hear any of that, and I stopped trying to get him to see the lighter side of things. He'd sit there in the rented house we shared in Augusta, drink a Crown Royal and Coke, and watch Alex Trebek host *Jeopardy!*

He also felt that he was wronged in the 1958 Masters when Arnold Palmer played a second ball on the 12th hole due to a question about an imbedded-ball ruling. It turned out that Arnold's decision to play that second ball to score a par three instead of the double-bogey with the first ball meant the difference between winning by a stroke and tying Venturi. Ken disagreed with the ruling and bitterness festered between the two for years. After Ken died in 2013, Arnold spoke up and said that he regretted how things had transpired between them. He still believed he was justified in doing what he'd done on the golf course, but not in how he'd responded to Ken's complaints. It was a case of life being too short.

Ken suffered various hand injuries that cut his career short, and that added to his sense that things just hadn't quite worked out for him.

I recently read where Rory McIlroy said that the Masters was the preeminent major in his and most players' estimation. He had to walk back his statement that he didn't "care about the U.S. Open and the [British] Open Championship." Maybe he feels that way because the Masters has so far eluded him, but those comments shed some light on Ken Venturi's attitude. Since he failed to win one of golf's biggest prizes, regardless of how it happened, he felt a void. The green jacket is that treasured an honor. After years of sharing quarters with Venturi, I went to Frank Chirkinian and asked for relief from the hazard. Frank said that he couldn't do that. I was one of the few guys from the on-air team who hadn't played professional golf. Ken was able to tolerate me as a result.

High on my list of favorite colleagues on CBS's golf coverage is David Feherty. David is the most spontaneously funny human being I've ever had the pleasure of being around. And that includes professional stand-up comedians. Of course, in mentioning a sense of humor, Gary McCord's name springs to mind. Part of having a good broadcast team is having a variety of different personality types. Gary is a good friend, and I know he won't mind me making this distinction. David can't help but say funny and at times inappropriate things. He has a wellspring of humor deep inside that sometimes overflows and drowns the internal editor in there, too, who would normally hit the button to delete a thought before it went out of his mouth and into the world. Gary, on the other hand, is a bit more practiced in his comedic arts—he's developed a shtick. It's a very popular and enter-taining routine and one that I really enjoy, but it's not as off the wall or out of the blue as David's extemporaneous expressions.

Early in my career I made a conscious decision to be judicious in how and what I expressed on air. I'm trying to be as equally judicious in selecting which of my favorite flamboyant Feherty tales to share. One that springs to mind has to do with my decision to ask David to come down to San Antonio to help me with one of my favorite events. I'm a loyal alumnus of Texas Lutheran. It's an NCAA Division III school, so it doesn't offer athletic scholarships. Budgets are tight to meet the demands of the fifteen intercollegiate sports the school offers to student-athletes. Each year for the past decade and a half or so, I've hosted what is called *Front Row with Verne*. I host it and do an interview and question-and-answer session with some celebrity from the world of sports. In 2015, David graciously agreed to come down to San Antonio to be the guest.

Nancy and I were sitting with David in an anteroom outside the main hall where we were going to do the show. This was before a brief meet and greet, dinner, and then the conversation. By this time I'd known David for more than twenty years and knew his propensity for getting caught up in the moment.

"David," I told him, "keep in mind your audience."

He looked at me quizzically. "What's your point?"

"This is Texas *L-u-t-h-e-r-a-n* University."

In my mind I envisioned the seven hundred or so prim and proper folks mouths agape in horror at some inappropriate remark.

David nodded. "You really think I would?"

"Yes," I said, "I'm afraid you really would. I don't want the F-word to come out."

"I'll try my best."

After dinner, I conducted the informal interview. He was funny, gregarious, and charming. So much so that I wasn't as calculated in my line of questioning as I should have been. I mentioned his wife, Anita, and how she saved him from his demons. David has been open about some of his substance abuse problems and he's also someone who dives deeply into whatever catches his fancy—cycling, collecting rifles. David spoke eloquently and lovingly of Anita and the positive impact she'd made on his life. Things were going along quite nicely until he decided to compare her to a previous wife who "made it a point to try to fuck every man in Tarrant County."

I felt my blood run cold and my vision narrowed to where the president of Texas Lutheran, Dr. Stuart Dorsey, was sitting with his wife, Michelle, at the head table. I couldn't make out Stuart's expression because he was bent over in laughter. My blood warmed—to match my heated, embarrassed cheeks—and we got through the rest of the evening. I apologized profusely to Stuart later and told him that if he got any complaints to forward them on to me. I never received any, and David was chagrinned but pleased to learn how well his appearance had been received.

David knew his limitations and that he had to conduct himself properly and hold his tongue while at Augusta National. The members provide the CBS crew with an area where we can have a catered breakfast, lunch, or dinner during tournament week in our compound. David dined there. We'd have a production meeting at some point in the morning and then most of us would head to the clubhouse dining room for lunch. David would never join us, knowing full well that he'd be hard-pressed not to utter something that might get him into trouble. "Know thyself" is a pretty good motto to follow.

I met him for the first time in 1990, fittingly, with Gary McCord. Gary and I were working at Butler National, outside Chicago, for the Western Open. We had privileges to go into the players' locker room and the players' dining room. So Gary said, "Let's go up and grab a bite of lunch." We walked in and David was sitting by himself. I had never met him. I had heard of him because he was on the European tour and a Ryder Cup competitor. And we had lunch with him, and I was belly laughing throughout the whole meal. On the way back to the course I said, "We've got to get him on the air at CBS."

Nodding, Gary said, "I'm trying."

I went to Frank Chirkinian and said, "I just met David Feherty. I don't know if you know him, but he is the most original, humorous guy I've ever met."

Frank scowled. "Aah, nobody in the world in America could understand him because of his Irish accent."

I know many people who tell me that David's accent is part of his charm. No one has ever complained about not being able to understand him.

It took a while, but CBS eventually did get around to bringing him on board—Irish accent and all.

I still like to tease David about his lousy abilities as a prognosticator. David is friendly with Rory McIlroy. In 2011, Rory had the lead going into the final day at the Masters. That Saturday night, Rory and David had dinner together. When David got back to our rented property he said to me, "Rory's going to win it. I guarantee it." That's the year that the young Irishman shot the infamous 80 in the final round and dropped off the leaderboard like a golf ball on a car's hood—that last bit is a tribute to Gary McCord and his wonderful analogies. Rory wasn't the only one to suffer through an ignominious final round. Ken Venturi nearly won the Masters as an amateur in 1956. He, too, held the lead after 54 holes only to shoot an 80 in the final round. Greg Norman's so-called collapse in 1996 saw him lose the largest third-round lead (six strokes) to my colleague Nick Faldo. The rise and fall of one player and another is always a fascinating story line. Personally, I prefer a comeback to a fall from grace.

David's a hard worker and we not only roomed together for a decade at the Masters, but we did our homework together. It became a routine for us to walk the holes that we covered. On the greens, David would take a putter and a few golf balls and stroke them from various locations to get a better sense of the speed and breaks on the putting surfaces. I would act as his caddy, rolling the balls back to him. I never wanted to presume to be anything more than what I was—a broadcaster. I couldn't see going out there and putting them myself. I was able to learn by watching and that was enough for me. For David, and others, I'm sure that what their hands felt was as important as what their eyes saw, but I was never a good enough golfer to develop that kind of sense. Eventually, and not only because David left CBS, I ended that routine. After so many years of covering the same holes, I felt like I knew the greens pretty well, and the pin placements were always only incrementally different each year if at all.

I miss having David around. I know that he enjoys his new role with the Golf Channel and NBC. He's ideally suited to doing that kind of programming. I'm a big believer that people need to do in life what best suits their nature. I can't say that David was held back in any way by anyone at CBS or at Augusta National. It's just that talent and inclination will naturally find their best outlet. I could no more be like David than Tiger Woods could be like David. I've only met Tiger in person once. He's lived his life under a microscope and he's a guarded individual. I don't know if he changed to become that way or that's just how he is. I have no problem with that. I don't understand why we expect the athletes we most admire and prize to be all things to all people. That's enormously unfair. Tiger has to be true to himself, just as you and I do.

We all know people who are chameleon-like. Call them insincere, phony, or what have you, but those individuals are more irksome than someone who is authentically his or her self. Like a lot of people, I admire Fred Couples. He is a genuinely nice man. He lived near Houston for a while. Texas Lutheran's men's golf team was playing in a tournament nearby. The TLU coach knew Fred's coach. He made a call and Fred agreed to meet with that group of young guys. That exchange made their day and likely their golf careers. He could have just stopped by for a quick few minutes, but he spent a good forty-five minutes with them talking about how he prepared for a major. He also let them ask questions and was very receptive. That conversation took place in the spring of 1992. One week later Fred won the Masters. I know that a lot is made of golf being a gentleman's game and its self-policing and etiquette may seem out of keeping with today's society, but in my experience, there are far more stories like this one than the Singh versus Mickelson battle.

I like doing golf because it does offer a change of pace for me. Basketball has more continuous action than football, but each of the sports I've covered has its own rhythms. I've seen condensed versions of football games, but I don't know if anyone has ever done the same for a round of golf. Viewers have gotten used to the product we present to them on our telecasts, and moving around the course to different players feels natural. I like stretching and utilizing different broadcasting muscles. Variety keeps you fresh, but every spring, come Master's time, I'm happy to get back to my accustomed spot on 16, fill my lungs with magnolia-sweetened air, and feel like I've found another home.

I've played Augusta National only twice. The course is open to selected members of the media on the Monday after the final round. A limited number of slots are available and in the early 1990s, I got to play for the second time. I was in a foursome with Rick Gentile of CBS, Frank Chirkinian, Jr., and the LPGA legend Jan Stephenson. We had a very early tee time. The sun was just starting to show its stuff when we teed off on No. 1. By the time we got to the tee box on 2, the sun had taken fuller effect. The mist was set aflame and everything was cast in a lovely golden light. Jan and I were walking down the fairway and we both sighed. I turned to her and said, "I feel like I'm walking into a commercial." Inadequate words, really, but she understood and I think most readers will as well.

I've been asked, if I had only one round of golf left to play in my life, would I choose Augusta National or the Pebble Beach Golf Course. Boy, that is a tough one, and since I can't say both, because of the long association I've had with the people at Augusta National and all the memories I have associated with it, I'd choose the site of the Masters. Bobby Jones had a pretty good feel for what makes a golf course special.

It has to be an exquisite place to play golf to make me choose it over Pebble Beach. I played that course once with a friend, Larry Bookman, from Steamboat Springs, Colorado. We came to 18 after having the course take its toll on us. Larry looked to his left and out over Stillwater Cove. We could hear the waves crash and the screech of gulls. Larry turned back to me and said, "I never dreamed in my life I would pay this much money for a round of golf. But I've got to tell you, it was worth it."

Amen to that.

Number 16 at Augusta produced another lasting memory for me. In 2009, another player with a number of years under his belt was taking on what some used to refer as the "flat bellies"—the lean and hungry youngsters. Post-Tiger, they brought a ferocity of competitiveness and fitness to the game. At forty-eight, Kenny Perry had never won a major. He was poised to do so. He came to 16 with a one-shot lead over another player who belied the weight room workout look—Angel Carbrera, Jr. Perry took out an eight-iron for a shot that rose majestically and then settled on the putting surface and nearly rolled in for an ace. Perry later said that it was the greatest eight-iron shot he'd struck in his life, and if things had turned out different for him, many of us would be talking about that tap-in birdie that put him two up with two to play.

I didn't get to see live what happened to him next, but later saw the skulled chip shot at 17 and the bogey at 18 that put him in a sudden-death playoff with Cabrera. Perry lost that playoff and a chance at the green jacket. Six weeks later at Congressional in Washington D.C. before the coverage of the final round of the AT&T Classic began, Jim Nantz and Nick Faldo debated whether Perry would ever win a major. Nantz believed that he could; Kenny was that talented. Nick believed that the last and best chance had passed him by. Nantz continued to press his point when Nick said, "He can't win a major. You have to be a bit of an asshole to win a major. I should know, I won six of them."

Kevin McHale, one of the sound crew, immediately piped up, "In that case, you should have won a lot more."

Nick roared along with the rest of us, but forgotten in all of that was the fact that what Nick wasn't quite saying directly was that Kenny was a great guy, one of those for whom you rooted. It wasn't meant to be for him and, worse, as Kenny himself later pointed out, his struggle at the Masters was eerily similar to his loss at the PGA ten years earlier. Kenny earned his PGA tour card on his third try and then kept it without interruption for thirty straight years and fourteen PGA tour victories. Quite a remarkable story of perseverance.

I don't think that I could have persevered enough to have an acting career, but I had a second brush with fame later in life similar to my *BFD* experience back in Dallas. The attention I receive from having hosted that bowling show so long ago has waxed and waned. Today I'm known among a certain set for having appeared in Adam Sandler's *Happy Gilmore*. This tender coming-of-age story is about a wannabe hockey player who learns he has a gift for golf.

My agent, Bob Rosen, called me and said, "There is a part for an announcer in this Adam Sandler movie, and I'm asking you if you want to go." And I said, "Well, sure, of course. When and where?" He said, "Well, in a month, and they want you in Vancouver, and they're only going to need a day." The producer sent a script to me.

I filmed it in one day. They had taken over an empty hospital that had been closed forever, and they did the crowd scenes in the backyard. And they did it the way you'd expect. I mean, they built a broadcast booth, and it was very comparable to what we use on the tour. I was there probably until four or five in the afternoon. And every scene I shot was done in that one day.

Believe me, I don't take my movie "stardom" too seriously. I didn't even back then in 1996, when I received the script. I opened it to find my lines and saw that the producers wanted to use Pat Summerall in the picture. How did I know that? Well, some poor production assistant had to use Wite-Out to get rid of Pat's name and then scribble in mine before sending it off. The shoot went well but the movie didn't do much at the box office.

That didn't stop my friends in Steamboat Springs from planning a premiere for me at our local cinema, a somewhat dingy remnant of the past when downtown theaters were popular. They planned to gather on the sidewalk in front of the place, wave flashlights into the air to simulate those huge spotlights. Nancy and I were to be driven to the location and get out of the car to the popping of flashbulbs or whatever the 1996 equivalent of that might have been. And speaking of what might have been, the movie never came to Steamboat, but I appreciated the thought and planning.

Years later, I was working for Turner Sports. I was in New York on a Sunday night to do a game with Pat Haden as my partner. Pat and I walked down toward one of the endzone tunnels to go up to our perch to do the broadcast. As we were walking, Pat said to me, "I'm really embarrassed for you."

I asked him why. He told me that he couldn't believe I took part in that horrible movie. I knew he was kidding but I played along.

"It's not horrible. It's just ahead of its time. You'll see. One day that thing is going to take off in popularity."

We kept walking and just as we were about to duck our heads to go into the tunnel, three teenage girls rose from their seats and shouted in unison, "Hey, Verne! Who the hell is Happy Gilmore?"

I looked at Pat and said, "What did I tell you?"

By the time 2005 rolled around and I was doing a North Carolina versus Arizona basketball game with Billy Packer in Tucson, I was nearly sick to death of hearing young people yell at me, "Who the hell is Happy Gilmore?" At a practice in the McHale Center, Billy and I were seated midway up the first section. Roy Williams was the coach and insisted that we media types keep our distance so we couldn't hear some of the things he said to his players. At the conclusion of practice, the team was on the court doing some stretching. I looked up and saw one of the assistants climbing the stairs toward our position. He said that the team hoped that "you" would come down to the court to answer a question. I assumed that the "you" in question was Billy Packer and said so. He shook his head. They wanted me. Unsuspecting, I followed the young man down. Tyler Hansbrough, an All-American on the team, looked up at me and said, "Mr. Lundquist, as a team, we would like to know your thoughts on Happy Gilmore, the golfer."

I knew what was up and said, "Who the hell is Happy Gilmore?!"

I facetiously added, "Now, if you win the national championship this year, I do expect a shout-out for having given you your first motivational speech."

They all laughed, and they did win the national title.

And I didn't get the shout-out.

It doesn't really matter. Every three or four months for the last thirteen years since then, I've gotten the shout-out in hotel lobbies, on the street, in airports, in stadiums, and field houses. *Happy Gilmore* is the gift that keeps on giving.

CHAPTER 14

Lasting Memories of the SEC

As a broadcaster you can't dwell for very long on any one event you cover. You always have to look forward and not back. Once a game is over, you have to take a kind of mental shower and let all the facts and figures, stories and images, wash from your brain. Like the athletes themselves, you can't dwell on a game for very long. Pat Haden called it the "game dump." You've got to clear the decks for the next one coming up. That was especially true during my time covering SEC football. Those weekly broadcasts and in general the high caliber of the play and the closeness of the competition made it impossible to dwell too long on any team or any one matchup. Certainly, some plays stood out, but in a game that saw coaches accelerating the pace of play, it was hard enough to fit in any commentary between plays, let alone sort them into mental folders for retrieval later.

I can't tell you the number of times I've been approached by someone who will mention a particular play from a particular game and ask me if I remember it. I'm sure I disappoint them when I get a bit glassy-eyed and blank of face. The thing about rat packing is that what seems valuable to one may not be of any particular use to another. As I said about that 2001 Florida versus Tennessee game, my lasting image is of Casey Clausen leading the band. When someone mentions one of his near interceptions in the game, I draw a bit of a blank and don't know what to say.

Perhaps it's because it's hard to remember everything that happens during four quarters of any game, or perhaps it's because as a broadcaster I'm always taking in what's going on both in front of the camera and behind the scenes. Part of being a broadcaster is recognizing what your audience wants and delivering as much of that to them as you can. I know, for instance, that some fans really like when we show a player's family and I deliver some story about that individual. I do a lot of research, reading, talking to players and coaches, hoping to glean from them nuggets that I can use that I think will add dimension to the broadcast.

In reviewing archival footage of the broadcasts, I've been struck by several things. Among them: We really do have to fill in quite a bit of time during a broadcast. Plays last a few seconds, many seconds lapse between plays, and with various time-outs, etc., the games themselves could take on a stuttering nature—like those old reel-to-reel films our teachers used to show us when the camera jittered and jumped. Our job is to steady that image, make the action feel continuous, give the appearance of spontaneity when much of it is planned out ahead of time, and make adjustments on the fly, since the action on the field is something we can't possibly anticipate fully beforehand.

I have to return to Gary Danielson and the role he plays in the broadcast. As is true of the coaches' meetings we hold, Gary is the one who drives the bus in our production meeting late on Friday before game day. I use that term in jest. We literally are on a bus converted to a television studio (driven by a very nice man named Mike Spears) that contains the needed electronics as well as a couple of couches. This rolling remote television studio goes from site to site and every Friday night during the season, our entire production crew gathers there for the meeting that Craig Silver leads.

Some of what's on the agenda is completely mundane—the schedule for the next day, how we're all getting out of town following the game. The highlight of the meeting is Gary giving us his insights, what he expects, based on his knowledge of both teams. What are their strengths? Where does he expect any opening opportunities to occur? Who might, for example, Auburn exploit or Alabama exploit? And that's usually a half an hour, and Gary does that every week. And then they ask me, "Do you have any particular stories you want to get in, and we'll try to fit them in." The director, Steve Milton, makes note of what I've come up with and during the game will cue me when appropriate to go to one of those stories. If it is one of those mom-in-the-stands stories, he gets the camera operator on board as well.

I'm often asked if it is hard to do a telecast with all those other voices in my head. The well-intentioned people who ask that don't fully understand the process. Yes, the producer, the director, the camera operators, the broadcasters, and nearly everyone else involved in the broadcast are all looped together in the same communications system. That doesn't mean that we're all able to hear and to speak with one another simultaneously. The technology allows for only certain communications to go to specific people at any one time. For example, Craig Silver, whom I worked with all seventeen years on the SEC broadcasts, when necessary communicates with Gary while I'm speaking on air. He may ask Gary what he wants to isolate for a particular play and he'll get the cameras to cover that. He may tell Gary that a ground-level shot is coming up on the replay. When he needs to speak with me, he does it while Gary is offering his commentary. I can't hear what he's saying to Gary, and vice versa. So, when Gary is delivering his analysis of a replay, Craig may be telling me that we need to do a promo after the following play if it isn't of any real significance. If it's a big play, we go to replay instead of the promo. Yes, I need to listen to what Gary has said about the play and what Craig has said to me, yet nearly everyone I know has the ability to filter and to focus. I hate to disappoint, but it's not as difficult as it seems. Conversations are taking place all around me, but I can dip into and blank them out with ease. We all do that all the time; I just get paid to do it.

My radio broadcasts were entirely different in this respect—I had no other communications going on except that between Brad Sham and me. It was similar in that during almost my entire Cowboy radio days, Gary Brandt was my producer. As I've pointed out before, continuity builds trust and comfort. As much as we could routinize things, the better. In that regard, we are very much like the athletes we cover. In so many other ways we are not like them at all. I never believed that I could do what they do. Athletes have demonstrated time and time again that they can do what I do, and I think that one of the reasons for that, besides their knowledge of the game, is their ability to focus, develop routines, and execute under pressure.

One former SEC athlete turned broadcaster whom I admire and respect and has become a friend is Charles Barkley. He absolutely loves Auburn athletics. I've done a bunch of Auburn football and basketball games and seen Charles there in the stands or along the sidelines. I would say that 50 percent of the time he would make the trek down. We always saw him at the bar the night before the game. And then if I stayed overnight following the game, especially if they won, I'd see him at the bar the night after the game.

I've heard Charles on the air stating unequivocally that there's no greater rivalry in sports than Alabama versus Auburn. What I love about Charles is that he's a passionate sports fan, as so many of the athletes I've worked with and covered are, and he's not afraid (surprise!) to express his opinion about it. His statement is quite something when you consider those who believe that in baseball the Yankees versus the Red Sox or the Chicago Cubs and the St. Louis Cardinals form *the* rivalry that defines all rivalries. I'll stop my list there because I know that everyone has their list of the fiercest rivalries in sports. We love to debate that issue. What I found most engaging about Charles's point is that he's a fan and in one particular instance decried the fact that Marshall and West Virginia flat-out refuse to schedule one another.

That intrastate rivalry would be wonderful to see and would generate incredible interest. Why they don't engage in it is complicated but the bottom line, as Charles pointed out and I agree, is that those games help keep interest alive and in fact grow the sport. He also said that schools not playing those kinds of games cheat the fans. With advertising revenues what they are, it is sometimes easy for networks to forget that the fans are truly the ones whose needs and desires should be served. At the end of the day, we all make our living off their passionate devotion.

Charles understands that these are athletic contests but also entertainment. As our technological capabilities have advanced, fans have many more options regarding when and to what they will devote their time. I think that is why the NCAA basketball tournament is such a huge draw for so many. To see teams from different conferences mixing it up has huge appeal. Most football programs schedule nonconference games that guarantee wins for the bigger program. The little guys benefit financially and gain some exposure, but the competition is seldom compelling. The rare upsets are wonderful, but it is the conference schedule that really matters. I can't envision the NCAA conducting a full-scale championship-determining tournament to crown a winner in football. They've made strides toward doing that, and that's a good thing. It helps preserve some of the traditional rivalries. I'm a sports fan, too, and I have fond memories of the bowl games as they once were, with conference champion taking on conference champion. The powers that be have made progress in clarifying as much as possible who will end up the national champion in football, and that's a good thing, but I sometimes wonder, at what cost?

One of the benefits of not having a national tournament is that with there being no second season, as the playoffs are often referred to in other sports, what you do during the regular season carries enormous consequences. As I've said before, when I'm asked about my most memorable games, the so-called classics, I always choose games that have a direct impact on the ultimate results in the SEC race and for the national championship. Given the SEC's track record, those two are frequently entwined. A battle that comes to mind that is nearly the opposite of the Tennessee–Florida game is one that the Volunteers waged against the Crimson Tide in 2009.

Tennessee was down a bit that year under Lane Kiffin. They came into the late October contest at Bryant-Denny Stadium with a record of three wins and three losses. That, plus the fact that Alabama was the consensus No. 1 team in the country and coming off a great 2008 season, meant few expected Alabama to have any trouble toppling Tennessee in this third week in October game. Again, as much as we talked about matchups and tendencies and all the rest, I was eager to let the game unfold and tell the story that it wanted to be told. What it stated was that this was going to be one of those defensive struggles that some find fascinating and others dismiss as boring. It was definitely not the latter.

Kirby Smart, now the head coach at Georgia, was Nick Saban's defensive coordinator. He had a talented bunch to work with, including Butkis and Lambert award–winning linebacker Roland McClain. As fast and tough as they come, the All-American McClain epitomized the SEC players' best qualities. Along with him, defensive lineman Terrence Cody was another anchor of a stout defense that wound up as the second-ranked overall defensive unit in Division I football. Tennessee's defense finished the season with the 22nd-rated overall defense. Among those they had to contend with was running back Mark Ingram, who was the first Crimson Tide player to win the Heisman Trophy. On the strength of three Leigh Tiffin (no relation to the Tennessee coach Lane Tiffin) field goals, Alabama was up, 9–3, at the half. The third period was scoreless, but in the fourth, Tennessee's Jonathan Crompton hooked up with Denarius Moore on a 31-yard pass play to set up a Daniel Lincoln field goal attempt of 43 yards. Big number 62, Terrence Cody, got a hand on it to block it. The ball wound up in the arms of the holder, who was swarmed under, and Alabama took over. They kicked another field goal to make the score 12–3.

The Vols recovered a Mark Ingram fumble and scored a touchdown with 1:19 left in the game. The extra point pulled them within two at 12–10. I love onside-kick scenarios going all the way back to my days with the Cowboys and their Austrian kicker Toni Fritsch. Most often you know the onside kick is coming, both teams line up for it, and depending upon how that oblong ball bounces, or doesn't, the future of the game is up for grabs. In this case, Tennessee managed to recover. A couple of Crompton passes, one to Gerald Jones (who earlier caught a touchdown pass) and another to Luke Stocker, set them at the Alabama 28. With four ticks left on the clock, Kiffin sent out his kicker for a 44-yard attempt to take the lead.

My simple call told the story: "Blocked again! Cody again! Alabama wins!"

As Nick Saban would say after, "That's how fragile a season can be."

On the depth chart and on our boards, he was listed as Terrence Cody, but everybody in Tuscaloosa referred to him as Mount Cody. At six feet, five inches and 345 pounds, Terrence certainly was a man-mountain. Alabama was in its "max block" mode and unlike the first one, when Cody leaped in the air, he simply overpowered his blocker. Cory Sullins weighed 84 pounds less than Mount Cody and was leveled by the avalanche.

Replays showed that Mount Cody didn't even have to leave his feet in order to block his second kick of the game. He pulled off his helmet and ran downfield with his dreadlocks flying behind him looking very much like *he* was fleeing an avalanche. As we wrapped the game up and then prepared to leave the stadium, it sounded as if no one had left the stadium yet. They chanted their hero's last name loud and long. After speaking briefly with Tracy Wolfson he made his way toward the tunnel with his left index finger in the air. He understood the moment and in a locker room interview told a reporter, "After I blocked the thing, I knew I was like a big hero."

A Florida native and a product of Gulf Coast Community College, Mount Cody was always too big to play in his local Pop Warner league. As a high school freshman, he was already six feet, two inches tall and weighed nearly 300 pounds. He played as a ninth grader but then sat out for the next two years due to poor grades. One of eight kids, according to his high school coach, Cody fell in with the wrong crowd. He righted himself and was able to play again as a senior. As a result of his limited experience, he attended that community college before accepting a scholarship offer at Alabama. Nick Saban personally visited him, telling him how invaluable he would be in the middle of their 3-4 defense. He went on to become a second-round draft pick of the Baltimore Ravens and played for them for three years before ending his career.

Alabama fans loved him, and one reporter fondly recalled Cody picking him up (the man weighed 275 pounds himself), tossing him on his shoulder, and carrying him into the Alabama locker room. I dislike stereotypes and the jolly fat man is one of those, but by all accounts Terrence was as jovial a presence in the locker room as he was fierce on the playing field. Alabama fans have dubbed his last-second effort "the Rocky Block," another indication of the bitterness of the SEC rivalries. He's become another of the legends and I appreciate the fact that I was there to see his efforts in person. In sports we often talk about how the little things made a difference in a game; in the case of Mount Cody it was two big things that clearly made the difference between a win and a loss, producing a profound impact on Bama's season. The Crimson Tide would go on to their first-ever BCS championship and their thirteenth national championship. They also ran the table, going 14-0.

Some might wonder how such a low-scoring contest could fit into my best of all-time SEC games. I think it's pretty clear that the dramatic ending had a lot to do with it. I recall that as the Alabama team celebrated and the Tennessee players looked disconsolate or stunned, we let the pictures tell the story. That's become a bit of a cliché, but as is the case with other clichés, it has become one because of its essential truth. The first words that Gary Danielson uttered after that long string of images wasn't the most articulate expression ever. He said, "Wow." I think his echoing of what a lot of fans were saying and thinking was appropriate and linked him to them. I appreciate and admire that style. There's always the temptation to go for the profound or the insightful, but I learned that letting the moment sink in, letting the viewers have a chance to just see the events unfold, reproduces to a degree what happens when you're at the game itself.

I also know that you won't please all the viewers, and that's okay. I do take it personally when I hear criticisms of other commentators. We're a relatively small bunch and to one degree or another we all know one another. So when a sports fan goes after one of us, I feel like he or she is coming after all of us. I don't always agree with the approach that my colleagues take but I defend their right to take it. For example, Brent Musburger, one of the biggest figures we've had in the profession, would frequently make references related to gambling—even direct mentions of the point spread. I would not do that, but he would. So would another great, Al Michaels. That doesn't detract from their legacy and consummate skill.

I'm especially protective of my broadcast partners. They made that job easier by so seldom doing anything that needed defending. Danielson is one of the finest analysts to ever work a college football game, and we were privileged to be on hand to cover so many extraordinary games. I also know that I've never done a game in which I didn't commit some error or two. Fortunately, with all the high-quality games the SEC produced, those bobbles won't go down in history; the play on the field will.

The 2011 LSU versus Alabama game, touted as a "Game of the Century" because No. 1 LSU squared off against No. 2 Alabama, ended with a score of 9–6. As one of my top five, this game didn't feature a lot of offensive production, but because it was of such great consequence for the national title picture and featured so many compelling moments, I find it extremely memorable. Gary and I both scratched our heads when we heard from other people and read about it being boring. The outcome was in doubt until the very end, and for me, that counts for a lot. There are many forms of drama and this battle had great tension.

It should have come as no surprise to anyone, really, that it was a low-scoring affair. Both teams came into the first week of November with outstanding defenses. Alabama would finish out the season ranked first in total defense, scoring defense, passing defense, and rushing defense. LSU would finish ranked second in those first two categories and not far behind in the others. Gary and I got our first look at Alabama on September 24 when they took on a very good Arkansas team at home. They won, 38–14, to open their SEC conference play. On their first scoring drive, Nick Saban and his staff rolled the dice on a field goal attempt with holder (and quarterback) A. J. McCarron taking the snap and then rising up to throw a 37-yard touchdown pass to Michael Williams. The Crimson Tide broke it open in the third quarter.

The following week, we were in Gainesville and watched as Saban took on his former assistant Will Muschamp and his Gators. After a tight 10–10 first quarter, Alabama rolled to a 38–10 victory over the No. 12 team in the country. Gary and I were both very impressed with

Alabama, especially considering they were coming off what was for them a subpar 2010 season that saw them finish with a 10–3 record and outside the top ten in the final Coaches' Poll and only No. 16 in the end of the regular season BCS standings. Clearly Alabama had reloaded and matured.

LSU's previous season told a similar tale, with an 11–2 record and hovering at or just outside of the top ten in the major polls and standings. With Alabama moving on to play Vanderbilt and Ole Miss, we got our first look at LSU on October 8 in Baton Rogue against Florida. LSU got a lot of people's attention early in the season. Their opening game, rather than taking on a nonconference creampuff, was against Oregon. The Ducks were coming off an undefeated regular season in 2010 and, at No. 3, were ranked one slot ahead of the Tigers in the preseason polls. They participated in the Cowboy Classic in Arlington, with LSU coming out on top, 40–27. They held the vaunted Ducks' running game to fewer than 100 yards. After a breather against Northwestern State, they defeated two ranked teams on the road. Those victories propelled them to the top of the AP poll.

That afternoon in Gainesville, they dismantled another ranked team, tromping on Florida, 41–11. They then beat Tennessee and Auburn, the previous year's undefeated BCS national champion, by a combined score of 83–17. For the season, their average margin of victory was 27.5 points. The Tide were even better, mixing in two shutouts; they had beaten their previous 8 opponents by an average of 32.5 points. They had not allowed more than 14 points; LSU had surrendered 48 points in its wins over Oregon and West Virginia, but in their other six games had only given up 54.

As is so often said, something had to give.

CBS also had to give. We'd previously shown the Alabama–Florida game in prime time. With so much anticipation about this "Game of the Century," originally scheduled for a two thirty kickoff, the powers that be made a deal with other networks to get the game moved into prime time. The move would prove to be a wise one, some 20 million viewers tuned in, and the game earned a 11.5 Nielsen rating, the highest non-bowl-game rating the company had since 1989.

I said earlier in recounting some of my first days onstage and on the air that I never got nervous. People have frequently asked me if I got a case of the jitters before a big game like this one. The answer is no. I feel some of the anticipation that comes from having a great matchup, but after so many games, and doing so much preparation work, I'm too busy focusing and have done this enough times that I come into the game calm.

For as much preparation work as we all do, I also come into the game without expectations of what kind of contest it is going to be. Sure, we talk about tendencies and provide our audience with a set of elements to watch out for, but personally, as a play-by-play guy I have to do what many players say about participating in the game itself: I have to let the game come to me. That means that I never "rehearse" a line that I hope I can squeeze in or anything like that. The ebb and flow of the game encourages a kind of spontaneity and that's what I hope to bring to every broadcast. That's true for whenever the game is being played.

I do know this: if the game had been played in Baton Rogue, the LSU faithful would have been grateful for the opportunity to spend a few more hours consuming before kickoff. As it was, I'm sure they did so in the southern comfort of their own homes or a local establishment. Whenever we were in Baton Rogue, we prepared for a certain level of rowdiness that was seldom exceeded anywhere else we traveled.

In acknowledgment of the extensive buildup to the game, as the Tigers' place-kicker approached the football for the opening kickoff, I timed my words with his steps: "At . . . long . . . last!"

To illustrate my point about letting the game come to me, I didn't enter the booth that Saturday prepared with a bunch of statistics or stories about the two kickers who would ultimately figure so largely in the game's outcome. I didn't prepare some memorable lines related to kicking, booting, shanking, or anything of that kind. No one could have predicted how the game would be determined by missed field goals. That's part of the joy of watching and broadcasting a game—the unexpected. If I had the ability to see into the future, I might have made more of the fact that Odell Beckham—I didn't use the "junior" part of his name—made a catch early in the game.

Of course, the story line for the game as it unfolded proved to be the kicking game. Alabama's Cade Foster missed field goals on Alabama's first two drives. Forgotten in that is that on the first two plays of the game, Alabama gained 40 yards on a Trent Richardson run and Trent Richardson reception. The drive stalled and Foster pushed his kick wide right. Before that, Gary pointed out that in their previous matchup in 2010 only three points had been scored—by LSU. Foster's next miss was a 50-yarder that was also wide right. Gary questioned whether it had the length and we agreed it was short. Alabama was moving the ball with Richardson and Eddie Lacey and a few McCarron passes sprinkled in, but they just couldn't convert on crucial third downs.

Early in the second quarter, Alabama looked to take advantage of the first turnover the Tigers had committed in five games—a Jarrett Lee interception. Gary and I wondered on-air if the first-quarter issues would affect Alabama's play call on third-and-18 from the LSU thirty-one. They appeared to want to go deep, but good coverage combined with a nice rush forced McCarron out of the pocket and he threw the ball away, setting up the field goal attempt.

Following Cade Foster's two misses, Nick Saban used his other place-kicker, Jeremy Shelley, to attempt a 49-yarder. Shelley was 11 of 13 on the season and was generally used on shorter attempts. The kick never had a chance. LSU blocked it and Ed Reid picked the ball out of the air and returned the miss into Alabama territory. Gary pointed out that this was a case of expecting a player to do too much. Shelley was their short guy and in trying to extend his range, he kicked the ball too low. As we went to commercial, Gary said that Nick had gone for the field goal three times and was 0-3.

In isolation, I suppose, Alabama fans could use that as an example of their view that Gary was biased against them or against Nick. I have no idea how many words either of us spoke during that broadcast, and I pull them out of context here just to give you some sense of how these things get done all the time. I suppose that timing is everything. Having gone to commercial more of a period was put on the statement that went out to 20 million people with just as many opinions and perspectives. In any case, while it is literally true that Nick didn't make those attempts, his players had and the game remained scoreless.

Finally, with exactly five minutes to go before halftime, Jeremy Shelley made a 34-yard field goal to break the scoreless tie. Alabama had been pinned back on their own four-yard line and their most sustained drive of the day turned into three points. LSU came right back. Jordan Jefferson came in to relieve Lee at quarterback. Les Miles had inserted Jefferson into the game at a similar point the previous year and Gary speculated that with time dwindling in the first half, the LSU coach was hoping that Jefferson could "get his sea legs."

The Tigers, again employing some fourth-down magic, had bested Alabama in a stirring comeback to win that game, 24–21. After that one, the quirky Miles explained why he chewed and swallowed some LSU grass just before that fourth-down gamble. He said it humbled him and made him feel like he was part of the game, the field. He also added that he did that all the time and LSU's was the most flavorful.

Mainly sticking to the ground game, Jefferson got the Tigers into field goal position with time nearly expired in the half. The quarterback's big play was a 29-yarder that got the Tigers down to the Alabama four-yard line with forty-five seconds left. Even with an Alabama penalty getting them to the two-yard line, they couldn't punch it in. They settled for a 19-yard Drew Alleman field goal and went to the half knotted up at 3. It was as enjoyable a half of football as I could ask for.

Just before the action resumed, I asked Gary what had surprised him about the first half, and he pointed out three missed defensive assignments: two on LSU and one on Alabama that had resulted in long gains. Add in the three missed field goals and the two interceptions and I can agree that the level of execution wasn't outstanding, but the intensity of the game play and what was at stake overrode that. Lots of games are mistake filled but this one didn't lack for other outstanding plays—they just didn't produce points.

The second half played out much as the first one had. Alabama took the lead on a Cade Foster field goal following Lee's second interception. Foster missed another one. LSU had a tremendous opportunity following a Morris Claiborne interception and return set them up at the Alabama fifteen. Alabama's defense kept them out of the end zone but a Drew Alleman short field goal tied the game at 6–6 just as the fourth quarter had begun. On the ensuing drive, something curious took place. Trent Richardson, who had 104 total yards of offense in the first half, had been held to 10 in the second to that point. We made note of that just before he took a handoff and ripped a slashing, bruising run 24 yards down to the LSU twenty-eight.

Things got a bit weird after that. An LSU lineman was injured so we went to a commercial break during the official time-out. When we came back, we presented a package showing highlights of various turnovers that played a crucial role in the games played between the two clubs. On the very next play, on first down, Marquis Maze, who suffered a leg injury early on and was clearly slowed by it, took the snap from the wildcat formation. Instead of running, he looked downfield. Tight end Michael Williams broke free near the goal line, but Ed Reid hustled over and was able to take the ball away.

The interception call went to replay and was upheld. At first we had called it a reception, but upon review it was clear that Reid had taken the ball away while both players were going to the ground. It was debatable and we spent some time talking about the call as well as how it happened. The ball was in the air a bit too long. Reid was covering another Alabama receiver who crossed the field bringing Reid with him and enabling him to close the gap on Williams. All in all, it was a brilliant defensive play in a game filled with them. As Gary said, "a bit of unintended consequences" of the play's design brought Reid into the picture to defend the pass. What we didn't get into was to question the choice of call. Rather than second-guess, we praised Reid for coming off his man to make the pick. We left the Sunday morning coaching to the fans and the radio call-in men and women who no doubt burned up the phone lines and the airwaves questioning the wisdom of the play selection.

Coaching is a tough business. If Maze's pass had been complete and Alabama punched it in from inside the goal line, the play would have gone down in Alabama history, another golden moment. It didn't and Nick Saban and the rest of the Crimson Tide coaching staff and players had to live with the consequences. Imagine if every choice you make at work fell under the scrutiny of millions?

Still, Alabama was in great shape. They had the Tigers pinned against their own goal line. I said that we do a lot of preparation but you can't do too much anticipation. Here's where the two met. After two short running plays, the Tigers faced third down and six. Gary reminded viewers that in the previous year's game, LSU faced a similar kind of situation with Jefferson at quarterback. He threw then on third down. This time LSU ran and was stopped short. The punting unit came on the field. Gary pointed out that the defense was playing well and they couldn't afford a mistake that deep in their own territory. He agreed with the call to punt.

Alabama's Maze, who'd just thrown the interception, was back deep to receive. The Australian punter, Brad Wing, got his left foot into a beauty and sailed it over the head of Maze, who was standing just inside his own territory. The ball wound up at the Alabama eighteen. Credit Wing with a mammoth 73-yard punt. We both commented that Maze's bad ankle likely came into play. He had to catch that ball and he didn't. Later, in a locker room interview, Maze stated that his ankle had nothing to do with it. He said that the ball had hit a wire that ran across the field supporting one of our cameras. I don't want to question the young man's motives or sound like I'm defending the network, but what we saw was him struggling to make a turn on his bad leg. The resulting loss of thirty yards of field position was undeniable.

No matter the cause, strange and interesting things were taking place that night in Tuscaloosa.

We were going to overtime and there's always high drama inherent in that. LSU got to call the coin flip, chose tails, and won. They elected to go on defense. Unsurprisingly, Alabama chose to take the ball at the 25-yard line nearest their student section. We recapped some of the kicking foibles, Gary again praised Ed Reid for his remarkably alert play, and then he reminded everyone of the 2008 game that was tied at 21–21 when Jarrett Lee was intercepted on first down. The Crimson Tide came on the field.

Incompletion intended for Trent Richardson. (A drop.)

A five-yard illegal substitution infraction on Alabama.

Incompletion intended for Trent Richardson. (Richardson was open; the ball wasn't there.)

A sack of Trent Richardson at the Alabama thirty-five.

Alabama field goal attempt.

A bad snap.

Cade Foster hooked one. The ball traveled side to side instead of end to end, and the sad saga of Cade Foster continued.

We had a game to call and things to think about, but still, though the words went unspoken on-air, I had to feel for him. Four missed field goals. Can you imagine?

The rest was almost anticlimactic. LSU drove down to the eight. Alabama called time-out to freeze the kicker. LSU went for the field goal on third down so in case something happened they'd have another opportunity on fourth down.

Drew Alleman drilled the 25-yard field goal and the game was over.

All I could say was "LSU remains undefeated." And later, "My oh, my!"

Les was gracious and straightforward in his postgame interview with Tracy. When asked his feeling about a rematch with Alabama for it all, he said, "I would be honored to face that team again."

Everything fell in place for that to happen. The LSU–Alabama rematch for the BCS championship saw the Crimson Tide take the title, 21–0.

That was a story for someone else to tell.

When the joy of the unexpected, a game of critical importance to the national picture, and an intense rivalry combine, you get my favorite all-time classic SEC game. That happened in 2013 when Auburn and Alabama met in another Iron Bowl clash of the titans. Alabama came into the game as the two-time defending national championship, and apologies to the Los Angeles Lakers' Pat Riley, they were seeking a three-peat. It was the seventy-eighth edition of the confrontation between the intrastate rivals and a lot more than just bragging rights was on the line. Alabama was undefeated and ranked No. 1 in the nation. Auburn came in at No. 4. They were experiencing a remarkable turnaround season. In 2012 they'd finished at 3–9, including a hard-to-fathom 0–8 record in the SEC that had their fans sinking to the depths of despair. Perhaps worse than any of that, Alabama had wiped them out in the previous year's Iron Bowl by a score of 49–0. Add in the 2011 game and for the past two seasons Alabama had hammered their Iron Bowl opponents by a 91–14 margin.

Gene Chizik was fired after that lowly season and Gus Malzahn left Tulsa to take the helm of a ship that sank about as far as possible. Malzahn had spent much of his life as a high school coach, and when he was at Springdale High School in Arkansas he had a kid who was regarded as maybe the best quarterback in the country, Mitch Mustain. Mustain had been recruited by Houston Nutt at Arkansas. As these things sometimes go, Gus came along as part of the package as offensive coordinator. And that's when he had his first college football coaching job. Gus and Houston Nutt had a warm relationship, I think, for the most part. But then Gus decided to move on, and he wound up at Tulsa as head coach. I knew him pretty well and thought very highly of him.

Auburn came into the game with one loss, a 35–21 defeat at the hands of the LSU Tigers. Still, their fate was in their own hands. They could win the SEC West title if they beat Alabama. As the saying goes, they controlled their own destiny.

Barely.

On November 15, we were in Jordan Hare stadium as the Tigers took on 25th-ranked Georgia. Auburn blew a 27–7 lead and with only twenty-five seconds left to go, they trailed the Bulldogs, 38–37. From their own 27 on fourth-and-18, their quarterback, Nick Marshall, dropped back to pass. He stepped up in the pocket and instead of going for a first-down toss, he went deep into the Georgia secondary. Two men were back for the Bulldogs and the ball seemed certain to be intercepted or at least knocked down. Instead it bounced off one of the defenders and into the hands of Ricardo Louis at about the Georgia ten-yard line. He went in untouched. Gary and I were astounded.

"Talk about a Hail Mary," I said.

"Play of the year," Gary added.

Upon replay Gary saw that one of the Georgia defenders had knocked the ball out of the hands of his teammate and into the air, where Louis grabbed it.

As Gary said at the time, "It bounced into the air for the most improbable touchdown you'll ever see."

A few moments later, he called it "a miracle of miracles."

Some called it the Immaculate Deflection, others the Prayers at Jordan-Hare, but no matter what, it was a sight to see. One person who almost didn't see it was Ricardo Louis. He was beyond the two defenders when they collided and admitted that he lost sight of the ball. It seemed to descend from the heavens, then came over his shoulder and into his arms. He bobbled it for a moment but then hung on.

How could you top that ending to the game?

Georgia nearly did. They drove down to the Auburn twenty and only a game-saving tackle by Auburn's Dee Ford kept slogan makers from working double overtime. As we wrapped up the telecast, Gary said, "That's the greatest finish I've ever seen. You'll never see another one like it."

It took two weeks.

In the Iron Bowl, on a late November day that I described as one that could not be more perfect, Alabama took the opening kickoff. They drove down to the Auburn 34-yard line but were stopped. Cade Foster came in and missed a 44-yard field goal. It was only his second miss of the season. We didn't bring up his previous kicking troubles against LSU. The only score of the quarter was quarterback Nick Marshall's 45-yard touchdown run, Auburn's first offensive touchdown against the Tide since 2010.

Most of the second quarter belonged to Alabama. They ran off

21 straight points on their first three possessions of the period—two A. J. McCarron touchdown passes and a T. J. Yeldon one-yard plunge. Auburn came back with an impressive 7-play, 81-yard drive in just over two minutes. The half ended with them trailing, 21–14. To that point under Nick Saban, Alabama was 73–3 when leading at the half. Auburn didn't seem to care about those kinds of statistics. It took the opening drive of the second half and, mixing up Nick Marshall and Tre Mason rushes with the occasional pass, including a 13-yard touchdown to C. J. Uzomah, they quickly tied it. The quarter ended with Alabama poised to score in Auburn's red zone at the eleven-yard line. It was an impressive drive that began at their own one-yard line.

At the start of the final period, McCarron's two incompletions and a catch that only produced one yard brought out the field goal unit. Foster came on. The snap was good and he booted it through for what appeared to be a 28-yard field goal. It wasn't. Before the snap we'd heard the official's whistle. One of Alabama's interior linemen had moved on the play. After watching the replay, Gary and I both questioned whether there was movement.

Regardless, the five-yard penalty made Foster's next attempt a 33-yarder, still well within his range. He yanked it left by a wide margin. At those moments you have to stick to the game as it is happening on the field. I reminded viewers that if there was movement on the successful attempt, it was "imperceptible." At the time and in reviewing the game later, my heart did go out to Foster. How could it not? His struggles were nearly Sisyphean in scope. He finally made one in a big game and it was called back because of a penalty. He missed another. We didn't bring up that previous debacle, but I had to say something. When we went to replay, Gary talked about how poor the effort was, and it was poor, but I said, "I don't want to put too much on his shoulders, but—" And brought up the previous kick and the questionable penalty call.

I have to be impartial, and if that statement crossed a line, I can live with that. The young man would later receive death threats and other harassing and denigrating comments from so-called fans. He'd have another kick blocked in the fourth quarter. I hate to mention that, because it may sound as though that's further justification for him being vilified by some. It doesn't. It is just flat-out wrong for anyone to express his or her disappointment and anger in that way. We all make mistakes and we should accept criticism for that, but some carry things too far.

I got criticized on a talk show in Dallas when I was doing the Cowboys. The caller said, "You know, you assume a familiarity with the Cowboys that I find offensive. With the opposition, you always refer to the people on the other side of the ball by their last names or their full names. But you have familiarity with the Cowboys that is irritating and aggravating. It's never Staubach. It's always Roger. It's never Dorsett. It's always Tony. It's never Cliff Harris. It's always Cliff. Or Charlie Waters is Charlie." And I said, "No, I don't do that." And he said, "I challenge you to listen to a tape." For a while, I didn't do what he asked. Eventually I did. He was right.

When Jackie Smith dropped the pass against Pittsburgh in Super Bowl XIII, and I've heard it a hundred times, I kind of wince. I did say, "Roger takes the snap and drops back."

And later I said, "And Jackie drops it in the end zone, bless his heart."

So the guy was right, but I couldn't see it.

That's fair criticism on his part. I took it personally at the time, but it never got out of hand.

Enough said. I'd rather talk about the great things.

At 10:42 of the fourth quarter, Auburn's Steven Clark pinned the Tide deep in their own territory at the one-yard line with a punt. A great play, but that was the second time in a row he'd done that to Alabama, eliciting from me a drawn out "Oh-my-gosh." I love those moments when an unheralded player, not someone who you think might make a real difference in the game, comes on and seizes the moment.

Given the score and everything that was on the line, you'd have expected Alabama to play conservatively and run the ball out from beneath the proverbial shadow of their own goal line. Instead, they ran a play-action pass. McCarron faked the run, dropped back to pass. As the ball was in the air I said, "How about this call?" The ball settled into the arms of Amari Cooper, who shrugged off one defender and was gone. How the Tide had turned in the ball game. The longest pass play in Alabama history put them up, 28–21.

How could you top that?

Auburn took over following the kickoff with ten minutes remaining in the game. From their own twenty-six, they ran off three plays that netted nine yards. They appeared to be well short, but a measurement was called for to confirm that. While the official did that, Tracy reported from the sidelines that a sewing machine had been brought out so that an Auburn player's jersey could be repaired. As I told her, I've been doing this a long time and I'd never seen that before. From the sublime to the ridiculous.

"Only in the SEC," I added.

Gary asked aloud what he thought Auburn might do.

"Try to sew it up," I said.

Auburn was short of the marker. Facing fourth-and-one from their own 35, they went for it. Gary pointed out that they were the second-ranked rushing team in the nation and agreed with Gus Malzahn's decision.

Alabama stopped them.

Wow. With the game still 28–21, the Crimson Tide took over at the Auburn thirty-five. Even if they gained no yards, they were within field goal range. T. J. Yeldon got them 13 yards closer on a first-down run. He would get them only 9 more on the next two attempts. Auburn's defense rose up and stopped them for no gain. Facing fourth-and-one from the thirteen-yard line, Saban had a choice: attempt a field goal and extend the lead to ten points or go for it in hopes of administering a potential knockout punch. He went for it. We both agreed that we would have been shocked if he brought in Foster at that point. Gary for the first time made mention of the 9–6 loss. McCarron handed off to T. J. Yeldon. Auburn's interior line got a great push. Yeldon tried to bounce it outside but couldn't.

Auburn ball.

The Tigers couldn't move it. A huge sack on a first-down roll-of-the-dice blitz pushed them back to their own five-yard line. Marshall overthrew everybody on second down. On third they went for it all. Ricardo Louis broke free down the right sideline and Marshall saw him. The ball was barely long. No Prayer at Jordan-Hare this time, but miss by just a hair.

Stephen Clark's 39-yard punt was returned by Christian Jones 19 yards to the Auburn twenty-five. All the action seemed to be taking place on one end of the field. Could Alabama put it away? A Yeldon rush for no gain, an 8-yard completion to Cooper, a holding call on Alabama, and another incompletion put the ball on the Auburn twenty-seven. It was fourth down and 12. Too risky to try to convert, so Nick Saban sent Foster out onto the field to attempt the 44-yarder. It was blocked. We all love tales of redemption but this was not that story. As I said, "The nightmare continues for Cade Foster." To make matters worse for Alabama, they put a late hit on the man who recovered the ball. Auburn took over on their own 35 with about two and a half minutes left.

Auburn, which employed an up-tempo style, managed to get off six running plays in the next minute and a half. From the Alabama thirty-nine, on first down, Marshall faked a handoff up the middle, ran left, and just before reaching the line of scrimmage tossed one to Sammi Coates, who was all alone along the sideline. The frenetic pace, the relentless runs had the Alabama defense back on its heels, and the triple option worked to perfection for Auburn. The roar of the crowd at Jordan-Hare couldn't resurrect my hair, but it did Auburn's hopes of advancing to the SEC title game. The extra point knotted it, and most would have expected that the game was going to go to overtime.

How could you top that?

Following a short kickoff, twenty-five seconds were left. On first down, McCarron was pressured and had to throw the ball away. On the next play, a draw was good for nine yards. Rather than let the remaining seven seconds run off the clock, Alabama called a time-out. At that point it seemed like a case of no harm, no foul. An interception or a fumble might be ruinous, but this was a veteran Alabama team well schooled in the art of holding on to the ball. In reference to the Prayer at Jordan-Hare, Gary jokingly recommended that Alabama run the "tip play."

It seemed unlikely that the game would turn on these last seven seconds, so, as the coaches talked with their players, I filled in the time with a story about the passion of the SEC fan bases. One time Nancy and I were driving from Tuscaloosa to Atlanta. We stopped for lunch in a local eatery in Oxford, Alabama. After our meal, we bought two coffee mugs—an Auburn one and an Alabama one. When we brought them up to the register to pay, the young woman looked at them and then said, "Are these gifts or are you a split family?"

We laughed. We'd heard the expression before, and knew how true it rang in the Yellowhammer State.

Things turned more serious as we discussed Cade Foster as he prowled the sideline. Given his troubles in the game, Gary felt that in overtime Alabama would be at a disadvantage. Would they be forced to go for a touchdown instead of a field goal? How would that affect their strategy?

Out of time-outs, we expected the Hail Mary pass; instead, Yeldon ran right, found some daylight, and was knocked out of bounds by Chris Davis, seemingly in time. He'd picked up 24 yards and got the ball down to the Auburn thirty-eight. The officials, though, signaled that time had run out. I stated again that I thought that he'd crossed the boundary with a second to go. Gary reminded viewers that the call was reviewable. Saban challenged the ruling. While he was conferring with the officials and they were making their determination, Gary said, "If they put one second on, obviously, they'll get one Hail Mary throw into the end zone." He wasn't alone in making a premature statement. The public address announcer, Matt Olsen, announced that the game was going to overtime. The Auburn faithful held up five fingers, indicating the fifth quarter.

It wasn't going to overtime just yet.

Time dragged on as the play was reviewed. We watched it again in slow-motion replay. Gary believed that time had expired. He said that he saw that Yeldon's foot was in the air as zeroes showed on the clock. I agreed. The slow-motion replay finally got to the point Gary had mentioned. We were wrong. It showed one second left. Gary reminded viewers that the rules stated that time stopped not when a runner broke an imaginary plane rising from the boundary but when it came down to contact the ground.

Just as he was correcting himself, the lead official, referee Matt Austin, came on to tell much of America, a Nielsen-rated 11.8, that regulation play was in fact not concluded. The replay official would make the call.

We waited. Gary brought up the field goal misses. We waited. We reminded viewers that what was at stake was Alabama's Hail Mary attempt. The possibility to go to Atlanta. A third national championship?

Our synced split view showed that there was indeed one second left. The replay official concurred. First down Alabama at the Auburn thirty-nine. One second remained.

While we waited for Alabama's offense to come out, Gary stated that if any defense in the country should know to knock down a pass that late in the game, it was Auburn's. They'd seen what happened a few weeks earlier to Georgia's secondary.

Gary sounded incredulous when he learned that the kicking team was coming out.

I was glad that I'd done my homework and so had my spotter. I told viewers that Nick Saban had sent out Adrian Griffin instead of Cade Foster to do the kicking. I remembered that he was a red-shirt freshman out of Calhoun, Georgia. He was 1-for-2 in his career. This was to be his third-ever field goal attempt. (Astute readers will note that it was not Adrian Griffin, as I said on air, but Adam Griffith.)

Auburn called a timeout. My spotter, Butch Baird, reminded me of the fact that in 1985, Van Tiffen had kicked a 52-yarder to win the Iron Bowl, one of the legendary moments in that great sports tradition. Gary mentioned that a blocked kick could be returned. The ball was snapped, the kick went up, and only then did I mention the presence of Chris Davis. He caught the ball nine yards deep in the end zone just to the right of the left upright and took off. He got a couple of blocks, headed down the right sideline, and was off to Auburn glory.

"Touchdown Auburn! An answered prayer!" I shouted.

"There are no flags," I added.

My heart skipped a beat. Was that right? Had I fallen victim to the anticipation goblin?

A moment later I could resume normal operation. There were no flags.

For a minute and twenty-one seconds Gary and I let the pictures tell the story.

During that time, Steve Milton, who should have been given an Emmy for his work but was not, made twenty-one camera cuts in which he visually told an absolutely compelling story of victory and defeat. His brilliant sequence of camera cuts ranged from the elation of the Auburn fans to a young kid from Alabama sitting there with a dazed look on his face. The whole camera team captured the moments perfectly.

I have to give more credit where credit is due. Rob Bramblett of the Auburn IMG Sports Network nailed it. After the game was over, I heard his call. He told his listeners that Davis had gone back deep. He mentioned the possibility of the ball coming up short and being returned. He also let loose with an emotional recounting that was a classic. Do yourself a favor and listen to it sometime. I sent him a text that same night offering my congratulations on a great call.

After that minute and twenty-one lapsed, Craig said to me, "Let's start the replay sequence." The tape rolled and all I said was "You might want to see that again." And then Gary took over. We only showed it twice. On the second replay, Gary made the observation again that Alabama had chosen to have its protection team on the field. And he said, "Look at the guys who are chasing Chris Davis. No wonder he scored. They're not real athletes; they're all big fat guys." And it was perfect and it was right. You know, they didn't put an all-speed team out there.

After the game, I didn't follow Pat Haden's advice. I didn't do the brain dump immediately. None of us did. We all gathered at our trucks parked down at the bottom of a steep hill. We all, the tech crew, the on-camera, everybody, stood around high-fiving one another in amazement at what we'd seen, grateful that we'd been able to witness and bring to people such a great moment in sports.

Eventually, we had to break it up. The tech guys had hours of work ahead of them. The New York guys had to get to Atlanta to catch a flight home. Gary was headed to the airport, too. Nancy and I would be driving home. Normally, that would be it. We wouldn't talk much about the game and have our focus on the next one. Not with this one. Nancy and I drove home; instead of going to our apartment, we had a bite to eat at the restaurant in the Ritz-Carlton across the street from our place. To give you some idea of the extravagance of that choice, Nancy and I frequent and love Cracker Barrel restaurants.

The next day, we all got on the phone and talked about that 2013 Iron Bowl again. It's funny to me, but if a game is good, then people assume the broadcast was good. If the game is substandard, then we talk about all the things about the broadcast that weren't up to par. That happens all the time—all the time. So none of us made mention of the fact that we didn't identify Chris Davis being back there and deep. To show you how that principle of good game/good broadcast works, it wasn't until I watched the game again that I noticed this omission. If you had asked me after the game, I would have sworn that we had.

I didn't kick myself too much over that. I'm human. My only regret, and it's a very small one, is that I could have had the time to talk a bit more about the kicker I'd misidentified. Not only would I get his name right the first time, but I would have let viewers know that he had a great story as well. He was orphaned in Poland, got adopted by a couple in Georgia when he was thirteen, and earned his way on to the Alabama football team. He was honest about not getting a good leg into that kick. He was the team's main field goal kicker the following season and got off to a rough start and missed his first four attempts. He turned things around and contributed five field goals in 2014 against Auburn. He contributed greatly in the national championship game with an onside kick that Alabama recovered. Now that's somebody you can root for.

And Cade Foster? He was part of two national championship teams. Since then he has gone on to the University of Alabama's law school. He also had someone rooting for him. Former president George W. Bush sent him a letter of support.

Over the years, I've been asked about my favorite moments in sports. I've said that the 2013 Iron Bowl is my favorite SEC game. David Barron writes a media column for the *Houston Chronicle* and has become a good friend over the years. He called me immediately after the game. "Okay, where do you rank this?"

And I told him, "It's tied for second."

"Tied for second with what?"

"Well, Christian Laettner's winning shot and Tiger's chip shot at Sixteen."

Jack's putt at 17 in the Masters was still number one.

A short while later, I read Mike Vaccaro's column in the *New York Post* listing eight reasons why the Auburn-Alabama football game played on Saturday might have been the most exciting finish to any sporting event in the history of mankind. It wasn't that strong, but it was really strong. He also made a great case for his point.

He made me think, and today I'll tell you that the 2013 Iron Bowl ranks right up there to be tied with Jack in 1986. Six months later I ran into Mike and we spoke for the first time. He told me he had watched the game while on assignment somewhere. He was in a hotel lobby with strangers, and he said the reaction—and these weren't die-hard Auburn or Alabama fans—was so striking that he sat down and wrote that column. The reach of that game, the surprising and rare circumstances of its finish, and what was at stake changed my mind. It's a bit crowded atop that greatest-moment-I've-covered podium. I don't think that Jack will mind sharing with the 2013 squads from Alabama and Auburn. Unless he thinks his 2013 Ohio State Buckeyes should have been in the BCS bowl.

I wouldn't be surprised.

CHAPTER 15

Matters of Consequence

In the end, the games matter.

Enough said.

Perhaps nowhere is that clearer than in my experience covering the Army-Navy football game. The 2016 edition was the last game I covered. That it was, seemed entirely fitting. Ever since I was a kid listening on the radio, that traditional rivalry struck a chord in my heart. The game being held post-Thanksgiving on a Saturday seemed appropriate. A battle between two military academies coming on the heels of a celebration of gratitude seemed entirely appropriate. Though I was only five years old when the hostilities of World War II ended, I came of age during a period when that group of men and women went quietly about the business of firmly establishing our nation as a beacon of hope. The Army-Navy game served as a reminder of the great sacrifice many members of the Greatest Generation made to my freedom and my prosperity.

For many years, the football mattered greatly as well. Though I don't have clear recollections of the games in 1944 and 1945, those two years Army came into the game ranked number one in the country and Navy number two. Army won each time in games of great consequence. I have a far clearer recollection of the 1963 game. Shortly after I helped in our coverage of the assassination of President John F. Kennedy, his widow, Jacqueline, influenced the two academies decision to hold the game despite talks of its cancellation. President Kennedy, of course, was a Navy man himself, having served heroically in the war aboard PT-109. That game was moved back to December 7, fittingly Pearl Harbor Day. In Philadelphia's Municipal Stadium, 102,000 people gathered as did millions more via radio and television. As Roger Staubach, the quarterback of the Navy squad who came into the game ranked number two in the country later recalled, the game was as much a tribute to the country's fallen leader as it was a sporting event. It helped the nation heal.

The games matter.

The traditions matter.

One aspect of sports that draws us together is the pageantry involved. I don't know if this dates all the way back to the Romans and the Coliseum—and no, I wasn't there to cover the bread and circuses—but there's something deep inside us humans gathering together to watch a spectacle that pleases us. Whether it's the opening of an Olympics, the presentation of medals or a championship trophy, but the word ceremony frequently gets used. Most of us love tradition, long standing rivalry, and the rituals involved in games. Maybe its because in an often uncertain world, its nice to know that there are some things we can count on—an umpire saying, "Play ball!" to NHL hockey players shaking hands at the conclusion of a playoff series. From beginning to end, from opening day to a championship being decided, we mark our days as we mark our scorecards. Keeping a tally just somehow feels right.

Family, friends, and those who know me only by my occasional visits into their homes via television will tell you that I'm sentimental. I'm okay with that. More than okay, really, I'm proud of that. That means that I care. My career depended upon being impartial—that didn't mean that I didn't understand or feel what was at stake for everybody involved. Some of my favorite shots from various games are when our cameramen found someone in the crowd in the throes of tears or overcome with joy.

If you are not moved by the sight of the Cadets and the Midshipmen marching on before the game then you have no soul. I sensed that from seeing the game on television, but I truly felt that the first time I covered the game in 2000. The precision and the commitment of the students at those two service academies is truly something to behold. I was in awe. If I have one regret it is that I wasn't always able to do the game. Once it was moved to a stand-alone date to complete the regular season for college football, the second week in December, I was free of SEC commitments and could be in the booth.

That 2000 game says something about the appeal of the game. Army came into it with a record of 1-9; Navy stood at 0-9. Still, the game very much mattered and the Midshipmen pulled out a victory to prevent them from finishing with their worst record in their, to that point, more than 100-year history.

History was always an appeal to me—for that game and in my life. So, during the ceremonies that surround the Army-Navy game, I'm always deeply moved by the recognition of those who have made the ultimate sacrifice for our nation. The Army-Navy game serves as a reminder also that playing the game for the game's sake alone is important. The vast majority of those who play in that game have no real shot at playing the game professionally. They play for love of the game and to honor the traditions and put in practice the lessons that competition and teamwork teach and reinforce.

As much as we are entertained by major college football and may think of it as a kind of minor leagues for the NFL the reality is that fewer than two percent of its participants make it to the professional level. So what I said about the love of the game and the traditions above applies to the overwhelming majority of players we see on our screens and in person. That love, that dedication, that sacrifice is there in all games. Knowing, especially at times of war, that many of those involved in the Army-Navy game will serve their country in combat or in other ways has always added poignancy to an already deeply meaningful game. I can't help but be reminded that service and sacrifice extends beyond the academies as well. Pat Tillman's decision to forgo his career in the NFL after graduating from Arizona State University and playing for the Arizona Cardinals is only the most well known and dramatic of those stories.

When I think back on some of the players I've covered over the years, the number who served in the military in various capacities is another reminder of what sports teaches us and how those skills and character traits translate into other areas in the military and elsewhere. I also can't forget Texas A&M and its Corps of Cadets and its proud 12th Man tradition.

I was fortunate in my time here in Steamboat Springs to become dear, dear friends with Brigadier General Robin Olds. A West Point grad, he served in the US Air Force as a fighter pilot. A so-called "triple ace," (becoming an ace usually means confirmation of having downed five enemy aircraft) with sixteen "kills" combined during World War II and the Vietnam War, Robin was a genuine American hero. He recalled fondly his days on the football field playing for Army where he became an All-American in 1942. He is legendary for having lost two of his upper teeth in making a tackle in the '42 game. He returned to the field, saluted by the Navy midshipmen in attendance. Because travel was restricted in war time, Navy's Third and Fourth Classes were assigned to cheer for Army in place of the absent Army Corps of Cadets. How's that for sportsmanship?

Olds flew some of the most iconic aircraft of World War II, served for a time as an assistant football coach at West Point under Earl Blaik when Mr. Inside and Mr. Outside, Glenn Davis and Doc Blanchard, won Heisman Trophies. He flew precision maneuvers as part of the first aerobatic demonstration team to use jets, and later served as Commandant of Cadets at the US Air Force academy and helped restore honor following a major cheating scandal there. I was honored to know him in his later years when he remained a man of great integrity and vigor.

He was very much on my mind as I walked into the stadium in Baltimore for the game. Sadly, he'd passed away in 2007, but he was still very much with me.

In our pregame, we of course had to mention that Army had last won the game in 2001, shortly after the attacks on New York City and the Pentagon. The streak had taken on almost mythic proportions, but in 2012, Army seemed on the verge of breaking the spell. Unfortunately, as so often happens, an Army turnover late in the game at the Navy fourteen yard line prevented that from happening. Quarterback Trent Streelman and fullback Larry Dixon got tangled up on a handoff and a fumble ensued. Navy recovered.

End of game. Navy's streak continued.

Afterward, Streelman was disconsolate. In the most moving scene I've ever witnessed at a sporting event, the Army quarterback openly sobbed as he joined his teammates as they walked toward the Navy fans to sing first. "Singing Second," when the victor's *alma mater* is played and sung with the losing team facing the opposition's fans, is one more stirring tradition.

As I've said, I always look to provide viewers with someone to root for. The Army squad was again an underdog in 2016, but they had a special incentive this time around. After the second game of the season, their cornerback Brandon Jackson had been killed in a car accident. His mother, Morna Davis, was in attendance for the first time since the tragic loss of her son. She joined the celebration in the locker room following Army's 21–17 comeback victory.

I'm not naïve enough to think that on its own a game can heal a mother's broken heart, help a nation deal with the loss of a president, or make us forget about a terrorist attack. They do matter, though. They do contribute to offering hope and healing. They can inspire us and infuriate us, but more often than not, we keep coming back to them.

I've been fortunate to play a part in bringing some great stories to viewers. It's been an honor and a privilege. I can only hope that I've brought some small measure of the enormous pleasure I've had in broadcasting them.

Radio and television brought the world to me. Being a part of that world and bringing it to others has meant the world to me.

Thanks for watching. Thanks for reading. Thanks, to borrow a phrase, for the memories.

ACKNOWLEDGMENTS

This book is the summation of my professional life. My gratitude is owed to a lot of people.

First to members of my family. Thanks to my brother David and his wife, Meche, of Guadalajara, Mexico. To my brother Dan and his wife, Herbie Kay, of Austin, Texas. To my sister-in-law Clarice Lundquist of Dallas, widow of my late brother, Tom. To my sister, Sharon Zinn, of Lincoln, Nebraska. And to their children and grandchildren, all beloved people in our lives.

Thanks to the members of the SEC on CBS Sports family. To Craig Silver, the producer and a friend and colleague for more than three decades. To Bob Fishman and Steve Milton, terrific directors during my tenure, and to the remaining members of our seventy-five person production and technical group. We traveled the cities and towns of the south together for seventeen years, the most significant assignment in my more than fifty years in sports television.

To my on-air pals. To Todd Blackledge and Gary Danielson, men with whom I shared three and a half hours in the booth every Saturday in the fall. To Jill Arrington, Tracy Wilson and Allie La Force, sideline reporters supreme. And thanks to Chuck Gardner, Butch Baird, and David Moulton, indispensable cogs in our on-air production. Their assistance in making our telecasts hum for fifteen weekends each fall was extremely important. And to Pat Haden, the former USC and Los Angeles Ram quarterback, with whom I shared both NFL and NCAA duties. Have I mentioned that he was also a Rhodes Scholar?

My thanks to some of my NFL partners. Hall of Famers Terry Bradshaw, Dan Fouts, Dan Dierdorf, and John Madden.

My gratitude to the late Steve Davis, QB of the Oklahoma Sooners in the early seventies, a team that went 34-1-1 with him under center. Steve and I worked together at ABC Sports and came to CBS together in 1982. He was a great friend and a wonderful broadcaster.

A shout-out to some of the men and women with whom I enjoyed televising both the NCAA college and NBA games. In college, gifted analysts such as Bill Raftery, Jim Spanarkel, Billy Packer, Len Elmore, Al McGuire, and Lesley Visser. In the NBA, Tom Heinsohn, Billy Cunningham, Hubie Brown, Chuck Daly, Danny Ainge, Clark Kellogg, and Doc Rivers. And the folks in the truck, producers Bob Dekas and Mark Wolf, directors Bob Fishman and Suzanne Smith.

Golf television remains an important part of my life, especially the Masters, where I've been perched at the 16th hole since 2000. The late producer Frank Chirkinian put me there and Lance Barrow, the current producer, has kept me there.

Scott Hamilton and Tracy Wilson taught me to love figure skating and we worked together through three memorable Winter Olympics in France, Norway, and Japan. And were so ably produced during the last two by my friend David Winner.

Thanks to the presidents of CBS Sports during my time in the saddle: Neal Pilson, Peter Lund, and Sean McManus.

A special shoutout to Kevin O'Malley, executive producer of college sports in the early eighties. He made a decision about my possibilities in October of 1982 and made a phone call to me that changed my life. And to the late Dave Lane, General Manager at WFAA-TV in Dallas, the man who recommended that I succeed him as the sports director at the station in 1967 and whose willingness to accommodate my wishes to be involved in network television made my career possible.

To Bob Rosen, who has been my agent since 1983.

During my life, I've had an equal passion for sports television and an appreciation for music, thus I have great memories of singing in the Texas Lutheran University choir and of the more than three decades that Nancy and I have been involved in the Strings Music Festival in Steamboat Springs. Both connections have affected my life in an extremely meaningful way.

To Gary Brozek, whose love of words and whose ability to string them together until they become sentences and paragraphs and chapters has resulted in this book of memories. My thanks.

To Lisa Sharkey and Matt Harper of HarperCollins in New York City. Lisa, thanks for providing me with the opportunity to share my life in broadcasting. Matt, I truly appreciate your guiding vision for the book and handling all phases of what was once a mysterious process. I'm indebted to you both for your faith in me.

It's been a joyous experience to share these stories of a lifetime in sports television.

There are more.

Let's do it again sometime.

Verne Lundquist